divorced

shattering the myths

dads

Sanford L. Braver, Ph.D.
with Diane O'Connell

Jeremy P. Tarcher / Putnam

a member of Penguin Putnam Inc.

New York

Most Tarcher/Putnam books are available at special quantity discounts for bulk purchases for sales promotions, premiums, fund-raising, and educational needs. Special books or book excerpts also can be created to fit specific needs. For details, write Putnam Special Markets, 375 Hudson Street, New York, NY 10014.

Jeremy P. Tarcher/Putnam
a member of
Penguin Putnam Inc.
375 Hudson Street
New York, NY 10014
www.penguinputnam.com

Library of Congress Cataloging-in-Publication Data
Braver, Sanford L.
    Divorced dads : shattering the myths : the surprising truth about fathers, children, and divorce / by
Sanford L. Braver, with Diane O'Connell.
      p.   cm.
    ISBN 0-87477-862-X
     1. Divorced fathers—United States—Psychology.   2. Divorced fathers—United States—Attitudes.
  3. Divorced fathers—United States—Public opinion.   4. Public opinion—United States.
  I. O'Connell, Diane.   II. Title.
  HQ756.B733   1998
  306.874'2—dc21   98-23183 CIP

Printed in the United States of America

1 2 3 4 5 6 7 8 9 10

This book is printed on acid-free paper. ♾

Book design by Ralph Fowler

To my own parents,
Sadie and Allen Braver,
for teaching me the importance of fathers,
and to my children,
Todd, Devra, Chris, Matt, and Carrie,
for the daily dose they provide me of paternal pride, and to Jodi
—Sanford L. Braver

To my parents, Mae and Joe, whose love has guided me
through these many years
—Diane O'Connell

Contents

Acknowledgments

Braver

My foremost debt is to the many hundreds of families who served over the years as our informants, sharing their intimate lives with us. We know we asked a lot of questions at a difficult time, and are profoundly grateful that so many people willingly shared their lives with us for the sake of helping gain knowledge that could help future divorcing families.

My most stalwart collaborators, Drs. Sharlene A. Wolchik and Irwin N. Sandler, have been a source of wisdom, guidance, perspective, and deep friendship that has made the research enterprise over the last fifteen years a joy and a blessing. My thanks.

Many other professionals contributed in profound ways to the work presented here. Dr. William Griffin has been my valued collaborator on *Dads for Life*. Others whose contribution to this program were substantial were Joe Rassulo, Dr. Steve Spaccarrelli, and Dr. Lillie Weiss, the colleague who, at a workshop I presented, recognized that my work could be knit into a nonacademic book.

Many former graduate students, most of whom are now Ph.D.s, made immense contributions to the research presented here. Of these, Virgil Sheets, Curt Bay, and Bruce Fogas were major collaborators over many critical phases of the project. In addition, I'd like to acknowledge the assistance of Marjie Gunnoe, Robin Whetstone Dion, Nancy Gonzalez, Pam Fitzpatrick, Andrea Fenaughty, Daria Zvetina, Stephanie DeLusé, Marnie Whitney, and Christine Ng, who were all co-authors of papers cited herein, and Kathy Wilcox, Melanie Trost, Melanie Smith, Lilly Lengua, Art Martin, Debra Troyer, and Julie Lustig, who were co-authors on other related articles, and Jill Sundie, Marcia Taborga, Jonathon Cohen, Debora Hepps, Rick Poulin, Felicia Brenoe, and Leslie Turner, who all helped out in other ways.

Profs. Elizabeth Peters, Ira Ellman, Judi Bartfeld, and Greg Duncan made important suggestions on the economic analyses, while Peter Salem and Drs. Bob Cialdini, Jessica Pearson, Judith Seltzer, and Joan Kelly made critical suggestions on other topics. A deep debt is due Karen DeCrow and Drs. Bill Fabricius, Irwin Sandler, Kay Pasley, and Richard Warshak, who took the time from their busy schedules to read the entire manuscript and offer excellent suggestions for improvement. If any technical errors or unsupportable conclusions remain after the invaluable feedback of these wise colleagues, they are entirely my responsibility.

The competent support staff at Arizona State University could always be depended upon. Thanks to Linda Harris, Betty Barwegen, Sterlene Itule, Ernest Fairchild, Kathryn Pomeroy, Mary Redondo, Evelyn Anderson, and Janice Duffey.

Many officials in our community provided a climate that was open and highly facilitative of our research efforts. These include the Hon. Barry Schneider, Dr. Russ Schoeneman, Joel Bankes, Judith Allen, the Hon. Kenneth Fields, the Hon. Sylvan Brown, Dr. Cheryl Lee, Alice Rose Thatch, and Kat Cooper; I also appreciate the insights of Drs. Ronn Lavitt and Brian Yee. I also appreciate the occasional help of Drs. Todd Braver, Deanna Barch, and Mary Walton.

Several Washington officials were especially helpful, most important, Dr. Jeffery V. Evans, who administered the Noncustodial Parent grant for NICHD. I also thank David Arnaudo and Dr. Doreen Koretz.

This book would not have been written, at least in its present form, except for the incredibly supportive efforts of many talented literary professionals. A deep debt is owed to my agent, Janet Spencer King, who knows the hurdles she got me over, and Tarcher editors Irene Prokop and Mitch Horowitz.

My co-author, the incredibly talented Diane O'Connell, also knows what I put her through. The book would probably never have been finished, and certainly would have been of far lower quality without her journalistic gifts. As she notes, our collaboration began via long distance phone calls, long before we ever met. I am proud that now she is my friend as well as my co-writer.

The deft influence of my beloved, Jodi M. Bernstein, is recognizable on every page. No words suffice to express my gratitude for her loyalty and support through the dark days, as well as for the very real and very substantial improvements she contributed to the writing.

O'Connell

I'm especially grateful to my agent, Janet Spencer King, not only for bringing Sanford Braver and me together, but for her unwavering belief in my abilities, her always on-target advice, and, most of all, her friendship.

A special thanks goes to my co-author, Sanford Braver, for his impeccable research, sound judgment, flexibility, respect, and kind nature. What began as two strangers separated by the width of the country blossomed into a close collaboration in which the whole was greater than the sum of its parts.

Our editor, Irene Prokop, couldn't have been better. I will always appreciate her sharp editorial vision, patience, and good humor during the rough patches. Also, thanks to Mitch Horowitz for doing such a good job shepherding the book to publication.

I owe a special debt of gratitude to all the fathers and mothers who so generously opened their hearts and shared their stories. This book could not have been written without them.

There were also many experts who took time out of their hectic schedules to talk to me: Joel Bankes, Jimmy Boyd, Minna R. Buck, Bruce R. Cohen, Bahney Dedolph, Mary Ann Forgatch, John Gray, Evelyn J. Hall, Elizabeth Hickey, Cheryl D. Lee, Anne Mitchell, Karen DeCrow, Jessica Pearson, Douglas Schoenberg, Andrew Sheppard, Ralph Underwager, Richard Warshak, and Cathy Young. Special thanks to William B. Hess for his resourcefulness and efforts on behalf of this project.

Finally, I wish to thank my husband, Larry, for his never-ending support, encouragement, and honesty in responding to my work, for shoring me up when I allowed doubt to creep in, and for celebrating my successes. I can imagine no better life partner.

Divorced Dads

Introduction

In October 1996, I served on a panel at a conference in Washington, D.C., devoted to the role of fathers in their children's lives. The conference was called in response to President Clinton's Fatherhood Initiative, an effort headed by Vice-President Albert Gore, to examine whether the Federal government's policies were inadvertently "father unfriendly." The panel included various experts, academics, think-tank researchers, and federal agency heads. Each of them offered their perspective, and together they brainstormed ideas about policies that could be implemented to better promote fathers' effectiveness in their children's lives.

I was invited because I had led the largest federally funded study ever attempted on issues confronting divorced fathers (a constituency of paramount concern in policy circles). In 1985, with my long-time friends, colleagues, and fellow psychology professors at Arizona State University, Sharlene Wolchik, Ph.D., and Irwin Sandler, Ph.D., I began an eight-year study to examine in detail the lives of these men and their former spouses and children. This study was called the Noncustodial Parent: Parents Without Children project (PWC). I had taken another four years to analyze and compile our findings and present them in scientific journal articles to my fellow social scientists. Now, faced with this panel of distinguished Washington officials, I felt the responsibility of making these findings and their implications understood.

What especially worried me was the fact that our findings were a direct challenge to the current thinking about divorced fathers. I worried because I was single-handedly, it seemed, taking on nearly twenty years of views based on seriously flawed research. How would what I had to say be received? Would I be pilloried and assailed? Would what I had to say be dismissed without a hearing? I tried to shrug off the pressure and just present the facts.

Why a Conference on the Value of Fathers?

For our country's highest leaders and policymakers to assemble a blue-ribbon panel of experts to examine the worth of fatherhood now seems a matter of the highest irony. On reflection, it seems ludicrous that we would need such a panel of luminaries to affirm something that should be so self-evident: *fathers matter*. At any other time in our history, the importance of fathers' roles would never have been questioned. From caveman days, through biblical times, until about thirty years ago, we simply assumed that fathers, like mothers, were indispensable to children's well-being.

But during the late 1960s, driven by various cultural developments I will discuss in subsequent chapters, we somehow departed from the wisdom of the ages and of our forefathers. Our society appeared to move to a position in which it was commonly believed that fathers were superfluous, dispensable, ineffectual. According to Washington, D.C., attorney Ronald Henry, an adviser to the prestigious American Law Institute's project recommending Principles of the Law of Family Dissolution, it came to be "considered impolite"[1] to suggest that children needed the influence of a father in their lives. To rediscover what we had instinctively always known required nothing less than a distinguished panel of experts assembled by the President of the United States.

A Professional Journey

When I returned home after my talk, someone had placed on my desk a copy of *The Washington Post,* in which I knew a story about the conference would appear. I nervously turned the pages to the story, wondering what the reporter's take would be on my presentation. Would he assail my views? Would he dismiss me as naive? Had I been too academic, too technical in what I had said, so that he wouldn't even understand? I breathed a sigh of relief when I read the headline:

Turnaround on Role of Dads
Conference Marks a Sea Change

Thankfully, the accompanying news story was very favorable to the facts I had presented in my testimony.[2] I *had* gotten my point across, after all, it seemed. My findings and views had been very well received by my fellow academics and professional researchers; similarly, the federal officials on the panel had been highly sympathetic to what I had reported. To complete the picture, it now appeared the media were going to participate in the reformation of views, as well.

This "sea change" in the thinking regarding fathers' roles marked the culmination of a long professional odyssey for me. I had started out fifteen years ago studying divorced families at the request of colleagues Sharlene Wolchik and Irwin Sandler. They were launching into a new area of research, studying the effects of divorce on children, and wanted my expertise as a methodologist and statistician. Since my previous area of research on the dynamics of interpersonal conflict was drawing to its own natural conclusion, I was searching for new projects on which to turn my professional attention. At the time I knew relatively little, other than what generally educated people knew, about children of divorce.

As I got more involved with the project, I couldn't fail to recognize both that divorce rates have reached epidemic proportions—demographers Carol Martin and Larry Bumpass estimate that from 50 to 66 percent of all new marriages will end in divorce[3]—and that the breakups of such families had devastating personal as well as social consequences for the family members, especially the mothers and children. But I quickly became most disturbed by the research findings regarding fathers' roles in divorce: it appeared they weren't paying child support, they were absent from their kids' lives, they were abdicating their roles as fathers.

It was this appalling record of irresponsibility of the fathers that had gotten the most attention in the media. Headlines in newspapers and weekly news magazines screamed their outrage at these offenses:

Declaring War on America's Deadbeat Dads
—*Detroit News,* April 28, 1995

Clinton Takes Aim at Deadbeat Dads
—*USA Today*, June 19, 1996

A World Without Fathers
—*Newsweek*, August 30, 1993

The stories that followed the headlines boasted studies and statistics to back up their claims. These news reports painted a detailed picture of divorced fathers as deadbeats and runaways, throwing their ex-wives and children into a life of poverty through their irresponsibility.

The news stories and opinion pieces on the editorial pages also made it clear what we, as a society, must (and have been trying to) do. *Get tough!* We simply make it too easy for fathers to relinquish their responsibilities. We need stronger laws, more enforcement personnel, collection policies without loopholes, and longer jail terms.

Thus, three years into the project on children of divorce, my work took a fateful turn: I decided to devote most of my attention to the fathers in divorced families.

I readily admit that I *expected* to confirm the negative portrayal of divorced fathers when I started to pursue my own angle on this research. After all, the portrait was based on solid findings from respected research organizations such as the U.S. Census Bureau. And while the subject of divorced dads was discussed in such forums as the *U.S. News & World Report* cover story "Why Fathers Count,"[4] and recent television specials on the topic by *48 Hours* and *20/20* correspondent John Stossel, the underlying issues were little debated or questioned.

My rigorous professional education at the Institute for Social Research at the University of Michigan, however, along with my ten years of subsequent experience as a professional social psychologist, prompted me always to put conventional wisdom to scientific test and to regard accepted truisms with professional skepticism until supported with state-of-the-art scientific research methods. I would subject this area of inquiry to stringent critical scrutiny, too. And as I took a closer look at these studies and reports, another picture began to emerge.

I found that the studies from which all of our thinking about divorced fathers came were questionable because there were gaping holes in the information. Most notably, almost nothing was known about *why* fathers were abandoning their children in such overwhelming numbers. Why did this information not exist? Because no one had bothered to ask fathers questions that would reveal the real reasons for their irresponsibility. In fact, almost none of the studies had ever bothered asking fathers about anything at all.

I believed it was imperative that this void be filled if we wanted some real answers as to what was driving fathers away from their responsibilities. For this reason I developed a grant application for a new project, proposing a study of several hundred families, in which my colleagues and I would interview matched pairs of mothers *and* fathers, as well as their children. Moreover, we would begin the study at a very early point in time, right after the divorce was legally sought (immediately after the filing of the Petition for Dissolution), and before the divorce was final. By starting near the beginning, we could get a better sense about how the processes we identified became set into motion. We would also follow these families for three years after the divorce was final. This would allow us to track patterns that developed with the divorce. While a wide range of issues would be covered in the study and in the questions asked of each family member, the primary purpose of the proposed project was to learn what was going through the minds of these fathers that would cause so many of them to break the bonds with their children, with such devastating consequences.

Both the grant agency and the scientists it enlisted as reviewers had to acknowledge that there was a serious deficiency in what we knew about fathers and divorce. As a result, our grant application for this project was approved, and we were fast-tracked for our funding start.[5] The agency also realized that getting a window into fathers' viewpoints concerning their motivations, their problems, and their difficulties post-divorce would help to establish a more solid platform for policymaking. Finally, the grant agency apparently appreciated the scientific merit and the rigor of the methodology of the proposed project on divorced fathers.

So began the professional journey that culminates with the publication of this book. Altogether, my colleagues and I have surveyed over 1,000 divorcing couples. The research has been supported by over $10 million of federal grants, primarily from the National Institute of Child Health and Human Development, and from the National Institute of Mental Health.[6] We have reported our findings in numerous professional articles and countless talks. I believe this research has put me in a unique position to understand the existing view about divorcing fathers, as well as to suggest remedies to policymakers.

The study has now been completed, and the results are startling. While I began this research hoping to find answers to why so many fathers abandoned their responsibilities, I discovered that not only were the characterizations of divorced fathers misleading, they were often *completely opposite to the truth.*

In short, virtually every aspect of what I call the "bad divorced dad" image has turned out to be a *myth*, an inaccurate and damaging stereotype. Not only is this myth seriously inaccurate, it has led to harmful and dangerous social policies. The victims are not only the fathers, whose suffering, anger, and frustration is immense, and increasingly registered, but also the more than one million mothers per year who obtain divorces. Laboring under inaccurate stereotypes, they are being denied the help and support that only a cooperative co-parent could provide. Most important, our mistaken popular views have imperiled our nation's children, whom we are inadvertently depriving of the love and support, both emotional and financial, of involved fathers.

Having spent so long learning the truth, I am now in a position to shed some illumination on a sorry story. The pages that follow will expose the problems that created a kind of tunnel vision for past researchers, which ultimately resulted in findings that were virtually molded to be perfectly compatible with the prevailing beliefs, values, and views. You will learn how our need for the bad divorced dad myth has led to a travesty. And you will learn what we can do about it.

1.

The "Bad Divorced Dad" Image

No one who has read newspapers or magazines, watched TV, listened to radio, or gone to the movies in the last couple of decades could fail to come to the conclusion that divorced fathers are generally irresponsible people. Just look at the phrases used to describe them: Runaway Dads. Absentee Dads. Disappearing Dads. Bad Dads. And the granddaddy of them all: Deadbeat Dads. These are the dad buzzwords for the '90s, supported by the images of the father who doesn't show up while his kids wait anxiously by the window for his visit. Or worse, the father who abandons his offspring altogether, refusing to support them, throwing them into a life of financial deprivation while he lives it up in high style. These stories make us clench our jaws in anger.

Engage in a casual conversation with any reasonably well-informed person and you're likely to find that this image of divorced fathers is not only firmly believed, but taken as almost a given. And those who hold these beliefs most strongly are policymakers—those legislators, judges, commissioners, and attorneys whose decisions regarding divorce affect millions of lives.

Furthering these images is the general belief that only bad dads get divorced in the first place. According to this view, fathers who are good family men, who participate actively in their children's lives, and who share child-rearing responsibilities with their wives only rarely would choose to divorce. They see too much value in their family life to jeopardize it in any way. This image is parallel to that of the gentle wife, who readily recognizes the immense value of such a man and works tirelessly to keep him satisfied and the rest of the family functioning healthily. Surely, only those men who are irresponsible, worthless, shifty, substance abusers, or batterers abandon their families. It is also only such men as these that wives would ever allow to walk out. And once these men leave the marriage, without the shackles of family life to constrain them, their irresponsibility only seems to grow.

The voices of other men readily join in this jeering chorus. Those fathers who remain good family men are among those who most strongly disparage divorced fathers, perhaps as a means of distancing themselves from what they see to be their moral inferiors. Politicians and the media have a field day badmouthing them since they are such an obvious and defenseless scapegoat for the ills of society. And few, until now, have spoken up in their defense or have questioned the image of the bad divorced dad.[1]

> ➤ **Once the detailed image of the villainous divorced dad became apparent, it was clear that our society had developed a full-blown mythology or stereotype.**

It is a human tendency that once we have identified a scapegoat, an evildoer or villain, we flesh out the image in detail. We fill in the portrayal with enough particulars to fully realize the "enemy" as a devil figure, completely different and more sinister than the rest of us. By vilifying the scapegoat and filling in the details of his alien nature, we comfort ourselves, because we feel we now "know" our enemy, and hopefully can better defend ourselves. In fact, it was only once my colleagues and I came to recognize how detailed the villainous image of divorced dads had become that we concluded our society had developed a full-blown mythology or stereotype.

As we progressed in our analyses of this image, we came to recognize that there were six distinguishable beliefs about divorced dads that together comprised the bad divorced dad image.

Myth 1: Divorced Dads Are Deadbeat Dads

According to this belief, divorced fathers, in overwhelming numbers, stop paying the child support the court orders them to pay. This notion is perhaps the very heart of the bad divorced dad image, and it goes like this: Very few divorced fathers can be trusted to meet their family obligations and to continue to financially support their families after its dissolution. Once divorced, they find "better" things to do with their money, such as lavishing it on their new girlfriends or buying new "toys" for themselves. Or they deviously hide their income in secret bank accounts or use tricky accounting practices to avoid parting with any of it for the good of their children.

Where would such a damning belief arise from? From the most respected data gathering organization in the country, the U.S. Census Bureau, which came to the conclusion in its set of special Census Studies entitled Child Support and Alimony (conducted every two to three years),[2] that only 50 percent of children receive the full amount of support to which they are entitled, while 25 percent receive only part of what they are owed, and 25 percent receive nothing at all. Thus, according to this account, at least half of divorced fathers are deadbeats, a sensational figure that the media have fully exploited in perpetuating this belief.

Myth 2: Divorced Dads Are Runaway Dads

This myth spins as follows: After divorce, fathers inevitably lose interest in their children, proving the old saying, "Out of sight, out of mind." Without the civilizing presence of wives and children in their daily lives, they migrate to different, less family-oriented interests. Their children increasingly become less and less of a priority, less of a concern. This process of drifting apart may not begin right away. At first, these fathers, who seem to have it so maddeningly easy on their visits—never having the burden of making the children do homework or chores, letting them stay up as late as they want, rarely needing to exert any discipline, as the mother does—might enjoy the thrill of being a "Disneyland Dad," able to take the children on exciting trips or buy them expensive gifts. But, all too quickly, the excitement wears away and the shine wears off. Disengagement begins innocuously, by missing a scheduled visit now and then. But inexorably, these divorced fathers come to a point of voluntarily discontinuing any kind of real involvement with their children, depriving them of a rich emotional connection with a father and the benefits of a male role model.

This myth can be largely attributed to one of the most influential sociologists in this country, Frank Furstenburg, Ph.D. Using a huge, representative national data set, Furstenburg and his fellow investigators reported in *American Sociological Review* and in the *Journal of Marriage and Family* that 49 percent of the children in their sample had not seen their noncustodial parent in the preceding year and that only one child in six averaged weekly contact or better.[3] These findings have been widely quoted in both the popular media and professional journals, and until recently have been regarded as definitive.

Myth 3: Divorced Fathers Impoverish Their Former Wives and Children

There is also widespread acceptance of the myth that divorce creates an economic calamity for women and children, both because the wives cannot support themselves and their children very well without the income of the primary breadwinner and because the primary breadwinner defaults on his child-support responsibilities, as in Myth 1. An overwhelming number of single divorced mothers and their children are believed to be catapulted into poverty by the irresponsibility of the fathers and the permissiveness of the system in allowing this to happen. Consequently these mothers are forced to rely on public assistance.

The impact of divorce on mothers is believed to be so profound we have coined the term "the feminization of poverty." Of course, once the remainder of the family is reduced to welfare status, the rest of the citizenry is unfairly asked to pick up the burden of supporting them. Thus, divorced fathers not only impoverish their own families, they cost everyone in society. A corollary belief is that fathers themselves actually *benefit* economically by divorce, since they now have only themselves to support.

This belief grew primarily out of the hugely influential 1985 book, *The Divorce Revolution: The Unexpected Social and Economic Consequences for Women and Children in America,* by well-respected sociologist Lenore Weitzman, Ph.D., which purported to show that women (and children) suffered a 73 percent decline in their standard of living post-divorce, while men enjoyed a 42 percent increase.[4]

Myth 4: Divorce Settlements Tilt Unfairly in Favor of Divorced Fathers

This belief is fueled by the writings of several respected gender scholars in largely influential books and articles, such as Lenore Weitzman (as stated above), Law Professor Martha Fineman *(The Illusion of Equality: Rhetoric and the Reality of Divorce Reform)*[5] and social scientist Mary Ann Mason *(The Equality Trap)*,[6] who have each come to the conclusion that fathers are favored in the divorce settlement, largely through their aggressive negotiating capabilities and because laws, though supposedly guaranteeing equity and fairness, are written *by* men *for* men. Men, after all, occupy most of the judgeships, men are the divorce lawyers, and men are the legislators who make the laws. How, the reasoning goes, can such men truly be sensitive to the needs of women and children? As a result of this male-dominated, clubby system, women and children are not fairly represented in the divorce settlement.

Furthering this myth is the corresponding stereotype that women are not adept at handling conflict, bargaining, or negotiation, which are all considered male-centered activities. Instead, women seek to look for compromise, to heal, to cooperate. These tendencies work completely to their disadvantage in divorce settlement negotiations.

Myth 5: Divorced Fathers Have It Easy Emotionally After Divorce; Only Their Ex-Wives and Children Are Distressed

This is perhaps the oldest part of the bad divorced dad image, which portrays fathers as recovering quicker emotionally after the divorce, becoming more content with their new lifestyle. Freed of responsibility, and flush with cash, they can pursue whatever interests they choose and grant themselves most of their wishes. Fathers are portrayed as personally fulfilled after divorce, in marked contrast to the mounting depression and gloom that envelops their overburdened ex-wives—and their troubled kids.

This was the one aspect of the image that grew without any support from social scientists. In fact, previous literature by a number of respected researchers, such as Judith Wallerstein, Ph.D., and Joan Berlin Kelly, Ph.D. *(Surviving the*

Breakup)[7] and Constance Ahrons, Ph.D. *(The Good Divorce)*[8] strongly and consistently suggested the opposite conclusion: that, while both parents suffer substantial emotional distress surrounding the divorce, it is in fact *mothers* who fare substantially better emotionally than fathers. And, according to a 1985 *USA Today* poll, 85 percent of divorced women claim to be happier post-divorce, compared with only 58 percent of divorced men.[9]

Myth 6: Fathers Initiate Most of the Family Breakups, Abandoning Their Families and Their Responsibilities

According to this last myth, the divorce was caused when fathers walked out on their marriage because, in their immaturity, they couldn't face the responsibilities of parenthood. The assumption that men are primarily responsible for dissolving families is widely shared among respected researchers, most notably David Blankenhorn in his book, *Fatherless America,*[10] and Marcia Guttentag and Paul Secord in their book, *Too Many Women.*[11]

In this portrait, bad dads quickly lose interest in being faithful to one wife and working hard to preserve the family unit. While wives sacrifice everything for the betterment of the husbands and children, many fathers are just too immature to handle the responsibilities in the same way. Walking out on their marriage is the result. And the abandoned wives and children are forced to bear all of the calamitous consequences.

Statistics Don't Always Tell the Truth

The six distinguishable beliefs just reviewed, the components of the bad divorced dad image, arose largely from media stories and television and movie portrayals that were, with few exceptions, consistent with most existing social scientific consensus. Yet our investigation revealed that the past studies had some serious problems that cast doubt on their accuracy—problems that were sometimes activated by the ideological gender views of the researchers. According to gender stereotypes currently popular in academic circles, if not society at large, women are basically good, gentle, self-sacrificing, and heroic. They are also seen as relatively powerless, and frequently victimized. Men, by contrast, are powerful, irresponsible, and deceitful brutes. As columnist Kathleen Parker noted in *The Denver Post,* "One can only conclude, judging from the news, that men are mean, small-minded, violent and stupid.... Men ... are fast replacing women as victims of negative messages. They're deadbeat dads. They're wife beaters. They're child abusers.[12] They are, as the former NBC sitcom so succinctly states, "Men Behaving Badly." Imagine trying to get a show called *"Women* Behaving Badly" produced. It would be unthinkable.

The image pendulum seems to have swung crazily, from the unfair and inappropriate assumption of the 1950s, in which women were seen as flighty and trivial, and men consequential and responsible, to its equally inappropriate polar opposite: Now, femaleness is inherently seen as good and maleness is implicitly bad. These new views are widely accepted in the current climate by both male and female researchers. Instead of a more balanced view, in which both genders are recognized as possessing a mixture of good and bad qualities, the current perspective is a serious distortion, an overcorrection from the old unbalanced views.

> The image pendulum seems to have swung crazily, from the unfair and inappropriate assumption of the 1950s, in which women were seen as flighty and trivial, and men consequential and responsible, to its equally inappropriate polar opposite: Now, femaleness is inherently seen as good and maleness is implicitly bad.

It is a testament to how deep-seated these views are that once I began to uncover and point out evidence that tended to exonerate fathers, some researchers were mistakenly led to infer that I myself must somehow be antifemale, antifeminist or antimother. The truth is the direct opposite: I have long identified with the goals of the women's movement to increase opportunities for women (and men as well), to treat the genders equally, and to end male domination in families. But somehow even to speak in defense of fathers is taken by some as the equivalent of bashing mothers. This shows how skewed we have become in our attitudes. Let it be clear: I *am* pro-father, because the evidence is compelling and incontrovertible that they benefit children; but I am also staunchly pro-mother, and most especially, I am pro-children.

Were these new invalid gender stereotypes strong enough to overcome the usual fair-minded methods that are the hallmarks of good science? Were the researchers blinded by their own biases, leading to sloppiness and lapses in their methods? Or did these new views serve a social need?

Why We Need the Bad Divorced Dads Myth

As the following chapters will demonstrate, we now have endowed the divorced father with all sorts of imaginary unpleasant attributes and assumed a divorce aftermath that is statistically fictitious. It is possible to think, say, and write negative things about divorced fathers that we could not say about any other group. It would be improper and inappropriate to denigrate other populations with the ferocity that we reserve for divorced fathers. To imagine an editorialist portraying Hispanics and African-Americans in the same kind of denigrating, stereotypical way that we routinely apply to divorced fathers is to imagine an editorialist out of work, rightly pilloried for prejudice.

Though the research findings served to create and reinforce these beliefs about divorced fathers, empirical evidence alone wouldn't be enough to create such a deeply held myth. For any myth as monolithic and powerful as the bad divorced dad myth to invade the popular understanding to the extent it has, society would have to be complicit. The myth would have to fill a need. But what is that need?

The answer is that we as a society are greatly troubled by the breakup of the American family. The devastation caused by the huge uptick in divorce compels us to find a villain in the drama. Clearly it cannot be the children's fault; nor is it fashionable or acceptable to blame mothers or the women's movement. But there is one group remaining in America that it is not socially unacceptable to derogate: Males. Rarely has a group had a poorer image.

And most men will not cry prejudice to ward off such attacks, as other groups do. Fathers seem to have no recourse but to plead guilty. Or no contest. And since no defense is ever raised, it has become socially acceptable to paint men in black and angry brushstrokes, as society fleshes in a detailed, if flawed, portrait. The result is the image we now hold so firmly about how well fathers fare after divorce and how irresponsible they are, compared with the bleakness of divorced mothers' and childrens' lives.

If belief in this myth was nothing more than bad press for fathers, we might dismiss it. They should be able to take the heat. But it is more than one of the worst public relations nightmares in memory; the stereotype is downright dangerous to our nation's health. (In the Epilogue, we review the evidence why fathers in general, and *divorced* fathers in particular, matter.) As we shall show in the following chapters, this portrait has led to societal perspectives and governmental policies doomed to failure, policies that have created even more hardship and suffering for children of divorce.

➤ Belief in the bad divorced dad myth is more than one of the worst public relations nightmares in memory; the stereotype is downright dangerous to our nation's health. It has led to policies that have created more hardship and suffering for children of divorce.

2.

Taking on Myth 1

Deadbeat Dads

Three True Stories

Story One

On the morning of March 30, 1995, *The Arizona Republic* ran a familiar type of story. It began with a case of a Maine truck driver who was welshing on his child-support payments. The report went on to describe a new law that passed the U.S. House of Representatives by a 426–5 vote for revoking the drivers' licenses of citizens who owed substantial back child support. The officials quoted were proud of this new weapon they had unfurled in their never-ending war to collect child support from deadbeat dads. One Congresswoman said it is "one of the simplest, most effective . . . tools we have." A Phoenix mother of three stated that her former husband owed her $82,000; she felt that if she "could have taken his driver's license away, he probably would have paid." The story did not quote the woman's ex-husband.

Story Two

During one of the interviews we conducted for our project, I met Barbara, a thirty-two-year-old divorced mother. (Except as noted, all parents' or children's names used in this book have been changed, to protect the privacy of the informants).[1] She and her seven-year-old daughter were managing pretty well since her divorce three years ago, I learned. But she was still furious at her ex-husband. She told me what a bad influence she thought he was on her little girl, because he was so irresponsible—especially about money. He was always behind on the child support he owed her. "He *knows* I have bills I have to pay at the first of each month, and that's when his child support is due," she lamented. "But he's always late or misses payments altogether." She estimated that during the last twelve months alone, he had paid only $1,400 of the $2,400 he had been ordered to pay by the court. "I never thought I would end up married to someone who would turn out to be a 'deadbeat dad.' "

Story Three

Jim, a father interviewed several times for our study, told us how much his daughter, Melissa, had always meant to him. When his wife divorced him, he was upset most of all by the loss of his everyday interaction with his child. He vowed he would do everything in his power to remain close to his "Bud."

The child support Jim had been ordered to pay was a financial hardship, he said, because his income as a self-employed electrician was highly variable. In recent months, the building recession in Phoenix had caused a dry time. But his responsibility to Melissa was foremost to him. She had her own room in his apartment, and it was well stocked with the toys and clothes he'd bought. Due to the irregularity of contractors' payments, he had been forced to make one or two child-support payments late now and then. But, he stressed, he always eventually paid all of it. He owed his daughter that. At that moment he was behind about $100. "No matter how tough it gets, I'll never be a 'deadbeat dad,' "Jim declared.

All these stories are, of course, related. The newspaper story on the new child-support collection procedure instituted was, as I said, a common story. News reports about child support and new enforcement mechanisms have mushroomed in recent years. The most popular mechanism is to jail the deadbeat dads. Several times a year, officials round up the most notorious or flagrant offenders, and with considerable press attention and lots of photo-ops, haul them before a willing magistrate, who orders them jailed for a few days, until a repayment plan is negotiated. These stories make good copy as well as good public relations for the officials. Who could possibly be sympathetic to men who abandon their own children? And what voter could fail to increase his or her admiration for any public official who had the gumption to bring such heinous offenders to justice?

Would it surprise you to learn that Barbara and Jim were formerly married to each other? What you read was what they each told us about the very same issue—how Jim was doing in meeting his child-support obligations. According to *him,* he was striving valiantly and nearly perfectly (only owing $100) to make his child-support payments and would never allow himself to become a deadbeat dad. But according to *her,* he already was one, and in her mind would forever be. *She* claimed he owed $1,000. How could two people have such discordant views of the same event? Is one lying and the other telling the truth? Or are their memories simply faulty?

> **If you have ever had the opportunity to talk to both spouses from a divorced couple, you could not fail to have recognized how absolutely common it is to have two completely different versions of the same event. It is as if you are hearing about two unconnected realities: his and hers.**

If you have ever had the opportunity to talk to both spouses from a divorced couple, you could not fail to have recognized how entirely common—how absolutely reliable—it is to have two completely different versions of the same event. It is as if you are hearing about two unconnected realities: his and hers. And generally, neither party is even aware that there is any other version but *his or her* own. Rarely are they conscious of the fact that they may be bending, enhancing, or diminishing real events to back up their own "truths." Thus, *he said/she said* is the rule among most divorced couples. In the drama told by each, there is both a clear hero (themselves), and a clear villain (the ex-spouse). But the starring roles switch, depending on whom you talk to.

The three stories I've just recounted point up one of the formidable problems in trying to get the facts about divorce issues. Any responsible researcher or
journalist simply can't rely on only one parent's side of the story as being the
whole truth. Do you think the father in the news story would have agreed that he
owed $82,000 in child support? And even if he did agree, could it be possible
that there was more to his story than simply callous withholding of child support?

It is not until you compare the stories of *both* of the parties that you are even
confronted with any disparity. Until recognizing that Jim and Barbara were talking about the same divorce, didn't you believe that Barbara's ex-husband was a
deadbeat? Didn't you think that Jim was one of the rare good dads, trying very
hard, and succeeding almost perfectly at meeting his financial obligation to his
daughter? Did both conclusions change when I revealed that you were hearing
two sides of the very same story? This is precisely why the myth of the deadbeat
dad persists.

The "Official" Story

How severe is our nation's problem concerning the payment of child support by
noncustodial parents? The statistics that answer this question are among the
most widely known facts about divorce. Most well-informed observers will tell
you that post-divorce child-support collections in the United States are so low
that they pose an overwhelming social problem. Hardly any divorced parents (almost always fathers), it seems, properly support their children.

➤ **Most well-informed observers will tell you that post-divorce**
child support collections in the United States are so low that
they pose an overwhelming social problem.

The data cited most regularly in the press, and by researchers and scholars,
is the set of special Census Studies, entitled Child Support and Alimony,[2] which

are regularly updated. According to these studies, which each investigate the situations of about 2,000 families, only about half of all women received all the child support they were awarded; another quarter received some but not all child support ordered, while the final quarter *received nothing at all.*

But these weren't the only figures that conveyed the impression that divorced dads were running out on the financial support of their kids. At least half a dozen other prominent studies came to the same basic conclusions as the Census Bureau findings, including the results found by the most well-known divorce researcher, psychologist and author Judith Wallerstein.[3] A great number of divorced dads were not paying the required amount of child support.

Think about it! According to these respected data sources, half of all divorced fathers break the law, depriving their children of their rightful future. Outrage at this flagrant denial of fathers' responsibilities prompted Margaret Heckler, then Secretary of the U.S. Department of Health and Human Services, to lobby Congress in 1983 to pass stricter enforcement legislation. She eloquently described:

> *the destitution, the desperation, and the simple human suffering of . . . children. . . . Frankly, it offends my conscience because I believe that a parent's first responsibility is to provide for the upbringing and welfare of his children. To deny that responsibility is a cowardly act. . . . Children deserve to be supported by both of their parents. For the sake of America's children, we must put an end to what has become a national disgrace.[4]*

➤ **The result of lobbying by the U.S. Department of Health and Human Services, backed up by the Census Bureau's "irrefutable" figures, led to a number of federal programs with billion-dollar budgets. Most notable is the Child Support Enforcement Act of 1975, which requires states to engage in more stringent enforcement efforts.**

The result of such lobbying, backed up by the Census Bureau's "irrefutable" figures, led to a number of federal programs, with federal-sized—that is, billion dollar—budgets. Most notable is the Child Support Enforcement Act of 1975, and particularly its amendments, especially those of 1984, which requires states to engage in more stringent enforcement efforts.

Implicit in these laws strengthening enforcement and others like them is the assumption that divorced men are not paying child support, not because they are *unable* to, but simply because they don't *want* to. No wonder the public gets angry! No wonder *Newsweek* once called child-support nonpayment "an epidemic of lawlessness that is rivaled, perhaps, only by income-tax cheating."[5]

Uncovering the Defects in the Census Bureau Surveys

When I began my own research program, the state of knowledge and conventional wisdom reflected the attitudes derived from the data cited by the Census Bureau. And why not? Who could doubt the U.S. Census Bureau—the most respected data gathering organization in the land? *I* certainly didn't question the figures when I first heard or read them. The findings seemed obvious and clear cut.

But then I began to study the research with my scientist's eye. My training, and what I teach my students, is not simply to look at *what* was found, but to take a critical look at *how* it was found. Thorough social scientists examine the methods both of gathering data and compiling figures and try to determine whether the researchers' conclusions are fully warranted. We know that there are many faulty ways to collect and analyze data and that not all "truth" or "received wisdom" is true when closely examined.

Before I get into the problems of the Census Bureau data, first let me ask you this: How do you *think* it was discovered that most divorced men don't pay all their child support? Perhaps you imagined, as I did, that there is a central national database containing official records of child-support payments made in all divorce cases. It would be similar to finding out how many traffic tickets were written and paid. All an analyst would have to do would be to click a mouse and have a computer churn out the percentages.

It turns out that this simple, believable idea is far from the truth. There *is* no actively maintained national database of child-support payments in divorce cases.

Lacking a trustworthy official national database logging in a divorced father's monthly child-support payments, Census officials relied instead on asking verbal questions in interviews or surveys of people in households previously found to have a minor child and a parent of that child who lives elsewhere. But wouldn't this method be just as reliable as an official database?

Well, no, it wouldn't. There are two conspicuous problems with the Census Bureau findings as well as the other survey findings I looked at.

The first problem is that in many of the analyses the researchers *combined* divorced people with never-married people. This mixing can badly skew results if the two groups behave in different ways—and there is certainly reason to expect they will. It would be like averaging a homeless person's income with a millionaire's and concluding that their average income is half a million. While it may not be technically wrong, it certainly describes neither party at all well. So it is when combining divorced families with never marrieds. The child-support compliance rate is known to be widely disparate for the two groups, for reasons that would be obvious even to the casual reader: the never-married group contains a high proportion of poorly educated teenage mothers living in urban ghettos. The fathers are deeply embedded in the underclass themselves. Moreover, the fathers often have failed to form any kind of bond with the mother or child, and even the paternity of the child is often likely to be in doubt.

In contrast, *divorced* fathers typically are from a better-educated, higher-earning group; they generally have no doubts about their paternity; and they could more reasonably be expected to have a deep bond of attachment to their children. In reality, their payment history is more reliable than never-married fathers.[6] It should be obvious that the two groups should always be separately addressed in any analyses or policy discussions. The distinction, however, has been too infrequently recognized or cited.

Allowing Bias to Determine "Truth"

As bad as lumping the never-married fathers with the divorced fathers is, the second deficiency in the findings reported is even more serious. It is that virtually all the researchers who arrived at the conclusion that fathers are overwhelmingly not paying child support used only one source of data in arriving at their findings: the custodial mothers. Since the results were based on answers to survey questions, rather than official records of payments, I was concerned about a problem inherent in all survey research: people's answers might reflect their biases and what they want the interviewer to think more than they reflect the truth. It is a matter of common sense, as well as professional training, that researchers need to be alert for these biases, and attempt to compensate for them appropriately; at the very least, paying attention to potential bias leads good researchers to insert appropriate qualifiers into their conclusions.

> Virtually all the researchers who arrived at the conclusion that fathers are overwhelmingly not paying child support used only one source of data in arriving at their findings: the custodial mothers.

Specifically, I was concerned in this instance about a particular kind of bias: people tend to slant their responses in a way that casts a positive light on themselves or people they like and that casts an unflattering light on those they don't like.[7]

For example, more people will tell you that they voted in the last presidential election than actually voted. More people will also tell you that they voted for the candidate who won. If the election was won by a 55/45 ratio, for instance, after polling voters, you'll get responses that would have put the outcome at 65/35.[8] It's the same with seatbelt use. More people will claim they use them than actually do.[9] Similarly, people will describe the behavior of those they don't like in highly negative ways.[10]

And that was precisely the trouble here: custodial mothers often don't like their ex-husbands very much, so there was ample reason to expect this bias would cloud the accuracy of their answers. But no child-support researcher seemed to acknowledge this problem.

Here is the exact question that's been asked in the Census study: "In total, how much in child support payments were you <u>SUPPOSED</u> to receive in (year) from the child support agreement for children covered by this award? How much child support payments did you <u>ACTUALLY</u> receive in (year) for children covered by this award?" (emphasis in original).

What's wrong with these questions? To answer them completely accurately, especially the second question, respondents would need to remember twelve to twenty-four different payments over the past year. In the absence of precise information readily at their fingertips, many if not most respondents will simply "make up a number," one which is simply a guess or "best estimate." This is exactly the circumstance ripe for one's bias to enter and distort the truth. The fact that former wives are often deeply angry with their ex-husbands (as we will discuss further in Chapter 6) makes it highly plausible that the mother's reports could be distorted by a bias to denigrate the activity and worth of the father—even if she's not deliberately lying or not aware of her bias. In all likelihood, she is simply going to remember better the payments he was late on or underpaid or missed entirely, than when he paid on time or paid more than he was supposed to. The net result is to render her answer an *under*estimate of how much or how well her ex-husband paid.[11]

The same bias, of course, would likely apply to any answers given by the non-custodial parent. He will tend to remember the payments he made, especially when it was a sacrifice to scrape up the money, and the times he threw in a little extra, and forget about the payments that were late or less than full. Remember Barbara and Jim at the beginning of this chapter? Recall the different impressions you may have had until learning they were formerly husband and wife.

For the Census officials and other researchers to come to their conclusions by asking only mothers and not allowing fathers to be heard, is equivalent to a judge making a decision in a case after denying one party to a disagreement the opportunity to take the stand. No judge would think of doing this, and our system of justice specifically precludes it, because we intuitively realize that people tend to tell their story in a way that makes themselves look good and their adversary look bad.

➤ Not a single one of the previous researchers or Census officials indicated that questioning only mothers may have been
a problem. Nowhere in any published reference to the figures
was the appropriate qualifying phrase "according to the custodial parent" included.

Why didn't the Census researchers take this fact of human nature into account? What perplexed me the most was that not a single one of the previous researchers or Census officials indicated in their writing that questioning only
mothers may have been a problem or a shortcoming of the data. Nowhere in any
published reference to the figures was the appropriate qualifying phrase "according to the custodial parent" included. Rather, the language used always im-
plied that the figures were to be regarded as factual, unbiased, and definitive. As
a result, the Census figures wield tremendous clout.

The Shortcomings of an Official Database

Though *no* national database of child support collections exists, in a very few select localities there *do* exist official court records of child-support payments
made. One of these is in the state of Wisconsin. There, a statute requires payments to be made through the county clerks. Respected University of Wisconsin Professor of Social Work Irving Garfinkle, Ph.D., analyzed these court records
of payment in 1985 for the state of Wisconsin, and his initial findings seemed to
substantiate the general thrust of the Census data. He found that noncustodial
parents paid only about half of what they owed, again, an alarmingly low result.[12]

But belatedly he realized that a problem existed with the court records:
They solely reflected payments made *through the clerk*. If some payers bypassed
the Clerk and paid their child support directly to the custodial parent, either because their decree failed to contain the stipulation to pay through the court, or
because they simply violated such a requirement, the clerk's records would *under*report the true amount being paid. Thus Garfinkle learned "from discus-

sions with some Clerk of the Court's staff" that "not infrequently" payments supposed to be made through the court were instead made directly to the custodial parent.[13] He eventually acknowledged that his figures underestimated, to an unknown degree, the true amount of child support paid.

Designing a Better Study

When we began our study at Arizona State University, we were determined to compensate for the limitations of the past research, and we believed our investigation could improve upon the child-support compliance rate picture in three ways. First, the county in which we conducted our study—Maricopa County, Arizona—was, like the state of Wisconsin, another of the very few jurisdictions in the country with "official" database court records of child support. By 1985, once the technology had become available to keep computerized records of child support paid, judges were instructed to approve divorce decrees only if they contained a provision that payments were to be made through the county clerk of the court.

The clerk's computerized records had disclosed that only about 30 percent of what noncustodial parents owed was actually paid—a figure even lower than the Census findings. But, cognizant of Garfinkle's experience in Wisconsin, I was alerted to the possibility that the records in Maricopa County might have contained the same flaw, an underreport due to some payments being made directly from payer to payee, bypassing the court. While Garfinkle was able to determine only that it happened, but not how frequently, we attempted to determine the extent of the direct payment by asking the parents in an interview.

Second, our study would also improve on the past research by separately interviewing *both* parents. Not only would we ask both mothers and fathers whether they actually paid through the court, but, third, we would also ask each how much was owed as well as paid in total, in a way that closely paralleled the Census questions.

Our sample consisted of families who were chosen randomly from court records of all couples with at least one minor child who filed Petitions for Dissolution (the first legal step in obtaining a divorce) in Maricopa County, Arizona, throughout calendar year 1986.[14] The first set of interviews, with 340 fathers and 271 mothers from 378 different families (about 70 percent of which featured interviews with *both* parents), took place within 2 ½ months of filing (before the divorce was final); these we refer to in what follows as the Wave 1 interviews. The Wave 2 interviews took place at the one-year anniversary date of the first interview (at this point 97 percent of the divorces were final). The Wave 3 interviews took place two years after the second, three years after Wave 1. Attrition from Wave to Wave was negligible. If the parent lived in Maricopa County, the interview was in person; if the parent resided elsewhere in the country, a full-length telephone interview was administered; if the parent resided out of the country, she or he was declared ineligible. Prospective participants were offered $20 for each interview.

We paid a great deal of attention to getting as representative a sample as possible. Our recruitment and location procedures resulted in an excellent interview rate as compared with other studies on divorcing families. In order to assess the representativeness of our sample of father respondents, we compared them to those who refused to be interviewed as well as to those we were unable to contact, on fifty-seven variables, such as demographic characteristics, specifications in the petitions, and provisions of their divorce decree. Only a few differences were found and these can be adjusted for. As a result of these findings, we can say that our sample is a good cross-section, neither over- nor underrepresenting various categories of families.

For this chapter, we concentrate on findings from our Wave 2 and Wave 3 interviews. The Wave 2 period was within a year after the formal divorce and so gives us a relatively early snapshot of child-support payments. Because there is mixed evidence as to whether payments decrease, increase, or stay constant in the years following divorce, we interviewed the couples again two years later.[15] Thus, Wave 3 provides a longer-term look at child-support compliance.

How Good Are the Official Records of Child-Support Payments?[16]

Although the divorce judges in Maricopa County had all been instructed not to approve divorce decrees unless they contained the provision that child support be paid through the clerk of the court,[17] a check of the divorce decrees of our sample families revealed that only 80 percent actually contained the provision; most of the remainder 20 percent didn't specify to whom payment should be made.

Even for those decrees that did specify that payments should be made through the clerk, however, the fathers might have paid the custodial parent directly. Why would fathers deliberately disregard the decree and circumvent the court? There were several reasons, we found. For starters, the clerk's office charged a small processing fee. Second, the clerk's office holds the funds for a day or two while logging in the payment.[18] Finally, many people simply didn't like the government getting involved in their personal business.

Additionally, the court or the clerk never initiated enforcement of the provision. They didn't regularly examine the files and bring to court anyone their records showed wasn't paying. Instead, enforcement waited until a custodial parent brought a complaint of arrearage. The case would then be prosecuted only if both the clerk's records substantiated the complaint and the noncustodial parent was unable to prove (by the production of canceled checks, for example) that he was paying directly.[19] As a result, mothers who regularly received child support payments directly wouldn't and couldn't easily make a change.

To investigate how frequent this direct payment practice was, we asked our respondents this question: "What percent of the child-support payments you have made (for custodial parents the phrase was 'your ex has made') were paid through the clerk of the court?" On the average, only 43 percent of the payments were reported to be made through the Clerk. In other words, over half of the funds were *paid directly* by the noncustodial parent to the custodial parent, once again bypassing the clerk and the court. In only 28 percent of the families did the mother and father both answer "100 percent" to the question. Once again, as in Garfinkle's study, we see that official records only reflect a part of the story explaining how much support is paid.

Our Survey Results

To get a more accurate estimate, we asked matched sets of custodial and noncustodial parents about child-support payments made and received after their divorce became final. To find out how much was *owed* in child support, we asked, "What is the total amount you were (your ex was) supposed to pay in child support in the last 12 months?" To find out how much child support was *paid*, we then asked, "How much money did you (your ex) actually pay in child support in the last twelve months?" Note that these were almost the identical questions

	As Reported by Custodial Parent	As Reported by Noncustodial Parent
Percent Paying None	13	4
Percent Paying Part	40	30
Percent Paying Full or More	47	66
Percent Paying More than Full	4	9
Percent Owing None	10	11

TABLE 2.1   Percentages Paying None, Full, Part, etc., as Reported by Custodial vs. Noncustodial Matched Parents

the Census Bureau asked. Table 2.1 presents the responses of both custodial and noncustodial parents in our sample.

A quick glance at our findings in Table 2.1 reveals what is hardly surprising once one recognizes the obvious: what mothers and fathers tell us diverges substantially. On all accounts, custodial parents—in most cases, mothers—report a much lower percentage of payments made than noncustodial parents—most often, fathers. For now, though, let's stay with only the custodial parents' responses. A closer examination of Table 2.1 reveals several points worth noting. In looking at the custodial parents' responses, we see that in 10 percent of families, the mother says there was no child support owed. Next, we see that, very similarly to the Census Bureau's finding that only half of all parents pay the full amount, we find 47 percent of custodial parents say they have received full child support. Of these, 4 percent said they were actually paid *more than* they were owed. Of the remainder, 13 percent of mothers claim to have received *no* child support, though they were owed some, and 40 percent claim to have received *partial* child support. Compared to the Census figures, our sample does a little better, in that about 15 percent less say they have received nothing, and a comparable amount more say they have received part.

But what about the "partial payments"? By this phrase do we really get an accurate account of how much child support was actually paid? Take the example of two mothers who were each supposed to receive $400 a month, for a total of $4,800 annually. Let's say one mother received $100 total for the year, and the other received $4,700 total. They would both be included in the "partial payment" group, yet obviously their situations are highly distinct. It makes a substantial difference whether the "percent paying part" paid hardly any, almost all,

Of Those Paying Part	As Reported by Custodial Parent	As Reported by Noncustodial Parent
Paid 1%–25%	30%	13%
Paid 26%–50%	20%	33%
Paid 51%–75%	23%	30%
Paid 76%–99%	28%	23%
Total	100%	100%
Median Percent Paid by Those Paying Part	49%	58%

TABLE 2.2 Breakdown of Those Paying Part (numbers rounded off), by Custodial vs. Noncustodial Matched Parents

or something in between. There are two ways to clarify this ambiguity. One way is to break down the group that made partial payments by what proportion they actually paid. This is done in the top of Table 2.2.

We see that roughly equal proportions of mothers who indicate that they have received partial payments report receiving up to 25 percent, up to 50 percent, up to 75 percent, and up to 99 percent, respectively. The bottom row of Table 2.2 shows that the median percent claimed to be received by custodial parents who reported receiving partial payments is 49 percent. (The median is the figure that half of the sample reports receiving more than and half reports receiving less than.) Thus it's fair to state that, on average, those who say they have received part of what they were owed report receiving half of what they were due.

Now let's turn our attention to the noncustodial parents' responses. When we look at what fathers have to say (in the second column of Table 2.1), the picture changes markedly. According to them, two-thirds report paying at least what they owed, and 9 percent claim they paid *more than* they were required to. According to fathers, only 4 percent pay nothing at all, and 30 percent report paying part. Looking at fathers' responses in the second column of Table 2.2, we see they report making partial payments in somewhat greater portions, with their median reported payment nearly 60 percent.

The next step we took was to calculate an overall payment statistic for the entire group of families by dividing the total dollar amount received by the total

	As Reported by Custodial Parent	As Reported by Noncustodial Parent
Average Amount Paid Annually	$2,718	$3,555
Average Amount Owed Annually	$3,692	$3,930
Ratio of Last Two Averages	.74	.91
Average of Paid Divided by Owed	.69[a]	.92[a]

[a]Excludes those reporting $0 owed.

TABLE 2.3   Average Amount of Child Support Paid and Owed and Compliance Rate, as Reported by Custodial vs. Noncustodial Matched Parents

amount they said was owed. Known as the "compliance rate," this figure expresses what percent of the amount owed was actually paid. These amounts are shown in Table 2.3.

The bottom figure is the compliance rate,[20] and shows that divorced mothers report receiving between two-thirds and three-quarters of what they are owed, a figure that is considerably less alarming than any previous portrayal of the extent of the nonpayment problem.

Turning next to what fathers report, it is interesting to note that they report that they *owe* even more than mothers say they do ($3,930 versus $3,692). However, they also report that they've *paid* much more ($3,555 versus $2,718). Putting these together into the compliance rate, we find that fathers report paying better than 90 percent of what is owed.

According to what divorced *fathers* tell us, then, child support nonpayment is barely a problem at all.

There remain two sides to the story when we ask mothers and fathers about child support paid two years later, at Wave 3. The results are in Table 2.4. Fifteen percent of custodial parents say their ex-husbands have paid nothing, but only six percent of noncustodial parents *agree* that they've paid nothing. The compliance figures are still disparate: 84 percent (down slightly from 92 percent two years earlier) according to fathers, 68 percent (down from 69 percent) according to mothers.

Viewing these results allows us to see what might have happened if the Census Bureau had made a decision to interview only fathers instead of only moth-

Child-Support Measures	As Reported by Custodial Parent	As Reported by Noncustodial Parent
Percent paying nothing	15%	6%
Average amount paid ($)	$2,462	$3,104
Average amount owed annually ($)	$3,439	$3,651
Average compliance ratio[a]	.68	.84
Sample N	155	
Percent owing nothing	13	12

[a]Excludes those reporting $0 owed.

TABLE 2.4 Child-Support Compliance as Reported by Noncustodial Parent and Custodial Parent at Wave 3

ers. Officials might then have gone before Congress and the media and reported that child-support compliance is a very small problem. Consequently, we would not be spending the billions that we are in child-support enforcement.

I am certainly not arguing that interviewing only fathers is what the Census Bureau *ought* to have done. I don't believe that noncustodial parents' reports should be uncritically accepted as truth, either. To me, it merely points out how erroneous the present practice of accepting the mother's report as truth without qualification is. When studying something as emotionally wrenching as divorce, it's nearly impossible for people to answer without bias. Indeed, *both* parents' reports are likely to be biased. In the absence of trustworthy objective official data to the contrary, it seems safest to assume that noncustodial parents are probably overstating child-support payments made, and custodial parents are probably understating. Thus, the truth lies somewhere in between, and our findings can best be thought of as "bracketing" true child-support compliance.[21] In short, we must conclude that how much child support is not being paid remains in substantial dispute, but the amount actually paid by divorced fathers is almost certainly higher than most official estimates. Deadbeat divorced dads are nowhere near as numerous as the stereotype portrays.

> ➤ In the absence of trustworthy objective official data to the
> contrary, it seems safest to assume that noncustodial parents
> are probably *overstating* child-support payments made, and
> custodial parents are probably *understating* it. Thus, the
> truth lies somewhere in between.

A point made early in this chapter and one that we will return to in subsequent chapters is made clear from these findings, and with hindsight is fairly obvious: *Asking any two divorced parents the same question about nearly anything will almost certainly garner far different responses.* There are two sides to every story, and up until now, it appears only one side has been recorded.

When Fathers Don't Pay

Though the compliance figures showed that more fathers were paying child support than believed, we wondered about the others. Why are these fathers not paying? Is it really that they simply *choose* not to, as the bad divorced dad image insists, or are they truly unable to pay?

In this chapter we present only one aspect of this answer, saving a more detailed discussion until Chapter 8. Briefly, we found that the single most important factor relating to nonpayment is losing one's job. For example, while the father-reported compliance rate at Wave 1 was 92 percent, this figure rises to 100 percent when fathers who experienced a period of unemployment are excluded from consideration. Thus, fully employed fathers tell us they pay every penny they owed. (According to the mothers' reports, the figure rises from 69 percent to 80 percent when including only those fathers who held their jobs for the entire year.)

This finding, that unemployment is the single most important factor relating to nonpayment, is consistent with virtually all past studies on the topic.[22] It belies the image that divorced fathers don't pay because they refuse to, though they are truly able to pay. As to be expected, when fathers lose their jobs, they temporarily cease providing for their children and families because they cannot afford to. It is a fascinating commentary on our view of divorced fathers that when fathers in intact families become unemployed, their financial support of their children similarly declines, but no one would ever think to accuse unemployed *married* fathers of irresponsibility. Instead, they get our sympathy.

Corroborating Our Results

How closely do the figures in the Maricopa County study represent *national* trends? The figures and conclusion we reached come very close to those found in the only other representative sample survey matching mothers and fathers, the two-state (Florida and Ohio) study entitled the Survey of Absent Parents (SOAP).[23] This project was commissioned in 1984 to the Urban Institute think-tank as a pilot study by the Office of Child Support Enforcement. The original intent was that a full-scale national survey would follow the pilot study. However, the sponsor subsequently withdrew funding for the full-scale national study after the pilot-study results, which strongly corroborated our findings, were released.

There has been speculation by fathers' rights groups that the full-scale study was decommissioned because of the controversy the pilot study, as well as my parallel findings, stirred up. Our convergent figures not only called into question how inconclusive the Census Bureau's findings have been, they cast doubt on the propriety of demonizing divorced fathers as we have. In 1988, when both my and the SOAP results were first made public, the idea that fathers were paying most of the child support they owed remained distinctly unpopular politically. Moreover, the far-flung federal bureaucracy involved with the child-support enforcement machinery would naturally feel threatened if the conviction became widespread that there might not really be a sizable problem with divorced fathers' child-support compliance, after all.

Early Reactions to Our Findings

While the pendulum seems finally to be swinging back to the point where it is acceptable for even the Office of Child Support Enforcement to question the bad divorced dad image, this wasn't yet true when we originally released this chapter's results, in 1988. At that time, we often encountered members of the academic community who dismissed or disparaged the findings. One incident illustrates particularly well this kind of prejudice.

I was in the audience at a 1988 conference at Arizona State University at which a well-known demographer—one of the most respected in the country—moderated the panel. One of the panelists, a researcher from the Census Bureau, spoke about her research on child support. Later, during the question-and-answer period, an audience member asked a question about Arizona's poor record in child-support collection. This posed a perfect opportunity for me to share my findings about the problems in trusting official records. I raised my hand and was given the opportunity to address the audience member's question. I explained how the official database statistics can be misleading and how I had taken the trouble to interview both mothers and fathers. I then repeated our results, which you've read earlier in this chapter.

At this point, the moderator stood up and said, "You know, I've heard about your findings. Our panel was discussing this very issue, of differences between mothers' and fathers' answers, over lunch. And what we concluded was if the mother tells you one thing and the father tells you something else, then the father is a God damned liar."

I was so flabbergasted, I could think of no response and sat down.

The demographer and panelists were hardly alone in this attitude. I found it was widely believed among mainstream social scientists in family research that fathers are not very good at reporting things. But I have yet to see any data that supports the belief that fathers either don't remember events as accurately as mothers or simply lie more. In the absence of convincing data that supports this view, those holding it are merely expressing their own prejudices, biases it would not be acceptable to express toward any other group. I can't imagine this man standing in a public setting and proclaiming that any racial, ethnic, or religious group—or even mothers, for that matter—were a bunch of "God damned liars." But until recently, it was socially acceptable even for academics to express such prejudices about fathers publicly.

The reaction of divorced fathers who learned of my findings was distinctly different. As one told me, "Up until now, I have felt like such a schlemiel; I thought I was the only man in America struggling to maintain my child support.

If no one else was paying, why was I? I can't tell you how encouraging your news was, that I was hardly alone, that many or most men were paying!"

Can We Eliminate Deadbeat Dads?

I am not arguing that there is *no such thing* as a deadbeat dad. To be sure, there remain some fathers in America who can afford to pay child support, yet withhold payment from their children. *Any* degree of child-support noncompliance creates a serious social problem. We certainly don't wish to be misconstrued as condoning *any* nonpayment of support whatsoever.

Yet, our findings demonstrate, more than was previously believed, that divorced fathers *are* voluntarily supporting their children financially, especially when they are fully employed. This fact runs counter to our society's insistence on perpetuating its divorced-dad image. Our knee-jerk reaction, to jail the deadbeat dads, may make us feel righteous, but we need to ask whether doing so is effective public policy, or merely an expression of outrage.

Policymakers understandably find irresistible the lure of forcing those rightfully responsible for children's financial status—the kids' fathers as well as their mothers—to pay their fair share. To the degree this can be accomplished, the tax-paying public is saved the responsibility of supporting these victims through welfare payments, and the policymakers reap a corresponding political dividend.

Perhaps that is why the federal Office of Child Support Enforcement has a $4 billion dollar budget,[24] and employs over 55,000 workers nationwide.[25] A recent child-support enforcement conference I attended featured thirty-nine private firms as "exhibitors," trying to woo the enforcement officials to expend some of their substantial enforcement budgets on the tools the company devised. But the coercive enforcement efforts we have gravitated toward have proven surprisingly ineffective in remedying the problem. We have become accustomed now to seeing headlines like that in the July 17, 1997, *New York Times* that reported "Child-Support Collection Net Usually Fails," noting that the General Accounting Office judged that "States have underestimated the magnitude, complexity, and costs of the projects and operations."

Even the seemingly surest method of guaranteeing payment, routine wage garnishment of child support, yields disappointing results. Professor Garfinkle (with Maria Klawitter, Ph.D.) reported in 1992 in the journal *Contemporary Pol-*

icy Issues that after instituting mandatory wage withholding of child support in Wisconsin, ten "pilot" counties collected only 2.89 percent more of what was owed than the ten "control" counties that didn't garnish. They "unfortunately" conclude that "routine income withholding has little effect."[26]

Apparently, the key to increasing the economic well-being of children of divorce remains the old and unglamorous one of solving unemployment and underemployment, both for the fathers and the mothers.

3.

Taking on Myth 2

The No-Show Dad

Donna was a student in one of my classes at Arizona State University. Once she heard about the kind of research I was doing, she volunteered to share her personal story.

> My parents divorced when I was nine. For a while, it wasn't so bad; I just lived in two houses instead of one, and I could never be with both parents together at the same time. But at least I still had two parents. My dad and I would spend a lot of time playing Monopoly and Risk. And charades—we loved charades.
>
> But things changed a lot about two years later. Dad found a girlfriend, Jennifer, and they started to live together. Dad pretty much stopped seeing me, then just disappeared from my life, like without warning.
>
> I can't tell you what that did to me. I was ten, and I felt the world had collapsed. What had I done wrong? Why did my father stop caring about me? How could he give me up for this woman? I stayed in my room and just cried and cried. I hid under the covers for days. Probably I would have killed myself, if I could have figured out how to do it. It really hurt bad and probably affected me most of the way through high school. I was a loner, and a stoner. I was just a sad, messed-up kid. And it started because I thought I wasn't worthy of my Dad's love.

Donna's story is a familiar one to anyone who has opened a book or newspaper, turned on the TV, or gone to the movies in the last decade or so. This image of the dad who simply stops showing up for his kids is reinforced regularly through our popular media. In the hugely popular sitcom "Grace Under Fire," about a blue-collar divorced mother, the father is almost never around, and when he schedules a visit with his kids, he more often than not fails to show up. On the rare occasions when he does make an appearance, it is usually disruptive, upsetting the whole family.

When we watch this and other shows that portray divorced dads as bumbling fools or worse—"no damn good"—we collectively nod our heads. "Yes, that's the way it is," we seem to be saying: "Divorced fathers *are* disconnected from their kids." Our beliefs are further reinforced by popular and respected books, such as *Fatherless America,* in which David Blankenhorn assails men for willingly abandoning their roles as fathers. "Historically, the principal cause of fatherlessness was paternal death. . . . Today, the principal cause of fatherlessness is paternal *choice . . . the rising rate of paternal abandonment,*"[1] he writes. (Italics added)

The Other Side of the Story

Have divorced fathers really voluntarily abdicated their role in their children's lives? How did such a popular belief take hold? As we looked closer at the past research, we came to the conclusion that this country has based its thinking on information provided by only one side of a two-sided story, as was the case with Donna's story. To get the broader picture, learn the rest of her tale.

> One day in my senior year in high school, I'm leaving to walk home after my last class, and who should drive by but Jennifer. She asks me to get into her car and go for a frozen yogurt. I have hated this lady almost all my life; she stole my daddy from me! But this time, for some reason, I just wanted to hear her out.
>
> She tells me that it really is sort of her fault that my dad stopped seeing me, but not the way I thought. It was mainly my mom: my mom hated the thought of dad being in love with another woman, and wouldn't let my dad visit me after he started with Jennifer. She says he tried to see me anyway; he even got a lawyer and called the police a few times. But my mom told him she'd never let him see me as long as he was with her. She told him she knew

there was nothing the police or the courts could really do if she hung tough, and she would. So my dad stopped seeing me.

I went home and asked my mom if the story was true. At first, she just lit up a cigarette and started to smoke it without speaking. Then she started to cry. When she finally spoke, she admitted it was true. She said that she became a little crazy after dad started living with Jennifer. She told me that after her anger wore off, a few years later, she felt really guilty for what she had done, but didn't know how to fix it. She was afraid I'd hate her, and she couldn't live with that; she'd rather I hated him.

I called my dad, and asked to see him. We had an incredibly emotional reunion. He told me it just about killed him when mom forbid him to see me, and he realized there was nothing he could really do about it. But he always kept up hope that someday I'd learn the truth, that mom would admit what she'd done, and that he'd get his little girl back. And now his prayers had been answered.

And I got my dad back!

The Conventional Wisdom

The idea that fathers were disappearing from their kids' lives partially stems from a study done in 1983 by Frank Furstenburg, Ph.D., and associates. Professor Furstenburg, who holds an endowed chair in Family Sociology at the University of Pennsylvania, is one of the most respected researchers on fatherhood issues in the nation. Using a huge, representative national sample, he and his fellow investigators reported that 49 percent of the children in their study had not seen their noncustodial parent *even once* in the preceding year and that only one child in six averaged weekly contact or better.[2] This eminent researcher speculates about why so many noncustodial parents withdraw from their children. "The significance of biological parenthood may be waning. . . . Biological ties to the child seem [now] to count for less."[3] He also believes it stems from "an unwillingness to provide child support."[4]

The media grabbed hold of this study and made it into a *cause célèbre*. In a *Newsweek* interview several years after his study, Furstenburg explained why so many fathers "just walk away . . . and take no responsibility for supporting the children they father." He argued that "the most intractable problem stems from the fact that many, if not most, noncustodial fathers are only weakly attached to their children. . . . There is a small group of fathers who are trying to do it all, and a much larger group of men who are doing very little."[5] This "much larger" group he gave the inciting term "bad dads."[6]

As these things tend to go, once the popular media report on a study in a big way, it takes on a life of its own. In the decade and a half that has followed Furstenburg's study, it continues to be quoted regularly in virtually every discussion on divorced fathers. It spawned the disparaging term "runaway dad," or as Furstenburg himself calls it, "disappearing dad."[7] As one academic paper gushed, "Considerable weight is given to these findings by . . . [those] . . . interested in the effects of divorce on children."[8] Furstenburg's findings, aided by his considerable credentials, gives academic and scholarly heft and weight to the media chorus deriding divorced fathers.

Examining Furstenburg's Findings

As influential as Furstenburg's findings were, in retrospect, a closer inspection reveals several points that must be considered when looking at the correspondence of his results with what we now know. First, similarly to the limitation of the U.S. Census Bureau survey on child-support compliance, Furstenburg's analysis does not distinguish between the never-married families and the divorced families.[9] As stated in the previous chapter, there is strong reason to believe that these two groups will behave differently. In fact, when Furstenburg's colleague Judith Seltzer[10] later broke down these groups into never-married fathers and divorced fathers in a 1991 article published in the *Journal of Marriage and the Family*,[11] she verified that their behavior was indeed vastly different. While 40 percent of the never-married fathers had no contact with their child in the past year, only 18 percent of divorced fathers had no contact.

The next point to examine is Furstenburg's source of information: his results are derived from the answers custodial mothers gave during surveys. As we discussed in Chapter 2, relying on only one parent's interpretation of events will lead to a conclusion that will be considerably different than if both sides of a story are given equal weight. In particular, the biases we discussed in the last chapter could easily lead mothers to underreport how much actual contact was taking place.

Furstenburg is not the only researcher to exclude the father from his studies. Almost every other respected researcher who has looked at the extent of contact with the father has based his or her findings exclusively on what the custodial mother reports in surveys.[12] As with the U.S. Census Bureau, few of the past researchers even mentioned the lack of fathers' answers as a limitation of the trustworthiness of their figures. Nor did they use any qualifying phrases, such as "according to the mother." They failed even to acknowledge that this one-sided reporting might potentially lead to bias.

Another issue occurs not in Furstenburg's study itself, but in the media's and policymakers' continued reliance on his results. Imagine citing data on social practices or problems from thirty years ago—be it drugs, out-of-wedlock births, crime rates, or racial and sexual discrimination—to form opinions and policies for today! Furstenburg's study is woefully out-of-date. The families, interviewed in 1981, had been divorced mostly in the 1960s. Many commentators have noted that cultural practices with respect to sex roles changed appreciably in the 1970s and 1980s, and that the current generation of fathers are more involved with their children and spend much more time with them than fathers did in the past. Also, in earlier decades, noncustodial parents who discontinued contact with their children after divorce may not have experienced social disapproval. With all the media reports on "new" fathers these days, that's no longer the case. A June 17, 1996, *Newsweek* poll, for instance, found that 70 percent of today's fathers of minors say they spend more time with their children than their fathers spent with them.

He Said/She Said . . . Again[13]

As with our approach to finding out the true picture of child-support compliance, in the absence of objective data on how often fathers visit, we determined that obtaining the reports of *both* mothers and fathers could at least bring us closer to reality than the past research. While fathers' reports are likely to be just as biased as mothers' reports, the two statements could be used to indicate a range of contact that brackets the truth.[14]

We asked both fathers and mothers in our sample how much contact the fathers were having with their children after divorce. As with our findings for child support, the responses of custodial and noncustodial parents in Table 3.1 significantly differ. No matter how we measured it (e.g., number of days, number of visits, number of overnights), the fathers' claims about how much time they spent visiting their children exceeded the mothers' reports. By three years after divorce, fathers reported as much as 40 percent more contact than mothers said they had.

Even taking into account the discrepancy between mothers' and fathers' versions, our results show dramatically more contact by noncustodial fathers than Furstenburg's findings. While Furstenburg determined that only 49 percent of fathers had contact with their children within the preceding year, we found that 90 percent had contact—by *either* parent's account (Chart 3.1). When we restricted our analysis of whether there had been any father-child contact within the preceding year to families in which the father and mother lived within the same town (which we defined as within 60 miles of each other), we found virtually *universal* contact. Additionally, five out of six fathers living within the same town three years after the divorce reported the equivalent of weekly contact[15]—compared with Furstenburg's finding of only *one* out of six; that's *five times* his proportion. Even more startling, two thirds of mothers in our study concurred with the fathers' reports.[16]

What could possibly explain the reasons for such a huge difference between our findings and Furstenburg's findings? They are almost mirror opposites. We have already mentioned many of the differences:

> Our study focuses on the current generation of fathers, whereas Furstenburg's fathers were divorced mainly in the 1960s, when fathers *were* less involved. More recent studies have showed consistently more contact than Furstenburg found.[17]

> We studied only *divorced* fathers, who must be distinguished from never-married fathers, who might well be more "weakly attached" to their children.

> We also provided the fathers' as well as the mothers' reports of contact, and as we have seen from Chapter 2, there are appreciable differences.[18]

We are not advocating that fathers should be unequivocally believed, while mothers' reports should be dismissed. But past research has prevented fathers

Wave 1 (Within 2½ months of filing for divorce)			How much greater than mothers' is fathers' report
	What fathers say	What mothers say	
Percent of total time in father's care	16.82%	12.65%	32.9%
Average hours per week in father's care	16.57 hrs.	13.57 hrs.	22.1%
Number of distinct visits last month	6.61 visits	4.82 visits	37.1%
Average number of days visiting last month	7.51 days	6.14 days	22.3%
Average number of sleepovers last month	3.07 sleepovers	2.54 sleepovers	19.9%
Longest period of time without seeing last month	6.31 days	8.61 days	36.5%

Wave 3 (3 years after Wave 1)			How much greater than mother's is father's report
	What fathers say	What mothers say	
Percent of total time in father's care	14.05%	10.01%	40.4%
Average hours per week in father's care	12.40 hrs.	8.94 hrs.	38.7%
Number of distinct visits last month	3.54 visits	2.85 visits	24.2%
Average number of days visiting last month	5.73 days	4.20 days	36.4%
Average number of sleepovers last month	3.52 sleepovers	2.51 sleepovers	40.2%
Longest period of time without seeing last month	9.13 days	12.57 days	37.7%

TABLE 3.1 Visitation Frequency: Mothers' vs. Fathers' Report

from even having their day in court to speak in their own defense. To deny this opportunity makes it far more likely that we will fail to recognize that *both* mothers' and fathers' reports are likely biased.

One final—and important—difference exists between our study and Furstenburg's that may further contribute to the huge discrepancy in results. Furstenburg's sample consisted of families that had been divorced for as long as 20 years (60 percent of the families had been separated in excess of ten years). If the divorces were this old, it stands to reason that so were the offspring. These were not *young* children Furstenburg was talking about, but teenagers or even young adults, who may no longer have been living at home or who may have had activ-

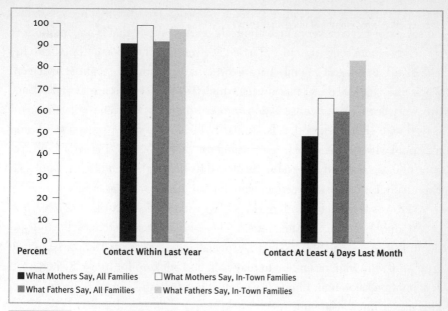

CHART 3.1   Amount of Father-Child Contact

ities they preferred to spending time with either their father *or* their mother. In contrast, we studied families who were divorced for only three years, and who had children age fifteen or younger.

Why Fathers Disappear

If our figures can be believed, between 67 percent and 83 percent of fathers living in the same town as their kids continue to see their children at least weekly three years after divorce. Such paternal devotion and tenacity is entirely at odds with the more popular image of the runaway, absentee, or disappearing dad.

Despite the vast difference in findings, it certainly remains true that at least some divorced fathers curtail or discontinue their contact as time progresses. Our research does, in fact, show what all previous studies have indicated: that contact drops off appreciably as time wears on.

According to the bad-dad myth, this invariably occurs because of only one reason: the father's lack of interest in his offspring. He stops visiting simply because he doesn't care very much about them. And surely that is one reason.

Gary is one such example. Married at twenty, he had been "roped into it," as he said, by Marcia's family because she had become pregnant at nineteen. Their marriage lasted six years, during which Trevor, now seven, and Melissa, age five, were born. Gary, a construction worker, admitted he had never been too involved with child-rearing details. Primarily, he liked to watch sports on TV and play pool with his friends. He felt cheated out of his youth by his early family responsibilities and had longed for the life led by his single friends at the pool hall. Eventually, his desire for freedom won out and he divorced Marcia.

"How is Gary doing with the kids?" we asked Marcia during her interview.

"Could be better," she answered. "He just doesn't seem to have the time for them. I'm concerned about Trevor, especially. He needs his Daddy. I can't do 'guy' stuff with him, teach him to play ball, and stick up for himself when a kid at school picks on him. I hope Gary gets it together and starts seeing these two kids more. They need him."

Gary confirmed most of what Marcia had said, when interviewed a few weeks later. "I try to see the kids a lot. I try. But things come up." He winked, conspiratorially. "Mostly females. I sure can't have the kids here when I have a babe over and we're up in my room, can I?" he asked, rhetorically. Although he was scheduled to have the children over for a visit the weekend after we talked, he was "going to have to reschedule it. Tiffany wants me to take her to the Grand Canyon."

Gary seemed unconcerned about any negative impact on his children of his cavalier attitude toward them. "Marcia's a great mom. She takes great care of the kids. With that kind of mother, the kids don't need to see me that much," he said, as if justifying his absence. "All they want to do when they come over is watch 'Power Rangers' on TV, anyway. They don't need me for that. And they know I love them. They know they can count on their Daddy."

But there is serious reason to doubt that Gary's kids really feel secure in their father's love. He has done little to demonstrate that "they can count on their Daddy." Gary's behavior is truly reprehensible. He is being irresponsible about his fatherhood, and in the process he is denying his children the benefits of a father. Of course, Gary is not the only one of his kind among the ranks of the recently divorced, and Marcia is not the only mother longing for her ex-husband to have more contact with his children. But for every Gary—the embodiment of the bad-dad image—we found many more fathers who were reliably seeing their children, often despite substantial obstacles. Though Gary's story fits the negative image, it is *not* the predominant scenario.

What Prevents Fathers from Seeing Their Kids More?

Complicating the whole picture is the often messy reality lurking behind the statistics. If a father sees his child only a very small percentage of the time, we know that merely as a fact. What we don't see are the myriad factors that may be outside his control that could prevent him from having the contact he may sincerely want.

> ➤ If a father sees his child only a very small percentage of the time, we know that merely as a fact. What we don't see are the myriad factors that may be outside his control that could prevent him from having the contact he may sincerely want.

One such factor, surprisingly overlooked by past researchers, is the divorce decree, which ordinarily spells out the "visitation privileges." While these privileges vary considerably from family to family, the most common provision is one that limits contact to every other weekend. What doesn't seem to have dawned on the promoters of the bad-dad image is the fact that to visit more could actually be a violation of the law. It took a divorced colleague to point out to me the double standard that divorce researchers (including myself) have used: while we routinely calculate the child-support percentage *compliance* (how much was paid *divided by* how much was owed), no research calculates percentage compliance for visitation (the number of visits taking place divided by the amount of contact allowed, by the decree or otherwise). We simply calculate visits, and leave the impression that anything less than a great deal must be the father's fault.

Yet regardless of what the decree says, a father's contact with his child *could in fact be* virtually limitless if the custodial mother permitted it to be so. She could easily—and with no outside interference—let him visit more than their decree stipulates. And some mothers, like Marcia, clearly want there to be more contact. But are these mothers the vast majority, as the bad divorced dad stereotype would have us believe?

Brian, one of the fathers I talked to while writing this book, told a far different story about his divorce.

According to Brian, he has battled with his ex-wife's interference of his visits with his six-and-a-half-year-old son for over five years. His ex-wife has sole custody of their son, who has Down's syndrome. Currently, Brian is allowed to have visits with his son for twenty-four hours a month. The arrangement is four hours on Thursdays and four hours every other Saturday. On Thursdays his allotted time is from three to seven P.M., an awkward time for most working people. In order to ensure he did not lose those hours, he had to make a number of adjustments in his work schedule.

Even with so little time allotted, Brian claimed he has had difficulty getting his ex-wife to uphold his visitation rights. In fact, since 1991, he said he registered with the police over eighty cases of visitation being denied. "On many occasions I've gone to pick up my son at his house and my ex-wife either doesn't answer the door or simply flat out refuses to allow me to see him. Other times she's simply not even home," he told me.

Brian said he has tried to get some redress from the police and the courts, and feels that they are truly sympathetic to him and his son, but has reluctantly come to the conclusion that the court has few tools to ensure that mothers permit visitation, as they do to ensure that fathers pay child support. When he's called the police, "That entails waiting two or three hours for the police to show up and then another hour with them. But because it's a civil and not a criminal matter, there's not much they can do. In a few cases, they'll write a report, but the court system can't really follow through on it. So I've given up on trying to get the courts to do anything."

If we can believe Brian's version of the facts (we were not able to interview his ex-wife in this case), his ex-wife prevents, restricts, interferes with, and otherwise makes it difficult for him to have contact with his child. In such cases, it would be difficult to blame the father for the low amount of contact. To use the term "bad dads" or to talk of "fathers' weak and waning ties to their children," as Furstenburg does, would be totally inappropriate. To justify using such terms, we'd have to know: When fathers do discontinue regular visits, why do they do so? How big a role does their own choice play? We will explore more subtle varieties of discouragement in Chapter 8. Here, however, we will address the question in the most blatant way: How often does an ex-wife actively block all or most visits or otherwise interfere? How many fathers could easily be visiting more if they chose to, like Gary, and how many are actively hindered by their ex-wives from more child-contact, as Brian claimed?[19]

To answer this question in our study, we asked both parents how many scheduled visits by the noncustodial parent were missed, and whether the custodial parent ever denied visitation. Knowing that custodial parents might be reluctant to admit denying visitation, we framed the question to them by asking if they "ever found it necessary to deny visitation." This way, we figured, they would be encouraged to admit the behavior more easily.

When we asked parents what proportion of scheduled visits were missed voluntarily by the noncustodial parents, we found that fathers claim they had missed only 3 percent of all scheduled visits, while mothers claim the fathers missed more, but still only 12 percent. However, when we asked whether the custodial parent had ever denied visitation, we found it is more frequent than previously believed. Fully a third of the noncustodial fathers claim they have been denied visitation privileges at least once, and—even more significant—*a quarter of custodial parents admit the denial.*

> When we asked whether the custodial parent had ever denied visitation, we found it is more frequent than previously believed. Fully a third of the noncustodial fathers claim they have been denied visitation privileges at least once, and— even more significant—*a quarter of custodial parents admit the denial.*

These findings are hardly unique and are, in fact, echoed in other studies.[20] Wallerstein and Kelly found that many mothers in their sample said they saw no value in visitation.[21] Sociologist Robert Weiss, author of the landmark book

Going It Alone, explains why that might be: Many custodial mothers "find non-custodial parents more nearly a burden than a resource. . . . He is someone to worry about. . . . The ways the other parent can be useful to the single parent are limited." This is especially true when the custodial parent remarries.[22]

In her research on the Expedited Visitation Service of Maricopa County, Arizona, a court program that enforces noncustodial parents' access to their children, published in *Family and Conciliation Courts Review* in 1995,[23] Cheryl D. Lee, Ph.D., has seen many instances of custodial parents interfering with visitation. While working in the service, she conducted research on visitation, interviewing over one hundred children. "In most cases, where the nonresidential parent claimed that visitation was being blocked, it was true," Lee related to me.[24] "While there were some instances where the interference was warranted, in many other circumstances the custodial parent had no justification for blocking visitation." Lee shared a couple of cases, which she believed were typical of many she came into contact with.

> *One of the cases involved a mother who was engaged to be married. The child, a very bright, very precocious boy of eight, persisted in expressing his need to see his father. But the mother not only discouraged visitation, she went as far as calling the police when he did come to pick up the boy. But there was no reason for it; there was no domestic violence involved. She just wanted her child to bond with his new father. The mother simply wanted to erase the boy's real father.*

In many cases, the custodial parent may not only block visitation, she may try to program her child's mind against the noncustodial parent. This practice even has a name: parental alienation syndrome.[25] Lee related a case that demonstrates this in action.

> *In this case, the mother completely alienated her daughter from the father. She didn't want him to have any place in her life. When it came time for visitation, she'd find all sorts of excuses to prevent the father from seeing his kid. When I interviewed the girl, she had been totally brainwashed against her father. She told me she didn't want to visit him. She didn't really have any reason, just that she had no interest in seeing him and didn't see why there was any reason she should do so. But I knew she wasn't expressing her*

own beliefs. She was actually parroting her mother, who had no use for her ex-husband.

Less Obvious Ways to Impede Visitation

A custodial parent who does not support the noncustodial parent's visits can find any number of ways of hindering them, short of outright refusal and parental alienation. She could insist on unacceptable conditions attached to the visit. ("Only if you don't allow your girlfriend to be over when they visit." "As long as you keep your mother away from the kid." "You want to see Jason, you tell him *you're* the one to blame for why our marriage broke up." "Only if you take them to church on Sunday"—said to an atheist father.) She could require him to pick up the child at an inappropriate place or an inconvenient time, like Brian was forced to do. Or she could attach additional unreasonable financial demands. For instance, one mother, who lives in Helena, Montana, was supposed to put her child on a plane for a summer visit with his father, who lives in Phoenix, Arizona. The cost of the fare was $300, which the father had agreed to pay. At the last minute, the mother decided to drive down to Albuquerque, New Mexico, for a vacation. She was going to take the child with her, where she would put him on a plane to Phoenix. However, she demanded that her ex-husband pay for all of her costs of the car trip, including *her* hotel bills, and *her* meals, or she would not let the child visit.

> ➤ **A custodial parent who does not support the noncustodial parent's visits can find any number of ways of hindering them, from outright refusal to insisting on unacceptable conditions or unreasonable financial demands.**

Another explanation we heard from some mothers as to why they block visitation is that they can't bear to be separated from their child. That was the situation that Geoffrey experienced with his ex-wife. "My daughter and I would have a trip planned that my ex-wife knew about ahead of time," he related. "At the last minute she would say, 'Oh, I just can't possibly be separated from her that long. She can't go.' "

Still another common obstacle occurs when the mother claims that the visits are too disruptive for the child or that the child does not *want* to visit. Sometimes when this happens, of course, the child will truly be reluctant to visit for natural and appropriate reasons, such as having extracurricular activities, plans with friends, or the occasional unpleasant experience during visits. But other times, the child has been brainwashed or programmed to refuse visitation, as we saw with the case Lee described earlier. And still other times, the mother has put a constant, subtle pressure on the child to drift away from the father. Such was the case with Marcy, one of the mothers in our study.

Marcy admitted how devastated she was when her husband Dan left her for his secretary.

> *I know I should have been bigger about this, a better sport. But you have to understand how it shattered me. So I encouraged the children to sympathize with me and to dislike their dad and Ruth, his new girlfriend. Whenever they said they thought Ruth wore too much makeup, I agreed and smiled. When they said they didn't like her cooking, I showed my pleasure. Eventually, as I'd secretly hoped, they allied with me against their father. And then they never wanted to go over when they were supposed to visit, and I didn't force them, and neither did Dan and Ruth. But later, the kids really needed a father figure and a male role model, and they no longer had one.*

Surely there are instances when it is in the child's best interests for the mother to act to limit visitation with their father, such as when there has been evidence of sexual abuse, drug or alcohol abuse, child abuse, or neglect. But according to our findings, and those of agencies like Cheryl Lee's, most cases don't come close to proving they have reached this threshold. They appear to involve either or both of two things: the custodial parent's efforts to control, punish or threaten the ex-spouse, which we have discussed earlier, or honest disagreements about child-rearing.

> ➤ Some custodial parents in our study became so concerned
> about minor differences in household routines that they used
> them as justification for a decision to prevent or hamper visi-
> tation.

Many custodial parents complained to us about minor differences in household routines, such as leniency about bedtimes, making sure homework was
done, eating routines, and the like. And some custodial parents became so concerned about these matters that they used them as justification for a decision to
prevent or hamper visitation. But we found that this tendency occurred primarily in mothers who were deeply angry at the fathers for hurts that occurred during or at the end of the marriage.[26] When a mother felt relatively little hostility
toward her ex-husband, she did not tend to get as upset by these child-rearing differences. Mothers who had better rapport with their ex-husbands were more
likely to see differences in parenting style as tolerable. I believe that many of the
mothers who hindered visitation because they disapproved of the father's child-
rearing actions would probably have been more accepting of the same practices
had it been a loving aunt's or grandparent's actions. In short, we found that many
mothers appeared to deny the fathers their right of access to their children arbitrarily.

A Double Standard?

While fathers who don't pay their child support risk criminal action and are typically punished and/or made to pay (and rightly so), in most cases mothers who
choose to can deny or hinder visitation without any repercussions. It's hard to
justify this disturbing double standard, pointed out particularly well by the following story.

A television news report was documenting the complicated and punitive
enforcement machinery the government has arrayed to ensure child-support
compliance. The truck driver father being interviewed admitted he was behind,

but said he stopped paying only after his wife arbitrarily refused to let him visit his children. He said he wanted to support his kids and would happily pay every penny he owed if he was allowed to see his children. But he said the children were exactly half his and half hers, and on principle he would rather go to jail than pay child support if his benefit in the bargain weren't upheld. The agency official who was interviewed confirmed that the father's facts were correct, but said the government hadn't developed any enforcement procedures to punish denial of visitation. He guessed that this imbalance was a reflection of current society's values: fathers should pay, and they will be seriously punished if they don't. Mothers should allow visitation, but . . . but nothing, at least for now.

According to the evidence we examined, vastly fewer fathers than conventional wisdom recognizes appear to have stopped seeing their children and become the runaway dads the bad divorced-dad image portrays. And what about the ones who *have* disconnected from their children?

The answer we have seen here and will explore further in Chapter 8 (where we will find strong evidence that withholding child support is substantially linked with visitation interference) suggests that nonvisitation, which is undeniably harmful to most children (as well as the father), is caused substantially by mothers' recalcitrance. Clearly, in the view of fathers, more contact is prevented by the choices of the custodial parent, not by their own choice. And most disturbing, many fathers whose visitation rights have been trampled on have little legal recourse to become what society loudly proclaims it wants of them: to be a father to their child.

4.

Taking on Myth 3
Standards of Living

What if one of the most significant pieces of social data of our time was flatly wrong, the result of a glaring arithmetic error?

In 1985, a book was published that immediately had a profound effect on how the general public viewed the economic impact that divorce had on women versus men, a book that, in the end, came to be recognized as having been based on flawed analyses, even according to its own author. Based on her comprehensive ten-year California study, the book, *The Divorce Revolution: The Unexpected Social and Economic Consequences for Women and Children in America,*[1] by Harvard[2] sociologist Lenore Weitzman, Ph.D., proclaimed that after a divorce, women and children suffer on average a 73 percent drop in their standard of living. Fathers, on the other hand, were actually found to *benefit* economically from the termination of their marriage, since whatever income they retained went to support only themselves. According to Weitzman, the average divorced man's standard of living increases by 42 percent. Weitzman's famous graph showing this disparity is reproduced in Chart 4.1.

If ever anyone needed any evidence to fuel their outrage against divorced fathers, to contribute to their bad divorced dad beliefs, or to inform them what is wrong with the divorce system and why so many men are moved to abandon their families, this was what they were waiting for. Social scientists, divorce professionals, some feminist writers, policymakers, and the media jumped on this news with all the zeal of a dog with a fresh bone. On the book jacket, the past President of the American Sociological Association called it "social science at its best"; a

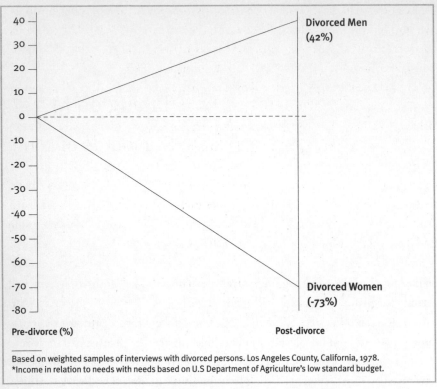

40 —
30 —
20 —
10 —
0 —
-10 —
-20 —
-30 —
-40 —
-50 —
-60 —
-70 —
-80 —

Divorced Men
(42%)

Divorced Women
(-73%)

Pre-divorce (%)   Post-divorce

Based on weighted samples of interviews with divorced persons. Los Angeles County, California, 1978.
*Income in relation to needs with needs based on U.S Department of Agriculture's low standard budget.

CHART 4.1 Professor Weitzman's Famous Graphic
Changes in Standards of Living* of Divorced Men and Women
(Approximately one year after divorce)

divorce judge was quoted as saying it would be "required reading for all lawyers and judges in family law"; and feminists Jessie Bernard and Betty Friedan gushed, respectively, "The book is a winner" and "I hope that Weitzman's compelling analysis and proposals will stimulate new legal thinking about the realities of equity and equality in divorce." An AP newswire story later printed widely in major newspapers around the country called Weitzman's findings "jaw-dropping, . . . [and] widely influential in the movement to change America's divorce and child support laws."[3]

It is probably impossible to overestimate how influential Weitzman's 73 percent figure was. Her data, for example, are widely cited in legislative debates, and she herself has testified before Congress. A search of databases found that over 175 newspaper and magazine stories have since cited Weitzman's numbers.[4]

Even this figure understates enormously the extent to which her findings have invaded popular culture. Like a virus out of control, Weitzman's results have surfaced in an unknown number of reports in which her figures are erroneously attributed to other sources. For example, in the January 24, 1993, edition of *The Arizona Republic* newspaper, an article stated, ". . . that observation is underscored by *U.S. Census figures,* which indicate that an average ex-husband's *income* increases 42 percent on average after a divorce, while an ex-wife's *income* declines 72 percent." The italicized words represent the errors in this quote. The writer provided the figure a bit inaccurately (72 percent, rather than 73 percent) and the statistic in question was misconstrued (it should have cited post-divorce *standard of living* rather than *income,* a distinction we'll return to later in this chapter); more important for our present point, the writer cited the wrong source (the U.S. Census Bureau rather than Weitzman's study). As a result, no database search keyed on Weitzman's name or her 73 percent number would have picked up this reference to her findings, which have so permeated the culture that journalists apparently regarded her conclusions as part of their store of "common knowledge," not requiring much in the way of verification.

When looking at academic sources, however, we are able to get a more accurate count of how widespread Weitzman's influence was. There were citations in 348 social science articles, 250 law review articles, and 24 appeals cases.[5] Her figures were characterized as "ranking among the most cited demographic statistics of the 1980s."[6] Furthermore, the U.S. Supreme Court cited Weitzman's figures in at least one of its cases, and even President Clinton cited the statistic in his 1996 budget request.

➤ If, according to Weitzman's findings, women experience a 73 percent decline in living standards, while men experience a 42 percent increase as a result of divorce, any fair-minded person has to agree there is something seriously askew with our divorce policies.

It would probably be fair to say that Weitzman's findings are the most widely known and influential social science results of the last twenty years. If women experience a 73 percent decline in living standards while men experience a 42 percent increase as a result of divorce, any fair-minded person has to agree there is something seriously askew with our divorce policies.

Weitzman's findings have prompted advocates to suggest that fathers must compensate mothers for this differential change in their relative economic prospects.[7] Proposals have ranged from a call for greater child support[8] or alimony levels[9] and/or disproportionate division of property favoring mothers,[10] to promoting far greater enforcement efforts to collect the child support ordered.[11] These calls have not gone unheeded. Secretary of the Department of Health and Human Services Margaret Heckler was quoted on the book jacket as saying that "Weitzman's insights and research were enormously valuable to us as we battled for a federal child support enforcement law with real bite." According to the AP newswire story, Weitzman's book "is credited with helping bring about stricter child-support enforcement and more flexible property-distribution laws around the country."[12]

Fathers Tell a Different Story

On the basis of Weitzman's figures, we expected to see fathers reaping a financial windfall from their divorces, or at the very least, living a rather comfortable existence. We hardly expected them to be complaining as much as mothers were about their financial condition. But as we began to talk to fathers for our own study, a vastly different picture began to emerge. These fathers were hardly describing a life of economic opportunity. Like many other fathers we talked to, Tom, a father of two young boys, lamented his reduced lifestyle after the dissolution of his marriage.

> *I lost the house. I lost the mini van. My wife got the furniture, she got the microwave, she got the TV and VCR. I had to dish out the money to replace almost everything in my life, starting with silverware, towels, and so on, all the stuff she already has. I don't have bicycles, games, video gear, or toys for the boys to play with unless I go out and buy them. And since I see the kids a*

lot, whenever they're over I have to pay for their food and entertainment, and whatever other expenses crop up—money never figured into the child-support calculation.

I take home $1,800 a month and pay $800 for child support. This may leave me with what sounds like a lot, but keep in mind: I am renting a one-bedroom apartment, while my ex-wife keeps the 1,700-square foot house with a swimming pool. Since we bought that house a long time ago, when housing prices were a lot lower, the two of us pay almost the same monthly payments for residences of far different quality. Plus, she's building equity, while I'm plunking down rent money and not getting the tax benefits of home ownership I used to get. I can tell you for sure, she's not so well off, but she's better off than I am. Don't believe the b.s. that fathers end up sitting pretty after divorce. I'm barely scraping by.

Can we believe Tom's story? Is he expressing a reality that many or even most divorced fathers face? Or do we believe Weitzman's figures that most fathers benefit from divorce while mothers and children face insurmountable odds in their struggle to get by?

The Mystery Data

As well-known and as influential as Lenore Weitzman's findings were to policy-makers and the general public, the professional research community was skeptical when the findings were first published. In particular, researchers, myself included, wondered how her results could depart so much from what others had found, findings with far less public attention. Chart 4.2 shows a graph of the economic decline other researchers have found for divorced women,[13] juxtaposed against Weitzman's findings. Despite the fact that Weitzman's findings disagreed with everyone else's, only her results were widely quoted by the press and politicians.

Two researchers who had conducted one of the related research studies depicted in Chart 4.2 were economists Greg Duncan, Ph.D., and Saul Hoffman, Ph.D. As noted, they had found only a 30 percent average decline in divorced women's standard of living. In an effort to understand the huge discrepancy, they attempted to contact Weitzman. Feminist writer Susan Faludi, in her provocative 1991 book *Backlash,* recounts an interchange between Hoffman and Weitzman.

> *Hoffman's letter [to Weitzman] wondered if he and Duncan might take a look at her data. No reply. Finally, Hoffman called. Weitzman told him "she didn't know how to get hold of her data," Hoffman recalls, because she was at Princeton and her data were at Harvard. The next time he called, he says, Weitzman said she couldn't give him the information because she had broken her arm on a ski vacation. "It sort of went on and on," Hoffman says of the next year and a half of letters and calls to Weitzman. "Sometimes she would have an excuse. Sometimes she just wouldn't respond at all. It was a little strange. Let's just say, it's not the way I'm used to a scholar normally behaving." Finally, after the demographers appealed to the National Science Foundation, which had helped fund her research, Weitzman relented and promised she would put her data tapes on reserve at Radcliffe's Murray Research Center. But six months later, they still weren't there. Again Hoffman appealed to NSF officials. Finally, in late 1990, the library began receiving Weitzman's data. As of 1991 the archive's researchers were still sorting through the files and they weren't yet in shape to be reviewed.[14]*

When I read this passage in *Backlash,* it seemed like déjà vu. I, too, had been curious about Weitzman's findings, because, in some previous work,[15] I had attempted similar analyses, using the same method she and Hoffman and Duncan used (a method I now believe—and will later argue—has serious deficiencies), and got a figure of a 26 percent drop in standard of living for divorced mothers, very close to every other researcher's results except Weitzman's. I, too, had called her, in late 1989, to ask some questions about exactly how she had gotten her figures, since I wanted to replicate her procedures as closely as possible with my own sample. She told me she didn't remember or couldn't answer any of my questions because a graduate student had actually conducted the analyses, and the data tapes were in a state of disarray. She mentioned that other researchers around the country were in communication with her also, having trouble corroborating her findings.

Then I asked her the loaded question I had prepared. "You know, Dr. Weitzman, I have an idea I want to run by you about why your results were so different from everyone else's. When I first attempted my analyses on mothers and picked up my computer printout, I looked at the bottom line and saw the figure 74 percent. I thought to myself: 'a 74 percent drop—almost exactly the same figure Professor Weitzman found.' But then I paused a minute and remembered what figure I had programmed the computer to give me: 'What percent of the former, pre-divorce standard of living, is the present, post-divorce standard of living?' It was *that* figure that was 74 percent. But that figure means the *drop* is only 26 percent, much like what others have found. [If one's income was $10,000 and is *now* $7,400, it is currently 74 percent *of its former value*, which is a 26 percent *drop* in income.] I wondered: 'Is my mistake possibly one that Professor Weitzman made as well? Would that account for her weird finding?' What do you think, Dr. Weitzman, is that possibly a mistake you also made?"

There was silence, except for labored breathing on the other end of the phone. I determined not to say anything more. I waited a very, very long time. Finally she answered, "I'm not sure I can rule out what you said. I'll investigate it and get back to you." And she hung up.

But she never got back to me.

Seven years later, in June 1996, she was heard from in another way. Richard R. Peterson, Ph.D., a sociologist at the Social Science Research Council, was another researcher who was dubious about the finding. He was finally able to obtain Weitzman's computer files and the paper records she provided to Radcliffe's Murray Research Center. Upon reanalyzing Weitzman's very own data set, he writes, he could never duplicate a figure anywhere close to what Weitzman reported, and couldn't see where her number came from. Instead, the figure he arrived at showed that the divorced women in Weitzman's sample really experienced a 27 percent drop in standard of living, *exactly the figure she would have gotten if she corrected the potential error I specified.* He also noted that his reanalysis of her fathers' circumstances yielded a far milder 10 percent rise in standard of living. He published his article containing these findings in the *American Sociological Review.*[16] Dr. Weitzman was asked to write a rejoinder article. Amazingly, rather than contradict Peterson, Weitzman very belatedly acknowledged that her original figures were wrong.[17] According to the AP wire story accompanying the publication, "she blames a mistake in computer calculations performed by a Stanford University research assistant. But 'I'm responsible—I reported it,' she says."[18]

In light of her admission, it is astonishing to realize that arguably the most influential social scientific finding of the last twenty years, in terms of policies enacted in reaction, is in all probability the result of a simple mathematical mistake—a mistake that could have been corrected seven years earlier when first brought to Weitzman's attention.[19] It is most disturbing to me that a respected fellow social scientist took so long, and had to be "backed into a corner" by several critics, before she'd come forward with the admission that an error had been made, especially an error that was so consequential and affected as many lives as hers did.

I believe this error, like many of the other problems we document throughout this book, is partly the result of the ideological biases of the researcher. Mistakes can happen to anyone, even Harvard professors.[20] But instead of questioning and double-checking her anomalous finding, putting it under the normal scientific scrutiny, Weitzman apparently accepted the erroneous finding at face value because it fit with the woman-as-victim stereotype she preferred to believe. And despite the fact that it deviated so much from other findings, partisan writers such as Monica Allen,[21] Sandra Butler and Richard Weatherly,[22] Martha Fineman,[23] Martha Haffey and Phyllis Cohen,[24] Sylvia Hewlett,[25] Barbara Lonsdorf,[26] Marygold Melli,[27] Sharon Seiling and Harriet Harris,[28] Barbara Woodhouse,[29] Nancy Polikoff[30] (who wrote that "the serious research in this book should form the basis for much needed legal reforms"), and Susan Okin[31] (who wrote that the findings "are far less surprising than is the fact that people have been so surprised by them") cited them without question.[32] And it caught the popular imagination for the same reasons. It fit too well the image our society had adopted for us to question it. It "proved" what we wanted to believe: Divorced moms suffer, while bad divorced dads profit.

A Faulty Equation for Standard of Living

Even Peterson's *correction* of Weitzman's figures—that women experience a 27 percent drop in standard of living, while men experience a 10 percent rise—may be giving us a picture that seriously inflates the extent of the imbalance. To depict "standard of living" results, Weitzman, like virtually every other researcher, including ourselves,[33] had used the "needs adjusted" technique, a method based on federal government–published figures concerning what level of resources it takes to maintain identical living standards for families of different composition.

These figures are known as "equivalence scales." Before we get into how these equivalence scales work, let me first explain what is meant by "standard of living."

In its simplest definition, standard of living means how well people can afford to live. For instance, a family that can only afford to eat mostly starch-based meals has a lower standard of living than one that can frequently afford to buy prime cuts of meat or go out to fancy restaurants. Likewise, a person whose budget forces him to drive a 10-year-old economy car would have a much lower living standard than someone who buys brand-new luxury imports every three years.

In figuring equivalence scales for standards of living, many analysts, including Duncan and Hoffman, and Peterson,[34] have used the "poverty level" as a base line. And the poverty level varies depending on the family size and configuration. For instance, as of 1987, the year the parents in our study became divorced, the poverty level for a family comprised of two parents and two children (what the government considers the *base family*) was $11,519 a year; for a family of one parent and two children, it was $9,151 (79.4 percent of the base family's income); and for a single adult with no children it was $5,909 (51.3 percent of the base family's income).[35] (In 1997, the poverty levels were $16,276 for the base family, $8,350 for the single adult/no children family, and $12,931 for the one-parent/two-child family.[36] The latter two figures are virtually the identical proportions of the base family as in 1987.)

The reason the figures don't go down exactly in proportion to the number of people in the household (for example, why a one-person household is 51.3 percent and not 25 percent of the level for a four-person) is that the index takes into consideration the fact that while some expenses, such as food and clothing, are *variable,* that is, they're directly related to the number of people in the household, many other expenses, such as rent and utilities, are *fixed,* and would remain about the same no matter how many people were living in the household.

If we take a given family's income and put it in a ratio with (i.e., divide it by) the poverty level for a family of its exact size and composition, we get its income in relation to what a family of its size *needs* to barely escape poverty, or what's called the "needs adjusted income" index (also called the "income-to-needs ratio").

Using these figures, let's make up a hypothetical but typical family and see

	Jeff	Rachel	Combined
Pre-Divorce Salary	$31,000	$16,733	$47,733
Pre-Divorce Needs[a]			$11,519
Pre-Divorce Income-to-Needs Ratio			4.14
Post-Divorce Salary	$31,000	$20,000	
Child Support	($6,000)	$6,000	
Total Income after Child Support Paid	$25,000	$26,000	
Post-Divorce Needs[a]	$5,909	$9,151	
Post-Divorce Income-to-Needs Ratio	4.23	2.84	
Post-Divorce/Pre-Divorce	102%	69%	
Gain/Loss	2%	−31%	

[a]Our calculations use the 1987 poverty levels in both pre- and post-divorce needs computations.

TABLE 4.1   **Figuring Rachel & Jeff's Post-Divorce Changes in Standard of Living**

how divorce might affect their standard of living (the calculations are summarized in Table 4.1). Since our sample became divorced in 1987, we will be using 1987 figures throughout the chapter. Later, we'll report the computations on our *real* families.

Let's assume that Rachel and Jeff have two children. Before divorce, he earned $31,000, while she earned $16,733. Their combined family income was therefore $47,733, 4.14 times the poverty level, giving them an income-to-needs ratio of 4.14 ($47,733 divided by $11,519). They divorce, and Rachel gets custody of the two children. Suppose that after the divorce, Jeff pays $500 per month or $6,000 annually in child support, and Rachel increases her work hours (as most mothers in our sample in fact do) and now earns $20,000. Her combined income including child support she receives is $26,000. Hers is now a one-parent/two-child household; the poverty level for this sort of family is $9,151.

For Rachel's *standard of living* to remain the same, exactly 4.14 times the poverty level, she would have needed to take in $37,885 ($9,151 × 4.14) in total, in salary and child support. Instead, her income-to-needs ratio is now only 2.84 ($26,000 divided by $9,151). So her standard of living is now only 69 percent of what it was (2.84, the post-divorce income-to-needs ratio divided by 4.14, the pre-divorce income-to-needs ratio); it has declined 31 percent. (If the ratio of post-divorce divided by pre-divorce standard of living is less than 100 percent, subtract the number from 100 percent to get the percent drop or decline. If the ratio of post-divorce divided by pre-divorce standard of living is *more* than 100 percent, subtract 100 percent from the number to get the percent gain.)

Jeff's is now considered a single adult/no children household; the poverty level for him is $5,909. For Jeff's standard of living to stay the same, again exactly at 4.14 times the poverty level, he would need to have $24,463 ($5,909 × 4.14) left in income after paying child support. Instead, he actually has a little more, $25,000, left. His income-to-needs ratio is now 4.23 ($25,000 divided by $5,909). His standard of living is now 102 percent (4.23 divided by 4.14) of what it was before the divorce, a gain of 2 percent.

Although this method seems fairly straightforward in figuring out how divorce might affect standards of living, I came to recognize that the method used by Weitzman, and sometimes others (including us) in calculating the "needs adjusted income" was highly misleading and seriously inaccurate for several reasons, which I'll describe in detail next.

Problem 1: The Tables

Imagine that you wanted to buy a new car. First, you need to figure out what your budget can afford. Then you need to see what model car will fit your budget. Now suppose, instead of looking through your daily newspaper for prices of cars, you look at newspapers that were printed more than twenty years ago. Sounds silly, doesn't it? Well, that's exactly the problem Weitzman encountered in relying on the government-published tables she used in calculating "needs adjusted incomes." The equivalence scales she used were the Bureau of Labor Statistics "1977 Lower Standard Budget."[37] The problem is, these tables were prepared based on a 1960–61 survey, the Survey of Consumer Expenditures. A special government review panel was formed in 1980 to investigate these tables[38] and concluded that the equivalence scales were badly out of date. In particular, the panel recognized that fixed expenses, like housing costs, had risen disproportionately compared to variable expenses, like food costs. For example, according to the Lower Standard Budget tables published prior to

1980, single individuals (such as noncustodial parents) needed only 36 percent of the income of the base family to maintain the same living standard, but they found that a more accurate figure was slightly over 50 percent. They recommended phasing out the Lower Standard Budget reports; they were actually discontinued by 1982, and replaced by other equivalence scales, such as the poverty thresholds. Thus, Weitzman's comparison figures were already out of date by 1985, when she published her book. Even Peterson's reanalysis, attempting to exactly repeat what Weitzman had done, was based on the out-of-date equivalence scales.

How would this one change have affected Weitzman's/Peterson's analyses? Recall that when we used the appropriate poverty thresholds in Table 4.1, we found a 31 percent loss for Rachel and a 2 percent gain for Jeff. But had we used the out-of-date Lower Standard Budget tables instead, as Weitzman did, the comparative figures would have been far more disparate—a 20 percent loss for Rachel and a whopping 42 percent gain for Jeff.

No wonder she found such a discrepancy in the impact!

Problem 2: Taxes

As every taxpayer knows, it is only what's left after the IRS and the states have taken their cut from one's paycheck that can be spent to support the family. Clearly, then, it is the *after-tax* income, not the *gross* income that affects standard of living. And that's where another problem with the needs adjusted income method comes in. Weitzman's calculations were based on *gross* income, before taxes had been paid. Thus, they failed to take into account what we found out when we investigated the tax code, with the help of a professional accountant[39]: the fact that custodial parents are taxed differently, and more advantageously, than noncustodial parents in at least five respects. Renowned economist Thomas Espenshade, coming to a similar recognition in 1979,[40] called for a recalculation corrected for tax consequences, but until now no researcher, including Peterson (who, as we noted earlier in this chapter, recalculated Weitzman's data), has done so.[41]

Our analysis was completed using both our Wave 1 data (for before-divorce values) and our Wave 2 data (for after-divorce values.) Since our sample was based upon families divorcing in calendar year 1986, our Wave 2 data applied to income and expenses incurred in 1987. In 1987, Federal tax law provided custodial parents—usually mothers—with the following five distinct tax advantages either not available at all or not fully available to noncustodial parents—usually fathers. (In what follows, as is the book's convention, we will simply use the terms mothers and fathers to recognize the typical case, keeping in mind that it doesn't apply where custody is given to the father. We also give the 1997 figures for the various tax provisions.) Mothers benefit in the following ways:

1. Tax-free Child Support Income

When a father pays child support to his ex-spouse, he must pay federal (including social security or FICA), state, and local taxes on this amount. In contrast, when the mother *receives* the child support, she doesn't have to pay any taxes on it, unlike most other income. (Alimony has the opposite tax status.) Consequently, fathers pay all the taxes on the child support amounts while mothers get to keep the full amount.

2. A Tax Credit for Child Care

Mothers are allowed to credit a percentage of the amount they spend on child care each year "off the top" of their tax debt (as the "Child Care Credit"). This credit may cancel as much as $1,440 yearly (in either 1987 or 1997) of the mother's tax debt. Interestingly, fathers are not allowed to take advantage of this credit even when they are forced to pay for child care when the children are in *their* care, such as summer visitation.

3. A Lower Tax Rate

As a single parent, the mother receives the benefit of being classified as "head of the household." As such, the mother's income is taxed at a lower rate than the father's, whose tax status is now "single." For example, if both Jeff and Rachel had taxable income (after exemption and deductions) of $22,000, Jeff would have had to pay $707 more Federal tax on it than Rachel (in 1987; the differential was removed by 1996). This head-of-household versus single status applied to many state tax codes as well as federal.

The mother can be declared a head of the household even if she is not the one who is primarily providing for the children's material needs. So even if the father is the parent mainly supporting his children, it is the mother who benefits from this special tax status.

4. Extra Exemptions

Mothers are allowed to claim the children as "exemptions" (worth $1,900 each in 1987; $2,650 by 1997), whereas fathers generally can claim only the exemption for themselves.[42]

5. A Tax Credit for Low Earners

Many mothers (but no noncustodial fathers in 1987) qualify for the "earned income credit," if their "earned" income (exclusive of child support) is less than $15,432 (in 1987; $29,290 in 1997). This means a tax credit of up to $851 ($3,656 by 1997).

(As of this writing, Congress had just passed another substantial new tax benefit, a $500-per-child annual tax credit, available only to married parents or the divorced parent *with custody*.)

How would these benefits affect our typical family? (The calculations are summarized in Table 4.2.) First let's figure their pre-divorce after-tax standard of living. Assuming the family last lived together in 1985, resided in Arizona, and claimed the standard deduction, their pre-divorce Federal tax would have been $8,820; their state tax would have been $1,967; and they'd pay FICA of $3,365, leaving $33,581 after taxes. Now, dividing that figure by the 1987 poverty level, their after-tax-income-to-needs ratio would be 2.92.

Now let's see what happens to Rachel after divorce, in 1987. Her FICA would be $1,430. Assuming she paid about $100 per week for child care, her child care credit would be $1,200, reducing her Federal tax to only $464. (Her earned income would be too high to qualify for any of the earned income credit.) Her Arizona state tax would be $453. After subtracting these taxes, but adding her child support received, she would have $23,653 left as after-tax income. Now her after-tax-income-to-needs ratio (using the 1987 poverty values) would be 2.58 ($23,653 divided by $9,151). This is 89 percent of its former level (2.58 divided by 2.92); only an 11 percent drop, as compared to the 31 percent drop she showed before taking taxes into consideration.

What about Jeff? His FICA would be $2,217. His Federal Tax would be $5,185 and his state tax would be $1,285. After subtracting these taxes, as well as subtracting the child support he paid, he would have $16,313 left as after-tax income. His after-tax-income-to-needs ratio (using the 1987 poverty cutoffs) would be 2.76 ($16,313 divided by $5,909). This is 95 percent of its former level (2.76 divided by 2.92). So after taxes, he no longer enjoys a very slight standard of living *gain,* as he appeared to before-taxes; now he suffers a 5 percent *loss,* very comparable to her 11 percent after-tax drop.

Problem 3: Expense Allocation

Another big problem with the needs adjusted income method is that it makes what we labeled the "sacrosanct household" assumption. That is, it assumes that *all* the family units' income and *only* the family units' income goes to support only *that* household's members. Put another way, it assumes that a single person spends all after-tax income to support only him- or herself, and that a family provides for all its members' needs out of only its own after-tax income. This is an entirely reasonable assumption for unrelated households, for which the tables were originally designed.

But, when applied to a divorced family, as Weitzman and others did, the assumption is no longer valid at all. Supposedly, the issue was addressed by taking child support (and alimony) away from father's income and adding it to mother's income. But this would provide an appropriate corrective only if child support and alimony were the only monetary transfers between the households. In actuality, child support and alimony represent only a portion of the expenses for the children typically assumed by fathers. Divorced fathers almost always make a series of substantial financial expenditures for their children that are over and above or distinct from child support. They include but are not limited to:

Clothing Expenses

For example, two-thirds of our fathers report that they have bought some of their children's clothing themselves. In an intact family (which is the assumption of the government-published needs ratios), all such expenses would figure into that household's "needs"; in a divorced family, however, the mother's "needs" will actually be reduced (since she doesn't have to pay all her household's cloth-

	Jeff	Rachel	Combined
Pre-Divorce Salary	$31,000	$16,733	$47,733
Federal Tax[a]			($8,820)
State Tax[b]			($1,967)
FICA[c]			($3,365)
After-Tax Income			$33,581
Pre-Divorce Needs			$11,519
Pre-Divorce Income-to-Needs Ratio			2.92
Post-Divorce Salary	$31,000	$20,000	
Federal Tax	($5,185)	($464)	
State Tax	($1,381)	($453)	
FICA	($2,217)	($1,430)	
After-Tax Income	$22,313	$17,653	
Child Support	($6,000)	$6,000	
Total	$16,313	$23,653	
Post-Divorce Needs	$5,909	$9,151	
Post-Divorce Income-to-Needs Ratio	2.76	2.58	
Post-Divorce/Pre-Divorce	95%	89%	
Gain/Loss	-5%	-11%	

[a]The 1985 federal tax code provides a deduction for a two-earner married couple. However, since we did not obtain separate incomes for each spouse pre-divorce, we could not calculate it.
[b]The state tax gives a deduction for income taxes paid in 1985. We assumed the couple paid only what was owed.
[c]There is a cap on FICA. However, the cap applies to each wage-earner separately. We did not obtain this separate income.

CHART 4.2   **Figuring Rachel & Jeff's *After-Tax*
Post-Divorce Changes in Standard of Living**

ing expenses herself), and the father's "needs" will actually *increase* (since he is now paying the clothing expenses of a different household). This shifting of expenses across households is in no way taken into account by the needs adjustment method.

Visitation Expenses

Similarly, but with substantially greater monetary impact, during weekly visitation, fathers must bear food, child care, child transportation, and recreation expenses for the children. Mothers, during these times the children visit the father, don't have these expenses. And most fathers are ordered to continue paying child support to the ex-spouse even during lengthy summer visitation. If the children reside with the father six weeks to three months during the summer, the father may end up actually paying *twice* to support his children during these times. But the needs adjustment method gives *her* full credit for bearing child-oriented visitation expenses and gives him *no* credit.

A recent study was conducted by economist James Shockey, Ph.D., for the state of Arizona to correct the state's guidelines for child support calculations by taking into consideration the expenses borne by the father during visitation. Shockey observed, as we pointed out earlier, that the costs to the father of visitation had never been properly taken into account. For instance, a typical household would be responsible for twenty-one meals a week for each of its members. However, in a divorced family where a child spends Friday night to Sunday night with the father, they will eat seven meals under the father's care. The custodial mother will therefore be responsible for only 14 meals a week. Yet, typical child-support awards expect the father to compensate the mother for 21 meals.

Phoenix attorney Bruce R. Cohen, a family law specialist who served on the committee that recommended revisions to the Arizona state child support guidelines, explained how the committee approached the problem[43]: "In trying to identify how we can quantify the time that dad has with the children as it relates to child support, we looked at which expenses tend to 'travel with the children,' such as meals, recreation, and driving children to and from activities. We estimated that about 68.5 percent of the expenses for children are affected by visitation in one form or another. The way that breaks down is like this: If we know that the children's expenses are $1,000 a month under the statistical average, about $685 of that will be incurred based on which parent has the children on any given day. If the children are with the custodial parent 75 percent of that month, then 75 percent of that $685 will be incurred by her. Conversely, 25 percent of the $685 will be incurred by the noncustodial parent. The other $315 of that $1,000 is not affected by visitation. Those are fixed expenses, such as the custodial parent's mortgage payment."

As a result of these calculations, the child support guidelines were lowered by certain percentages effective October 1996. For instance, if the children spend between 20 and 30 percent of the time with the father, under the new guidelines, he will pay 18.7 percent *less* in child support a month than he did previously. As the father spends more or less time with the child, the adjustment goes up or down accordingly.

According to Cohen, "What we have historically seen, due to the fact that we did not adjust for these expenses that travel with the children, is that noncustodial parents are paying higher child support than the reality would dictate. These corrections come closer to mirroring reality than did the old guidelines." But, he emphasizes, "Until we get a statistical base that we can rely upon made up of *divorced* families rather than *intact* families, all we can hope for is that we're coming closer to reality. The bottom line is that these corrections have better recognized that noncustodial parents have expenses that should be accounted for when we determine the child support award."

A New York appeals court in March 1997 came to a similar conclusion in ruling in the case of Gregory and Diane Holmes. According to the *Albany Times Union* news story on the case, Gregory had "initially been ordered to pay 25 percent of his gross income ($236 per week or $12,272 per year) to support his two children." The children spent two nights a week with their father and three nights a week with their mother, and alternated weekends. Thus, the children spent 40 percent of their time in their father's care, and 60 percent in their mother's. The court noted that, had the couple changed only one more night per week to the father, *he* would have had the majority time and been considered the custodial parent, in which case he would *receive* child support from his ex-wife (about $200 per week or $10,400 per year), rather than *pay* it. Recognizing that this huge shift in payment (from *paying* $12,000 to *receiving* $10,000, a turnaround to each parent of $22,000 per year) was ludicrous in view of the fact that it was awarded on the basis of only one extra night per week, the court realized that the very foundation of the argument about how much child support was due was flawed and admitted it had to use a different standard. "The Appellate Division of the New York State Supreme Court found that the Holmeses are [both] simultaneously custodial and non-custodial parents. Therefore she is required to pay him 25 percent of her income and he is required to pay her 25 percent of his income." They ordered only the net difference to change hands as child support.

We shall not address in this book the debate about whether or by what amount child support ought to be adjusted depending upon how much time the father spends with the child, except to note that most states' payment guidelines do not take this sometimes very appreciable factor into account. Laws that don't do so raise the financial stakes enormously for being declared custodial parent, and thus encourage court battles over custody. Laws that *do* permit an adjustment, on the other hand, will typically, as in Arizona, lower the amount of child support to be paid, according to the amount of time the child spends with the father. This puts a double incentive on fathers to push for, and mothers to oppose, more visitation, and may well encourage court battles over visitation schedules. On the other hand, it should more fairly allocate the costs of raising the children between the parents.

A Better Approximation of Expenses

While it is not our purpose to choose a side in the debate about whether child support should be adjusted depending upon visitation, it *is* our purpose to assess the financial impact of divorce on fathers as compared to mothers. No previous economic analysis has attempted to allocate the visitation and clothing expenses between the households (presumably because previous analysts believed, on the basis of the erroneous findings detailed in Chapter 3, that visitation was hardly ever actually occurring). However, evidence cited in Chapter 3 indicates that visitation with the noncustodial parent is far more frequent than previously believed, which means that past analyses of gender differences in economic impact of divorce substantially overstated its relative harm to mothers and its relative benefit to fathers.

One method we devised to account for the visitation and clothing expenses on the parents' relative financial well-being after divorce was suggested by the Arizona analysis, which estimated that 68.5 percent of expenses due to children "travel with the children." The poverty level estimation of the cost of Rachel and Jeff's two children is $3,242 ($9,151—the poverty level for a one-parent/two-child household—minus $5,909—the poverty level for a single-adult household). Suppose Rachel and Jeff have a "typical" visitation schedule: One day a week and every other weekend. This means that the children are with Jeff for eight days in the typical month or 26.7 percent of the days. Of the $3,242 which the children cost the poverty level family, 68.5 percent (or $2,221) is for expenses that travel with the children, while the remaining 31.5 percent (or $1,021) stays with the residential parent, Rachel. Jeff cares for the children 26.7 percent of the time, so bears that proportion of the $2,221 children's expense that travels with them, or $593. This means that, for Jeff, the needs standard we should use is a combination composed of the single-adult level of $5,909, plus $593, i.e., the expense due to children that travel with them, for a total of $6,502. Rachel's needs standard, in turn, should be reduced by the $593, i.e., the expense due to the children that Jeff relieves her of, so her needs should be $9,151 minus $593 for a total of $8,558.

We may also need to take into account how much summer visitation is taking place. For example, if Jeff visited eight days per month during the school year, but had two weeks of visitation in the summer, for 50 out of 52 weeks he would have 26.7 percent of the expenses, but for two weeks he would have between 73.3 percent and 100 percent, depending on how much the children visited Rachel during this time. If it was 100 percent, he would be the custodial parent 29.5 percent of the total year, and Rachel the remainder, 70.5 percent, rather than the 26.7 percent–73.3 percent split we assumed above. This makes Jeff's needs $6,564 and Rachel's $8,496.

Now if we use these figures instead of the standard poverty levels, as we show in Table 4.3, Jeff's after-tax-income-to-needs ratio (using the above modification of the 1987 poverty values) would be 2.49 ($16,313 divided by $6,564). This is 85 percent of its pre-divorce level (2.49 divided by 2.92), for a drop of 15 percent. Meanwhile, Rachel's after-tax-income-to-needs ratio would be 2.78. This is 95 percent of its former level (2.78 divided by 2.92); a 5 percent drop, as compared to the 11 percent drop she showed without allocating visitation expenses, and the 31 percent drop she showed before taking taxes into consideration.

Thus, using these more realistic corrections on this hypothetical family, we change from the 20 percent drop for the mother and the 42 percent gain for the father that Weitzman's method would have shown, to the opposite pattern, *in which it appears that divorce economically benefits mothers noticeably more than fathers.*

One other way the needs-adjustment method may not to be applicable to divorced families should be discussed: that single-mother households have babysitting and other child-care expenses that a two-parent household might not because there the parents can share the child-care burdens. It is unclear whether the poverty levels account for this issue.[44]

Problem 4: Other Child-Related Expenses

Residential Expenses

While the expenses just cited are examples that decrease mothers' needs while inflating fathers' needs, other expenses inflate the fathers' needs, while having no effect on the mothers' needs. For example, many fathers maintain a larger residence than a truly "single" person would, with extra bedrooms and bathrooms, to accommodate visitation. This requires more substantial housing costs than are allowed in the government-published needs ratios for single persons, but wouldn't necessarily diminish the mother's needs.[45]

Transportation

Another example of an expense that inflates the fathers' needs while having no effect on the mothers' needs is the transportation costs for exercising visitation rights. According to our sample, fathers do most of the driving for picking up and dropping off. This factor is especially salient for fathers who reside a considerable distance from their children and must pay airfare several times per year.

Medical and Dental Expense and Insurance

Fifty-five percent of the fathers, but only 24 percent of mothers in our study, were ordered to pay directly for the children's medical and/or dental insurance. These insurance payments, which are sometimes very costly, are being made by the fathers for the children in a different household, and are in addition to child support, but the needs adjustment method's sacrosanct household assumption assumes the mother is paying all of it. Similarly, two-thirds of the decrees ordered the parents to split 50/50 the costs for any medical and dental care for the children that isn't covered by medical insurance. Again, the needs adjustment method's sacrosanct household assumption assumes the mother is paying all medical and dental costs.

	Jeff	Rachel	Combined
Pre-Divorce Salary	$31,000	$16,733	$47,733
Federal Tax			($8,820)
State Tax			($1,967)
FICA			($3,365)
After-Tax Income			$33,581
Pre-Divorce Needs			$11,519
Pre-Divorce Income-to-Needs Ratio			2.92
Post-Divorce Salary	$31,000	$20,000	
Federal Tax	($5,185)	($464)	
State Tax	($1,285)	($453)	
FICA	($2,217)	($1,430)	
After-Tax Income	$22,313	$17,653	
Child Support	($6,000)	$6,000	
Total	$16,313	$23,653	
Days Children Live with Father Per Month (Non-Summer)	8		
Weeks Lived with Father in Summer	2		
Proportion Time with Father	0.295		
Post-Divorce Needs	$6,564	$8,496	
Post-Divorce Income-to-Needs Ratio	2.49	2.78	
Post-Divorce/Pre-Divorce	85%	95%	
Gain/Loss	-15%	-5%	

TABLE 4.3 Figuring Jeff and Rachel's *After-Tax* Post-Divorce Changes in Standard of Living Taking into Account Visitation (Including Summer Visitation) Expenses

Problem 5: The Equivalence Scales

It was not clear to us how to correct the needs adjustment method for any of the expenses mentioned in Problem 4. But even if a method could be devised, there would be other problems that remain. For the needs adjusted income method to be definitive, the equivalence scales would have to be completely accurate. Yet there is hardly a consensus among economists about the methods of establishing poverty levels. In the National Academy of Science book, *Measuring Poverty: A*

New Approach,[46] edited by Constance Citro, Ph.D., and Robert Michael, Ph.D., many economists critique the poverty threshhold ideas, especially the methods of adjusting for differences in family structure. Concludes economist Elizabeth Peters, Ph.D., professor of policy analysis and management at Cornell University, "There is not one obviously right way to establish equivalance scales for different family sizes—many methods are defensible. Moreover, regardless of the general method used, it is likely not to take into account specific factors that may be important in individual cases."[47] In short, the equivalence scales are arbitrary and may be inaccurate.

Problem 6: The Expenses of Starting Over

Imagine that your house burned down and you had no insurance. You would have to come up with the money on your own to replace everything. That's the situation that many fathers such as Tom, who we read about at the beginning of this chapter, speak of but few economists take into account. The wife and children generally keep most of the costly items in the household (furniture, TVs, toys, video games, dishes, and soft furnishings), and the husband usually bears the costs of replacing these in order to retain the same standard of living and have the children visit. Most important, the wife and children typically retain the house itself (see Chapter 6).[48]

The father, then, is usually forced to seek new housing. In a rising real estate market, replacement housing costs more than original housing. For the father to maintain a comparable living standard, he may have to spend more on housing than the mother would. And many fathers, such as Tom, find themselves obliged to rent rather than own their residence, while the mother continues home ownership. When this difference appears, she alone reaps the twin benefits of home ownership: equity buildup and tax advantage (note that our tax analysis used the assumption of the standard deduction for both parents and didn't take into account any tax advantages relevant to home ownership).

How Are Mothers and Fathers *Really* Affected?

Recognition of the last three problems convinced me that the weaknesses in the needs adjustment method were virtually insurmountable. While the first three defects—out-of-date tables, failure to take taxes into consideration, and the assumption that all income stays within each household—could be remedied by tinkering, no amount of tinkering could fix the last three—other child-related expenses that traverse households, the possibility of inaccurate equivalence scales, and the fact that fathers usually bear most of the expenses of starting over. We therefore decided to tackle the issue of how divorce affects mothers versus fathers economically through multiple approaches. This would, we felt, compensate for any weaknesses in any single method.

First, we computed the relative economic impact of divorce on fathers versus mothers in our sample by modifying the needs adjustment method as much as possible. Specifically, we compared parents in our study in terms of the impact divorce has had on their *after-tax* incomes after correcting for visitation (including summer) expenses, as in Table 4.3.

In order to obtain the after-tax income figures (since we didn't wish to ask to see respondents' tax returns), we estimated the FICA tax and federal and state income tax each respondent would pay by calculating their tax return for them based on information, including child care expenses information, they provided during the interview. (The assumptions we made to estimate the taxes were the same as for the hypothetical family.) We calculated these taxes on their income both before and after separation.[49] Once we determined after-tax income, we calculated the after-tax-income-to-needs ratio (using the poverty levels in effect in 1987) for both pre- and post-separation income, correcting the needs figures for visitation by using the mixture approach described earlier based upon the amount of days each parent reported spending with the child. Since, as noted in Chapter 2, mothers and fathers gave us different information about child support paid, we used *both* of their child-support figures in separate analyses. Since they also gave us different information about visitation, as reported in Chapter 3, again we used both reports (including their reports of summer visitation), in separate analyses.

The results when we use fathers' reports of both child support paid and visitation are presented in Table 4.4. The figures shown are the averages (means) over all families. Using our sample's income and child support/alimony figures, had we not taken into account taxes and visitation, fathers would have shown a 23 percent gain, while mothers would have shown a 23 percent loss, which was similar to the range of all other studies. However, when we correct for visitation and taxes, mothers' standard of living increases one percent from its pre-divorce

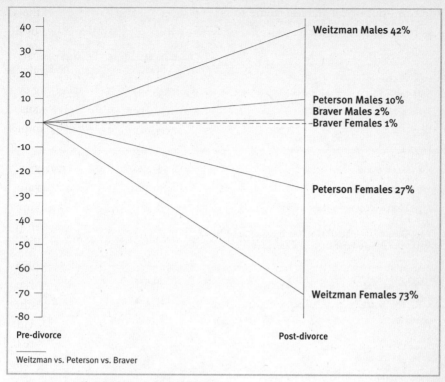

40 — Weitzman Males 42%

30 —

20 —

10 — Peterson Males 10%
Braver Males 2%
0 — Braver Females 1%

-10 —

-20 — Peterson Females 27%

-30 —

-40 —

-50 —

-60 —

-70 — Weitzman Females 73%

-80 —

Pre-divorce   Post-divorce

Weitzman vs. Peterson vs. Braver

CHART 4.3   **Change in Standards of Living for Divorced Men and Women**

level while fathers' increases two percent. This result, superimposed on both Weitzman's and Peterson's figures, is depicted in Chart 4.3. If we use instead mothers' reports of both child support paid and visitation frequency, the results are that mothers show a five percent decrease while fathers show a five percent increase from their pre-divorce standard of living.[50]

We are not suggesting that these figures be taken as the definitive analyses. There are a multitude of different ways of figuring the calculations, and a multitude of different assumptions an analyst can make.[51] In fact, one conclusion we advocate is that perhaps there is no one indisputable figure. However, by almost every way *we* used of calculating the needs-adjusted method, the results show that *economically fathers and mothers on average*[52] *fare almost exactly equal about one year after divorce, both quite close to their pre-divorce levels.*

Pre-Divorce (Family) Income, Taxes, Needs, and Income-to-Needs Ratio

	Noncustodial Fathers (N=89)	Custodial Mothers (N=84)
Salaries[a]	$38,767	$38,176
Federal Tax	($7,013)	($7,049)
State Tax	($1,460)	($1,412)
FICA	($2,733)	($2,692)
After-Tax Income	$27,561	$27,023
Pre-Divorce Needs	$11,161	$11,023
Pre-Divorce Income-to-Needs Ratio[b]	2.47	2.45

Post-Divorce Income, Taxes, Needs, Income-to-Needs Ratio and Pre- to Post-Divorce Gain/Loss

	Noncustodial Fathers	Custodial Mothers
Salary	$29,572[c]	$19,655[d]
Federal Tax	($5,384)	($1,733)
State Tax	($1,245)	($453)
FICA	($2,018)	($1,285)
After-Tax Income	$20,925	$16,184
Child Support Reported Paid/Received	($4,370)[e]	$4,683[f]
Total	$16,555	$20,867
Post-Divorce Needs[g]	$6,598	$8,458
Post-Divorce Income-to-Needs Ratio[h]	2.51	2.47
Post-Divorce/Pre-Divorce	102%	101%
Gain/Loss	2%	1%

[a]Pre-divorce figures may differ for fathers vs. mothers because fathers and mothers may answer differently about the family's pre-divorce income.
[b]The ratio of the above two averages; not an average itself; the averages are 2.51 and 2.50, respectively.
[c]Includes interest received, etc.
[d]Includes interest received, alimony received, etc.
[e]Includes child support plus alimony paid minus financial support from other family members, federal assistance and nontaxable sources of income. Child support alone equaled $4,212; alimony was $360.
[f]Includes financial support from other family members, federal assistance and nontaxable sources of income. Child support alone equaled $4,333.
[g]Based on reported averages of 8.87 days per month and 1.1 summer weeks. The needs figures *not* adjusted for visitation would be $5,909 and $9,107, respectively.
[h]The ratio of the above two averages; not an average itself; the averages are 2.42 and 2.61, respectively.

TABLE 4.4 Our Sample's Average After-Tax Post-Divorce Changes in Standard of Living Taking into Account Visitation (Including Summer Visitation) Expenses

Checking for Discretionary Income

The approach just described corrects the needs-adjustment technique as much as possible, but doesn't compensate for Problems 4 through 6 mentioned earlier. For that reason, we developed other ways of determining divorce's financial impact on mothers versus fathers. An alternative way of seeing how economically well-off a person is, is to find out how much of his or her income is discretionary (also known as disposable income), meaning that the person spends it at his/her discretion. To see if there was a difference between mothers and fathers, we asked the parents in our study how much money they had left over after all expenses, for such necessities as housing, clothing, food, utilities, transportation, medical needs, and child support, were paid. If fathers are economically better off after divorce than mothers, they should actually have a considerably larger amount of discretionary income left after meeting all expenses.

Of course, this approach has another problem: it leaves the parents to define themselves what is "necessary." It could also be true that, in some cases, parents are merely guessing, rather than providing accurate figures. However, there is no reason to believe these problems apply *unequally* to mothers and fathers, so whatever ambiguities this method introduces shouldn't mitigate or invalidate a cross-gender comparison.

All parents were simply asked, "After you've paid what you must pay for bills and necessary expenses, about how much money do you have left over each month to spend on whatever you want?" Fathers answered a median value of $100 per month. Mothers answered a median value of $75 per month. The difference of only $25 per month suggests that economically fathers and mothers fare almost identically one year after divorce.

Who Gets the Sports Car?

Our next approach looked at standard of living from yet another angle. One might argue that economic privation manifests itself in a variety of spending constraints; thus the more the economic hardship, the lower the quality and worth of what one tends to purchase. One particularly telling index of economic condition, according to this reasoning, is the brand and age of the vehicle a person owns. The age and financial value of the vehicle owned is a crude but not inappropriate index of discretionary income and hence standard of living. This particular possession was selected as such an index for two reasons. First, each parent is likely to be acutely aware of the approximate value of his or her own and the ex-spouse's automobile (at least more aware than for any rival material possession) and any perceived discrepancy will thus have rather compelling symbolic value. Second, this possession bears so directly on an adage that summarizes the popular image of the relative economic impact of divorce on fathers versus mothers: "She gets the kids; he gets the sports car!"

We asked each parent what year and make of car they drove in our Wave 2 interview, several months after the divorce was final. Then our staff went to the Blue Book and looked up its value. The results showed that while the father's car averaged $4,483 in value, 6 percent more than the mother's car, this difference was slight enough not to be statistically significant. Moreover, the mother's car was on average three years *newer* than the father's, again a difference not statistically reliable. Thus, again, there appears to be no appreciable difference in how mothers and fathers fare economically one year after divorce.

How Many Mothers Fall Below the Poverty Line?

Finally, we wanted to know how many mothers were actually thrown into poverty by divorce. The "feminization of poverty" has been a rallying cry for advocates who claim that having better child-support enforcement will help lift divorced women out of poverty. Indeed, much indisputable research demonstrates that living in poverty is disproportionately a problem for single mothers. For example, according to Census data, female-headed families with children constituted 10 percent of all households in 1980, but fully 43 percent of the families in poverty. Put another way, in 1980, 43 percent of single-mother families were in poverty, as opposed to only 14.7 percent of *all* families.[53]

Don't these statistics prove the advocates' point? Not necessarily. As we stated in previous chapters, one needs to refrain from mixing *never-married* single-mother families with *divorced* single-mother families, since never-married families with children come disproportionately from the lower socio-economic strata, with both mothers and fathers having low income capacity. In divorced families, however, with both parents having on average far higher education than

never-marrieds, as well as a stronger attachment of father to child, the poverty figures are far less dramatic. Yet, it is the rare poverty analysis that makes this distinction.

The analysis we performed with our sample, which was made up exclusively of divorced families, revealed that only 12.8 percent of our mothers report
their income (including child support received) to be below the poverty level.
Moreover, only 15.2 percent of our mothers reported being in government assistance programs at Wave 2. Note that these figures are nearly identical to the
overall poverty rate for 1980. Thus our divorced mothers seemed *not* disproportionately in poverty. The feminization of poverty may indeed be a special
problem for never-married mothers, but doesn't appear to be so for divorced
mothers.[54]

What about the argument that, even though divorced mothers might not be
disproportionately likely to go into poverty, hardly *any* of them would be if their
ex-husbands were fully paying their child support? For those mothers in poverty,
we actually found that a little more than half of them had ex-husbands who were
behind at all in their child support (according to the mothers' report). Finally, we
wanted to know the proportion of families with the wife having an income below
the poverty level, for which if the ex-husband had paid every cent his ex-wife said
he owed in child support, the wife's income would have risen above the poverty
level. We found only four such families in our entire sample, less than two percent.

➤ For those mothers who were in poverty, we actually found
that a little more than half of them had ex-husbands who
were behind at all in their child support (according to the
mothers' report). And in only four families—less than two
percent of our entire sample—was it true that if the ex-
husband had paid every cent his ex-wife said he owed in
child support, the wife would be lifted out of the poverty
level.

We conclude from all four of these methods that divorce impacts fathers and mothers approximately equally with regard to their economic status. Neither divorced mothers nor divorced fathers drop in economic status much, if at all, according to a needs-adjusted analysis that corrects for taxes and visitation. Mothers report having only $25 per month less discretionary income than divorced fathers. Mothers drive slightly newer, though slightly less expensive cars. And divorced mothers don't go disproportionately into poverty, and when they do, full child-support payment would hardly ever lift them out.

Needing to Go Further in Time

Even if we take as definitive any of the figures so far in this chapter, all of which attest to a reasonably equal impact of divorce on fathers and mothers, should we stop there? We argue that most analyses—ours included—are shortsighted, as well. Our post-divorce analyses, for example, are based on our Wave 2 data, about a year after the divorce became final. Even if it had been true that fathers fare far better than mothers shortly after divorce, is that the time point we want to use to develop social policies to redress the imbalance? As law professor Steven Sugarman wrote: "It is ... not clear that the most sensible time period for comparing financial circumstances of the former spouses is the first year after divorce.... Consider instead ... if we compared the living standards of former couples three or five or ten years after divorce. ... It is certainly possible that the differences between the ... men's and women's living standards would be considerably less than they appear to be one year after divorce."[55]

There are at least two reasons to believe that the earlier we study the economic impact, the more disproportionately disadvantageous to mothers it will appear. Put another way, the longer we wait before assessing the impact of the divorce, the less it will appear that mothers are disadvantaged. The first reason is that as time goes on, women will progressively upgrade or rehabilitate their education or job skills, earn promotions, and work more hours (as the children age), all of which will help them earn more.[56]

The second factor is remarriage. Statistics show that 75 percent of women and 80 percent of men will remarry, the vast majority within seven years after the divorce.[57] When a woman remarries, she tends to marry someone who brings substantial income, but relatively few expenses. When a man remarries, however, he tends to marry someone who brings expenses proportionately greater than income. Duncan and Hoffman found that five years after divorce, even the minority of women who had not remarried had risen from a 30 percent decline to within six percent of their pre-divorce standard of living, due to their enhanced salary, while those who *had* remarried now had a living standard 25 percent *higher* than in the year before their divorce.[58] And Randall Day and Stephen Day and Stephen Bahr[59] found that males who remarried suffered a 3 percent decline in per capita family income (compared to their predivorce levels) while females experienced a 14 percent increase.[60]

Something to Ponder

After presenting our conclusions at the 1993 Conference of the Association of Family and Conciliation Courts, a domestic relations judge from another state approached me and asked what we would have recommended if we *had* verified Weitzman's original results, instead of overturning them. Did I think that the law really "ought to be redressing any real differential in standard of living" that placed mothers at a disadvantage after divorce, by awarding more alimony, much higher child support, or uneven property divisions? I answered that I thought this was more a question for a philosopher, judge, or lawmaker, than for a researcher. He pressed me. "Suppose a woman (or a man for that matter) makes a decision to dissolve her marriage, in full knowledge that she will take a financial bath as a result. Supposedly, this anticipated financial decline has been part of her calculations in choosing to divorce, but she has decided that leaving the marriage is worth it anyhow, so she can have her freedom. She has taken the economic loss into account and decided it was more than compensated for by other benefits she would gain. As long as she was fully aware of what she was getting into, isn't it basically a lifestyle choice? Should we force her ex-husband to redress her loss, in those cases in which it was *her* and not his choice to divorce?"[61]

"There are two problems with that line of reasoning," I answered. "First, assuming he beat her, philandered, or otherwise drove her away through objectionable behavior, then it is not a lifestyle choice, but a matter of survival, or at least survival with one's basic human dignity attached."

"Granted," he replied. "In those cases in which she was driven away by such egregious behaviors, my reasoning wouldn't apply. But didn't you earlier report in your presentation that when the mother chooses to divorce the father, such cases are the minority? Isn't it primarily because she wasn't 'getting her needs met' or the communication wasn't good between them? Stuff like that?"[62]

I admitted he was right. So I turned to my other concern. "But it's not only *her* lifestyle we'd be protecting, it's their *children's* as well. Even if *she* is willing to make the tradeoff for her lifestyle choice, should we condemn the children to a lower standard of living after divorce?"

He was ready for this argument. "I understand your question. But, number one, we always let *married* parents make lifestyle choices that will lower their children's standard of living with no government intervention. If someone wants to leave a high-pressure job which pays lots of money for a more pastoral but poorer existence, and take his children with him, society won't lift a finger. It's his choice, and we let him make it, even applaud it, though he may take his kids to the poorhouse with him. Why should it be different in divorce? Second, if we're really so concerned about the children's standard of living, why don't we just typically award custody, when it's in dispute, to the parent with the higher income?" He concluded by saying the law would have no business trying to correct any financial inequities, even if Weitzman had been right, when the wife leaves the husband, unless there were proof of abuse, adultery, and so forth.

As was said earlier in the chapter, we don't want to take a position in this book about whether child support or alimony ought to be adjusted downward. But, this judge's comments are worthy of consideration. We will address some of his concerns, for example, about how often the wife chooses to leave the husband, as opposed to vice versa, the reasons wives divorce, and the issue of awarding custody to the parent who is the greatest earner, in later chapters.

5.

Taking on Myth 4
Terms of Divorce

A distraught father who had read an article in that day's *Phoenix Gazette* about the divorce system poured out his frustration over my phone line. "My wife, Myra, and I have worked two different shifts for a while. Because she wasn't home in the morning and I was, I've always taken care of Jenny then, giving her breakfast, dressing her, getting her ready for kindergarten at noon. We'd watch kid shows together on TV, read books, color, and play together. Now Myra and I are getting a divorce and the courts are telling me I can't see Jenny more than once every other weekend. It doesn't make sense that some baby-sitter will take care of Jenny in the morning now, and Myra will have to *pay* for it. I'm ready to do it for free, and it will be great for Jenny, for me, and for Myra, too. But the courts say 'no.' Does this make sense to you? Do you call that fair?"

This phone call came on the heels of an August 2, 1993, *Phoenix Gazette* story, accompanied by my picture, in which I was interviewed about the system this country has in place to deal with divorce. I had explained to the reporter that "the system isn't designed to deal with human misery on this scale," that keeping divorce in a legal setting lets couples "put on the lances and shields," and that I didn't think that an adversarial legal system designed for torts (personal injury) and criminal cases suited the problems of divorcing families with children. Almost all the other sources the reporter had quoted, including the judges of the divorce court, said similar things. I wondered if they were fielding as many calls as I was.

What has particularly struck me whenever divorced parents call after a newspaper story such as this is how frequently the issue of *fairness* is raised, as it was with the distraught father I just described. Most callers seem pretty convinced the system is unfair to them.

A woman: "I saw the figures you gave in the newspaper about the typical child-support award. Is $300 to $400 a month all I'll get? No one can live on that! My husband always wanted me to stay home with the children, so I haven't had any job experience in years. Now how can I support myself and my kids? And I believe it's better for them if I stay home with them, anyway. It's so *unfair*."

A man: "My kids are undergoing so much horror. I want joint custody, but my ex-wife resists it. And the courts back her. They won't force joint custody on a mother unless she wants it. And my lawyer tells me there's nothing I can do to stop her. It's just *unfair*!"

While most of my callers of either gender bemoan the system's lack of fairness to them, only mothers' cries seem accepted by society. It is a widespread belief and part of the bad divorced dad image that men fare far better than women concerning the terms of their divorce settlements. This point has been reinforced by many respected scholars in largely influential books and articles, such as those by law professors Martha Fineman *(The Illusion of Equality: Rhetoric and the Reality of Divorce Reform)* and Kathleen Mahoney ("Gender Issues in Family Law: Leveling the Playing Field for Women," *Family and Conciliation Courts Review*), sociologists Lenore Weitzman *(The Divorce Revolution)* and Terry Arendell *(Mothers and Divorce: Legal, Economic and Social Dilemmas* and *Fathers & Divorce)*, and social scientist Mary Ann Mason *(The Equality Trap)*.[1] These scholars have eloquently voiced their views that divorce laws, though ostensibly gender neutral, in fact are written *by* men *for* men. Judges, who dispense the law, are largely male as well. As they further write, these factors, combined with the more aggressive bargaining strategies and abilities men are known to have, and their capability to hire more expensive, shrewder, more aggressive attorneys, gives fathers an unmistakable edge in final settlements. Accordingly, we shall subsequently refer to these advocates as "gender scholars."

But are these claims true? This chapter will examine whether the evidence really supports the belief that men generally fare better than women concerning the terms of their divorce settlements. Before we address this issue, however, it helps to have some understanding of how divorces are currently settled.

How Are Divorce Arrangements Settled?

My mother used to watch a program on TV called "Divorce Court." There, warring parties would bring their tales of betrayal, infidelity, and pain to the judge, who would dispense wisdom and retribution to the guilty party. But I had to tell my mother, to her chagrin, that her program was fictional, that she wasn't watching real life, that since no-fault laws have come into existence, betrayal and infidelity don't matter much legally anymore (see Chapter 12 for an extended discussion of no-fault laws and their consequences), and that few divorces are settled by a decision handed down by a judge, commissioner, or other third party (a process known as "litigation" or "adjudication"). On the contrary, most divorce settlements are reached through some form of negotiation between ex-partners. (For a rundown of the issues that most commonly need to be resolved, see the box, "The Seven Issues Most Divorcing Parents Settle," on page 92.) In fact, fewer than 5 percent of divorce cases reach a level where a judge hands down a decision about any aspects of the settlement.

Rather, four other means of settlement predominate:

1. Default

This is when there are essentially no issues of difference between the parents, and/or where one party cares so little that he or she does not care to raise disputes, and/or where one party is so distraught or otherwise impaired that he or she *cannot* raise objections.

2. Negotiation Between Partners
Without the Involvement of Lawyers

What we call "self settling," this category includes those couples who hire a single lawyer once they've made all their agreements to make sure that what they've negotiated is expressed in proper legal language and is in conformity with the laws.

3. Negotiations Between the Partners with One or Both Spouses Represented by an Attorney

The couple may do some of their negotiations face to face, and others with, or through, an attorney. In many families, only one partner was represented by counsel.

4. Mediation

A trained neutral party (usually a mental health professional or an attorney) attempts to aid the couple in resolving their differences. Not infrequently, agreements reached by the couple in mediation are later brought to the parties' attorneys for approval.

Couples may fall into more than one category of settlement mode. For example, the couple may initially try to negotiate themselves, without attorneys, but fail to reach complete agreement. They may then hire one or two attorneys. If they're still unable to reach an agreement, they may next attempt mediation, and finally, adjudication. In our study, we ultimately categorized the couples by the highest level of intervention needed. Thus, a couple that we designated as a mediation case used a mediator who helped them successfully settle, so they did not need to have a judge decide. They may or may not also have had attorneys.

Table 5.1 shows how the couples in our sample fell into the categories. If only one in twenty couples relies on a judge to decide any issues—as shown by our sample—and the vast majority decide all matters themselves through negotiation and bargaining, it may at first be difficult to believe that *any* unfairness can exist for this majority: the divorce settlement is, after all, what the *couple* wanted and both willingly agreed to. Can't unfairness result only if decisions are imposed on people? If they decide things themselves, is it still possible for fathers to have the upper hand in divorce settlements, while mothers are severely disadvantaged, as gender scholars like Weitzman, Arendell, Mason, and the others contend? Before we can answer that, let's first take a look at how a bargaining session might conceivably go.

Method of Settling	Percent
Default	18%
Self-Setting	14%
Attorney(s)	53%
Mediation	9%
Adjudication	5%
Total	100%

TABLE 5.1 How Couples Settle the Terms of Divorce

The Optimistic Bargaining Session

While it's true that nineteen out of every twenty couples settle their divorce themselves through one or another form of negotiation, there is little research about the nature of the bargaining process. What really goes on in these negotiating sessions?

One optimistic possibility is that each spouse vies for an outcome most desirable to him or her. When disagreements arise, they are resolved through bargaining and negotiation, with both partners giving in a little on things they care less about to obtain concessions on matters they care more about. This continues until an agreement is reached. In the typical case, then, the final outcome should be equally—and moderately—satisfying to both parties, because each gave up some things valued less in order to obtain other things valued more.

Let's say the wife feels strongly about keeping the kitchen appliances and the living room furniture, and would also like to keep the power tools and the dining room furniture, but values them a bit less. The husband's preferences are the reverse. Each, presumably, would give up the items they valued less in order to get the items they valued more, and each, in the end, would be moderately satisfied.

In this example, where the divorce settlement is viewed as a negotiation similar to any other civil contract, the final agreement should not favor the desires of one partner more than the other. Rather, it should be a compromise that ultimately honors *both* interests. It should be a "win-win" situation, or perhaps more realistically, a "win somewhat" outcome.

The Seven Issues Most Divorcing Parents Settle

The issues that most couples settle in the divorce negotiations and that are formalized in the divorce settlement fall into seven categories:

1. **Physical or Residential Custody.** This is where the child (or children) will primarily live. Options include with the mother; with the father; "joint" or "shared," meaning *about equally with both parents;* split, meaning different children residing in different households; or "other," typically meaning with another relative.

2. **Legal Custody.** This refers to who has the legal authority to make decisions about the child regarding such things as medical care, schooling, and religious issues. The options are essentially the same as for residential custody.

3. **Visitation or Access.** This refers to how often and under what circumstances the child will have contact with the nonresident parent. Commonly, visitation involves some regular weekend and/or weekday contacts, with special schedules for holidays, vacations, the child's or parents' birthdays, and Mother's and Father's Day. It's also common for decrees simply to specify "reasonable," "fair," "generous," "open," or "liberal" visitation, without spelling out any details.

4. **Child Support.** Not only is the dollar amount typically specified, but frequently also how it is to be paid (by cash, check, through the court, to the lawyer, etc.), how often, and when, how, and why the schedule is to be revised. For example, some decrees will specify that the parents will exchange income and expense information no less frequently than every two years to assess whether changes are needed to accommodate the new financial circumstances. Also at issue is whether child support will temporarily cease if the child resides with the nonresident parent for an extended time period, such as summer vacation.

5. **Spousal Support/Maintenance or Alimony.** As with child support, dollar amounts, method of payment, and other particulars, are typically specified. The current trend is for spousal support to be ordered only rarely, and when it is, it is normally time limited, until the spouse receiving it "rehabilitates" her (or his) work skills to the point where it's no longer necessary. Among our sample, for example, only 7 percent of decrees examined contained an alimony award.[2] Of these, 2/3 were scheduled to terminate within a specified period of time.[3]

6. **Other Financial Issues Concerning the Child.** For example, who pays the medical insurance, who pays for medical expenses not covered by insurance, who pays for travel expenses associated with visitation when or if the parents move apart, and what, if any, college expenses will be covered?

7. **Property and Debt Division.** The decree may contain a list of assets and debts and specify who gets what. Among the most important and common such assets is a house, retirement accounts, and pensions. In our sample, 39 percent of decrees contained the mention of a house as property to be allocated. Of these cases, 16 percent required the house to be put up for sale immediately and for the equity to be divided. Of the remainder, in 58 percent of the families it was retained as a residence by the mother and in 41 percent of families, it was retained by the father.[4]

This idea suggests that any "inequities" a third party (e.g., an attorney, mediator, or family member) might recognize in the divorce settlement are not considered inequities in the eyes of the divorcing couple at the time. Rather, the trade-offs they've made demonstrate each of *their own* values and preferences.

Dissatisfaction may arise for one or both parents down the road, however, even with such an optimistic bargaining scenario, if experiences challenge some of the assumptions on which they had based their decisions. For instance, a mother may have underestimated the actual costs of child-rearing and, as a result, have accepted less than adequate child support awards; conversely, a father may have accepted nonspecific visitation terms (e.g., "fair and reasonable"), expecting greater flexibility than his ex-wife ends up accommodating. When reality dawns, the parties may realize the inadequacies of their settlement and experience a drop in satisfaction with the relevant decree provisions.[5]

The Gender-Biased Bargaining Session

While the previous bargaining scenario would be ideal and it *does* appear possible that divorce negotiations could be similar to any other contract negotiations where each party *wins somewhat,* according to his or her *own definitions of winning,* it is also possible that such a scenario does not at all reflect the realities of the divorce settlement process. In fact, law professors Robert Mnookin and Lewis Kornhauser noted in a 1979 article in the *Yale Law Review* that spouses likely bargain with some knowledge of the court's probable stance on various issues. For example, if both partners believe that the court is known to award custody of the children to mothers, the father might be less likely to "push" very hard for custody, knowing that if they end up going to court, he will probably lose.[6]

As a result, even if almost all couples resolve all issues through bargaining, their beliefs (or that of their attorneys) about what the court will do if they fail to reach an agreement poses strong constraints on their capacity to freely negotiate. If the couple takes the negotiating process to the next step—mediation—the mediator's beliefs about appropriate settlement arrangements or about what the judge might do if they fail to agree can cloud the negotiations, even though the mediator is merely supposed to facilitate the couple's own wishes.

This bargaining in "the shadow of the law" (as Mnookin and Kornhauser aptly call it) provides the legal backdrop for the couple's decision-making and allows considerations besides their own preferences to enter the process. And this is exactly what has led to most of the furor about gender bias or unfairness and to calls for policy changes to ensure greater equity and fairness in divorce outcomes for women vs. men. The gender scholars I cited earlier contend that even free bargaining tends to lead to outcomes that greatly disfavor mothers' interests in divorce settlements. If they are right, fathers should be greatly satisfied, while mothers should disproportionately experience unfairness.

"The Shadow of the Law": Gender Scholars Make Their Case

Professor Fineman and the other gender scholars mentioned earlier have been extremely outspoken and compelling in their arguments about gender bias in divorce law. They have unceasingly called for reforms that would, as law professor Kathleen Mahoney calls it, "level the playing field for women."

These arguments begin with the observation that laws tend to be written *by men for men and administered by men as well.* Mahoney articulated this view in 1995 in her keynote address to the Association of Family and Conciliation Courts Annual Conference in Montreal, called to examine gender bias in domestic relations law. Here is how she formulated the problem:

> *To begin to understand or respond to accusations of bias or privilege in the law . . . we must ask the following questions: What are the sources of law? Who has shaped it? Whose understanding, philosophy and world views are imprinted on the law?*

The answer, she concludes, is that:

> *. . . unfortunately for women . . . for centuries, male supremacist forms of organization were unquestioningly replicated and perpetrated in the common law. . . . The problem begins with the male centeredness of legal language. Consciously or unconsciously . . . the male standard predominates legal reasoning.*[7]

Mahoney acknowledges that a number of reforms such as no-fault divorce have been introduced that were "designed to create more equitable settlements for women," most with the strong backing or instigation of the feminist legal community. Unfortunately, she laments, they have ultimately turned out to be "disastrous."[8] Why? She points directly to the courts, and specifically to the judges.

The vast majority of judges are drawn from a very small unrepresentative group: a group of White, middle class, middle-aged, Christian, male, heterosexual, married lawyers. . . . For most judges . . . feminist theory did not exist in their law school curricula. When more than 90 percent of judges are married . . . how can they possibly understand the problems of . . . divorced persons? . . . Family law disputes usually involve intensely gender-specific, value-laden questions . . . [so we should] wonder whether judges can avoid being influenced by societally induced assumptions about the roles of men and women.[9]

This explains *why* mothers can be disadvantaged in litigation, and by extension, in bargaining and negotiations with their ex-spouse under the "shadow of the law." Mahoney, along with the other writers, also explains *in which respects* they are disadvantaged: primarily in financial areas such as child support, alimony, and division of property. Essentially, and based primarily upon professor Lenore Weitzman's incorrect analysis, which we reviewed in Chapter 4, these gender scholars claim that the introduction of no-fault laws brought economic disaster to women. In their view, child support was inadequately awarded, child-support compliance was spotty and poorly enforced, alimony was awarded hardly ever, and the couple's property, which was typically awarded "equitably," shouldn't have been. As they see it, the property should have been awarded disproportionately to the mother, who typically needs and deserves the extra resources to break even, given the financial burdens of caring for children.

➤ **In the view of gender scholars, under no-fault laws, the couple's property, which was typically awarded "equitably," shouldn't have been. As they see it, the property should have been awarded disproportionately to the mother, who typically needs and deserves the extra resources to break even, given the extra financial burdens of caring for children.**

In addition to this judicial backdrop, the gender scholars have noted at least two other factors they contend may reduce the power of women in the negotiation process.

1. Men Are Seen as More Experienced and More Aggressive Bargainers

As the general populace believes, men's life orientation and perspective makes them competitive and aggressive, while women will more likely avoid conflict and seek cooperative solutions, even those to their own disadvantage. Thus men are more likely expected to use "coercive" strategies to make women accept less child support, property, or spousal maintenance than they desire.[10]

2. Men's Generally More Secure Financial Status Is Seen As Allowing Them to More Easily Hire More Aggressive, Shrewder, and Expensive Attorneys

Whether or not this is statistically the case, this view is best expressed by one wife who told us:

> I desperately wanted to hire a lawyer to counter the cutthroat that represents James. I found out the guy has a reputation as the most ruthless and expensive divorce lawyer in town. He was using every tactic, every innuendo in the book. "Have you sought counseling for your drinking problem or gone to AA meetings?" he asked me. My God, I don't even drink! But all I could think to answer was No, which made it look like I was in denial about a drinking problem. If I'd had a lawyer, she could have objected, and spared me from looking like an alcoholic. But every lawyer I called wanted at least $1,000 as a retainer to go up against James's guy.

Considering both these factors together, the conventional wisdom is that divorce settlements will not honor the desires of both partners equally, unlike the optimistic bargaining scenario described earlier. Rather, according to the gender scholars, men's interests will tend to prevail at the expense of women and children. The result, in their view, is that fathers are typically greatly satisfied with the divorce settlements, while mothers overwhelmingly feel unfairly treated.

This perspective has clearly dominated recent divorce debate, with little or no responsible critique or rebuttal. The views of the gender scholars and the evidence they've cited have been unchallenged and unanswered in responsible commentary, rigorous research findings, or academic writing. Thus, policymakers have faced a one-sided discourse calling for reform.

Included in these calls are those from the gender scholars mentioned earlier, in addition to other social scientists, who have argued that it is best to impose constraints on both the bargaining parties and on judicial discretion.[11] According to these writers, we shouldn't simply allow men and women to bargain freely among themselves, because doing so will perpetuate the kinds of divorce settlements that have been so unfair to mothers. It is worthwhile noting that this is a paradoxical recommendation since it disempowers women as well as men. By taking away their prerogatives, such constraints disrespect women's abilities to look after their own welfare, and quite possibly sets the analysts' preferences against the preferences of the couple. The thinking goes, since women are apparently such overwhelmed, outmatched negotiators, it's necessary to "protect" them by barring them from negotiating. Left to their own inadequate resources, women might just continue to make too many or too large concessions. So, the thinking goes, discretion-removing reforms are desirable to "level the playing field" and to prevent men from once again taking advantage of their greater savvy to outbargain mothers.

As a result of these powerful voices, a number of reforms were quickly legislated. We will explore the impact of some of these reforms at the end of this chapter.

How Real Divorcing Women and Men Feel[12]

In reviewing the arguments just presented, my colleagues and I realized that the gender scholars had failed to do something we considered crucial in evaluating the validity of their argument: *they never bothered to ask the parties involved how they felt.* As a result, the scholars were substituting their own values and perceptions for those of the ones most intimately affected: the divorcing mothers and fathers. Without going directly to these sources, recommendations for policy changes designed to insure justice for divorcing women, especially those that disempower the parties by removing from them the power to negotiate freely, seemed premature at best and downright harmful at worst.

What *is* the reality? That's what we wanted to know. Instead of imposing our own—outsider's—values, our approach was simplicity itself: we asked the protagonists themselves to tell us how they felt.

We wanted to know how satisfied mothers and fathers really were with various aspects of their divorce settlements, both at Wave 2 and Wave 3, i.e., at one and at three years, respectively, after the divorce became final. We asked our sample of subjects[13] how satisfied they were with the custody, visitation, child-support, and property/debt provisions in their divorce decree. We also asked about their satisfaction with financial issues concerning children other than the child-support provisions, such as medical expenses and long-distance visitation. All answers were rated on a seven-point scale, with one being extremely dissatisfied and seven being extremely satisfied. Chart 5.1 presents the average Wave 2 satisfaction ratings of men and women for these divorce provisions.[14]

In direct contradiction to the claims of the gender scholars, women reported *greater* satisfaction than men with *all five* provisions.[15] In fact, women were relatively satisfied with their *entire* divorce settlement. Fathers' satisfaction was noticeably lower, hovering near the midpoint between satisfied and dissatisfied on each count.

> **In direct contradiction to the claims of the gender scholars, women in our survey reported *greater* satisfaction than men with custody, visitation, child support, and property/debt division.**

What happens as time passes and parents gain more experience with what they have agreed to? Do mothers finally and belatedly realize, as some writers proclaim,[16] that they have been outbargained by their ex-spouses, the more experienced, aggressive, and adept negotiators? Our Wave 3 interview (Chart 5.2), which occurred two years after the previous one, shows these long-term ratings. In general, parents felt much the same, even as they reassessed their agreements.[17]

In fact, only one substantive change in satisfaction ratings over the two-year interval was apparent: while women initially indicated greater satisfaction than

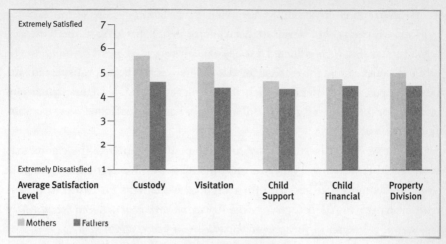

CHART 5.1 **Mothers' vs. Fathers' Satisfaction with the Provisions of Their Divorce Settlement (Wave 2)**

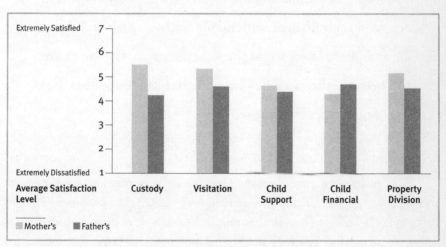

CHART 5.2 **Mother's vs. Father's Long-Term Satisfaction with the Provisions of Their Divorce Settlement (Wave 3)**

men with the child financial provisions of the decree (outside of child-support), this pattern reversed itself at the later interview.[18] Three years after filing for divorce, men claimed marginally more satisfaction with the financial provisions of their decree than women.[19]

We weren't content simply recognizing that mothers were so much more satisfied with most of the terms of their divorce than fathers. We wanted to know *why*. To that end, we conducted a series of analyses called *mediation analyses* to attempt to determine the reasons for this discrepancy. These sophisticated and complicated analyses identify which, if any, of several possible factors statistically account for the observed gender differences in decree satisfaction one year after filing for divorce.[20]

What we found is astonishing, and completely counter to the claims that women either are or feel misused and mistreated in the negotiation process. Women feel more satisfied with their divorce settlements for two reasons: *because they are more likely to get the deal they want than men are, and because they feel they have greater influence over the settlement process than men do.*

> ➤ **According to our findings, women typically feel more satisfied with their divorce settlements for two reasons: because they are more likely to get the deal they want than men are, and because they feel they have greater influence over the settlement process than men do.**

First, women were more satisfied with custody in part because they were more likely to get the custody arrangement they wanted than were men. The decrees overwhelmingly favored what mothers told us were their custody preferences before the divorce was final: 67 percent of mothers—but only 15 percent of fathers—obtained *both* the legal and residential custody arrangements that they preferred, and only 8 percent of mothers (as compared with 37 percent of fathers) found neither decree custody provision to correspond with their pre-divorce preferences.[21] But while that could explain satisfaction with the custody issue, it couldn't account for the fact that women were more satisfied with *the other* provisions, as well. To put it succinctly, the factor we found that could best explain the overall greater satisfaction was the mothers' belief that they pretty much *controlled the process.*

We asked parents to rate how much control (on a 1–5 scale, with 1 meaning no control and 5 meaning complete control) they felt they themselves had over (1) the way the divorce legal proceedings had gone, (2) the amounts of visitation awarded, (3) the child-support awarded, and (4) the final property distribution in the decree. Remarkably, women actually reported feeling *more control* over the divorce settlement process than men, as shown in Chart 5.3. Moreover, this greater empowerment appeared to be the factor that best accounted for females' greater satisfaction with the terms of their divorce in the mediation analyses we conducted.[22]

Women's greater feelings of control over the settlement contradicts the notion that they are the pawns in a settlement process controlled by men. The divorce settlement process does not appear to be one in which women feel helpless. On the contrary, they feel more in control—more "empowered"—than men. If any party feels he or she lacks empowerment, it is the fathers. Since previous studies did not question the participants themselves, but rather examined "objective" outcomes, it's obvious that the conclusions made by the writers followed their *own* values and did not reflect the values of the divorced men and women themselves.

And what of the charge of some writers that women win custody at the expense of other areas of settlement? If this were so, then the more satisfied a woman was with the custody arrangement, the less satisfied she should be with the other arrangements. Instead, our results show quite a different picture. We found that if she was happy with custody, she tended to be happy with the other provisions.[23] If women were indeed "trading off" desired custody outcomes for less abundant financial outcomes, they nevertheless remain happy with these tradeoffs, and feel they have them under their control.

By contrast, fathers' dissatisfaction stemmed from their perception that the process itself treated them unfairly, leaving them feeling helpless. One of the few other researchers to query fathers directly, Virginia Polytechnic University family researcher Dr. Joyce Arditti (together with Karen Allen), similarly noted in an article in *Family and Conciliation Courts Review* that divorcing fathers generally feel treated completely unfairly by the legal system.[24]

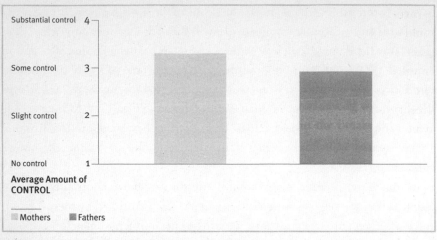

Amount of CONTROL Mothers and Fathers Felt
About the Divorce Settlement Process

Further Tilting the Playing Field?

As discussed earlier, divorce laws are constantly shifting, primarily in the direction that the gender scholars advocate. The study whose data has been presented here took place prior to two substantial policy changes, both of which shifted even more power to mothers.

The first change involved new federal laws that forced states to develop and apply firm "presumptive" guidelines for child-support awards. The guidelines that were adopted in 1988 in Arizona provided for somewhat more generous awards than had been the case previously and also removed most discretion from judges as well as couples regarding child-support award amounts.[25] As we've seen, however, in almost all cases, it is the parents who typically negotiate the settlements—not the judges. These new guidelines, in effect, have removed the authority of the divorcing couple to make their own decisions.

The second reform introduced mandatory withholding of child support from all fathers' paychecks by the employer. While Arizona was one of the first states to adopt this reform in 1988, all the 50 states have since followed suit. Prior to the passage of this law, wage garnishment was readily available, but only as a *remedy* against any father who failed to meet his child-support payments. If the father systematically met all his obligations, he continued to be allowed to pay on his own. However, if he was found to be as little as 30 days delinquent, the court would order wage withholding immediately. Since advocates convinced policy-makers that these remedies were inadequate, the new law sanctioned garnishing the wages of *all* newly divorced noncustodial parents, even those who never were and never would become negligent. In effect, this new reform declares divorced fathers "guilty" of being probable deadbeats simply by reason of being divorced.

We wondered how these changes would affect the divorced couple. Since both changes tended to favor mothers, we expected more recently divorced mothers and fathers to be even more imbalanced in how they viewed their settlements. Our more recent study was able to provide the answers. We first asked the questions, "How satisfied were you with the legal process itself?" The results reveal that mothers are on average satisfied, while fathers are not (Chart 5.4).[26]

We also asked, "How would you describe the slant of the Arizona legal system regarding divorced parents?" The options were "very slanted in favor of mothers," "somewhat slanted in favor of mothers," "slanted toward neither mothers nor fathers," "somewhat slanted in favor of fathers," and "very slanted in favor of fathers." The startling results are presented in Chart 5.5. Not a single father thought that the system favored them in the slightest, and 3/4 thought that it favored mothers. And mothers, albeit to a lesser extent, *agreed* that the system was slanted in their favor! While 2/3 thought it was balanced, *three times as many mothers thought it favored mothers as thought it favored fathers.*[27]

➤ Our study found that not a single father thought that the system favored them in the slightest, and 3/4 thought that it favored mothers. And mothers tended to *agree* that the system was slanted in their favor.

Indeed the newer reforms appear to have further tilted an already uneven playing field. Now even the advantaged party couldn't escape noticing that the system was slanted her way.

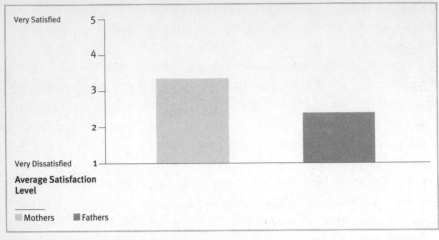

CHART 5.4 How Satisfied Were You with the Legal Process?

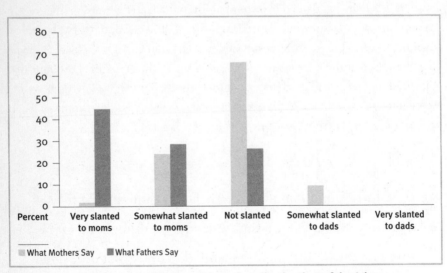

CHART 5.5 Responses to: "How would you describe the slant of the Arizona legal sysem regarding divorcing parents?"

A final finding of interest regards the speculation I referred to earlier that men are more likely to hire aggressive attorneys who bargain for their advantage. In fact, our recent study indicated that in 40 percent of our cases, the mother either hired the only attorney on the case, or hired her counsel first. In contrast, only 18 percent of the fathers were either the only party represented or had hired their attorneys first.

An informal survey of divorce attorneys conducted by the legislative sub-committee on which I sit indicated that this unequal representation accorded with the attorneys' own views. More believed that the current statutes and system favored women over men. In fact, the majority indicated that they preferred women clients, because mothers were more likely than fathers to be satisfied with their representation and the divorce system. Simply put, mothers were more likely to "win."

This lopsided outcome is exemplified by the case of Sheldon, a successful physical therapist. To look at Sheldon, one would think he would have all the advantages in a court battle: education, money, a lucrative business he built up himself, not to mention a well-paid attorney. Yet, according to court records, he was clearly on the losing end of a bitter court battle.

His ex-wife's attorney had written into the agreement a clause that even if the children decided to reside with Sheldon, she would still receive 50 percent of the child support. "That was supposedly to maintain her style of living *in case* they decided to come back to live with her," Sheldon explained. So when two of the children indeed decided to come live with him full time, as he had predicted, he still had to pay 50 percent to his ex-wife for them. He also paid full child support for the one child that resided with his ex-wife.

In addition to the child-support payments, Sheldon was also paying alimony. It was written into the decree that alimony would cease if his ex-wife either remarried, or cohabited with another man for nine consecutive months. She did begin to cohabit openly with a man, but the new couple skirted the intent of the cohabitation provision by virtue of the fact that the man always kept up another residence.

More than two years passed and the children were still living with Sheldon, who had remarried. He and his second wife, Linda, hired a new attorney, who recommended that they hire a private investigator. "The investigator attested to the fact that he saw the man's car outside the house and saw him coming into the house every evening and leaving every morning," Linda reported. This was not proof enough for the courts. "The courts say you can sleep over someone's house seven nights a week, but if you don't change your address [which the wife's lover hadn't] it is not considered a legal residence. In the eyes of the court, they were not considered cohabiting."

Sheldon went back to court to try to get a change in the divorce decree. He wanted both to stop the alimony payments because his ex-wife had been living with this man and cease paying 50 percent child support because the children were living exclusively with him. After the two attorneys and judge met in a settlement conference, however, Sheldon found he had given up the cohabiting clause *forever* in return for getting the 50 percent child-support clause struck from the decree. So even after his ex-wife's lover sold his house and moved to Florida with her, Sheldon was still forced to pay alimony. This went on for sixteen years and only stopped a few months ago when his ex-wife and her boyfriend finally married. Clearly, Sheldon could not be seen as having had any advantage in his divorce settlement. If anyone had "made out like a bandit," it was his ex-wife.

Sharpening the Lion's Teeth and Claws

I presented the results described in this chapter at a conference in Montreal in 1995. I spoke of the calls of many advocates[28] for reforms in the divorce law that would protect women from "unfair" settlement outcomes forced on them by men. But these calls contradicted the evidence I presented of the experiences of the parties themselves. If anything, I stressed, it is *fathers* who need to be protected. A member of the audience put it aptly, I thought, in the note he passed me after the presentation:

> *When both the lion and the slave it devours in the Coliseum would agree upon who won and who lost their particular contest, it seems both impudent and presumptuous for the spectator to superimpose his own judgments or to provide new instruments to sharpen the lion's teeth and claws.*

The Belief vs. the Reality

Myth 4, that divorced mothers are on the losing side of divorce settlements, has won widespread acceptance, perhaps because of the persuasive advocacy of so many talented gender scholars. But on examination of the most compelling evidence—the judgments of the parties themselves—this belief seems completely opposite of the truth. Whatever gender biases exist in the system appear to make *men* feel far less equitably treated than women. Moreover, mothers, by their own admission, seem to have their fingers more firmly on the levers of power within the system than fathers.

Indeed, policy changes recently put into effect by our judicial system may have over-armed women even where arms weren't necessarily needed. Our rapture with the bad divorced dad image has thus contributed to the enactment of lopsided policies that are inconsistent with the facts.

6.

Taking on Myth 5

Emotional Issues of Divorce

A distraught witness had come to address the subcommittee on which I had served for the past year. The mission of this subcommittee is to suggest reform to the Arizona divorce system. Composed of both experts and ordinary citizens, the committee was formed because of a statute passed by the Arizona state legislature.

The witness said her lawyer had both misrepresented her and served her badly. She didn't want the divorce in the first place, she claimed. She started to shake, then to weep. "I hate divorce!" she shrieked. "Even the word makes me cry. I hate that word!" She apologized and tried to compose herself. But she failed and couldn't continue her testimony.

We've seen a lot of this. Our subcommittee takes public testimony at every meeting. Any citizen who wishes to speak can get five minutes to address us (or they can submit written testimony). Only a handful of those who have testified orally have managed to get through their remarks without crying, yelling, screaming, using obscenities, or at least struggling mightily for self-control. They are dismayed, distraught, enraged, hurt, angry, depressed, and often in need of professional help.

Based on the bad divorced dad image, which professes that divorce devastates the lives of women more than men, one would think most of our distressed witnesses would be mothers, like the one whose testimony was just described. In fact, fathers easily outnumber mothers.

While divorce is generally considered modern life's most stressful event and has been found to cause more anguish than even the death of a spouse or serious illness,[1] most get through it without permanent impairment. Those who come to the state capital to testify are probably among the most damaged. The fact that most witnesses are men should not be construed as scientific evidence that fathers are more emotionally devastated by divorce.

But the fact remains that our society seems wedded to the image of the divorced father as comparatively content, coming through the whole divorce process with relatively few emotional scratches. This stereotype holds that these men are truly little boys who are relieved to be finally released from the oppressive responsibilities of fatherhood and family. Unburdened by these demands, they are free to pursue the single lifestyle they crave—even if it's only a subconscious craving. As a result, they get a chance to live a second childhood and are substantially at peace, content with their post-divorce lives.

The mothers, on the other hand, are seen as struggling valiantly to get their kids through their first childhood. Mothers still retain all the responsibilities for children they had before, but after divorce they must bear them alone, without the financial resources the father contributed, as well as child-care assistance and household help. According to this belief, these additional burdens, plus the crushing blow that being deserted causes, push the poor mothers to the brink of emotional calamity.

It's the image portrayed to stereotypical perfection in *First Wives Club,* a 1996 blockbuster movie about three middle-aged women who are dumped by their husbands and set out to get even by any means possible.

From the first images of a woman committing suicide because of the anguish her ex-husband has caused her, to the sad tale of the dowdy, overweight Brenda, who is traded in for a young, sexy model, the movie capitalizes on every negative stereotype of the divorced father. Brenda's ex-husband, in particular, is shown to be having the time of his life, driving around in a pricey sports car, dining in expensive restaurants with his new trophy on his arm, lavishing expensive clothes, jewelry, and furs on this nubile young thing. Meanwhile, Brenda is left to fend for herself, adrift in a sea of emotional and financial deprivation.

The movie not only did phenomenally well at the box office, making it the number-one box-office smash its debut weekend, but remained in the top ten for months,[2] despite middling to poor reviews, and has spawned a cultlike following among women. Why? Mostly, it has tapped into female anxieties about the stereotype—anxieties that say that when women reach "a certain age," their husbands will dump them and abandon their families without a second thought so they can be free to live the life they were meant to live, leaving their ex-wives emotionally scarred.

But is this aspect of the bad divorced dad image true? Are divorced mothers really emotionally disabled by the dissolution of their marriage, while fathers are happier, more content, and more actualized than while married? Or is it, like the other beliefs we have examined, simply another destructive and untrue myth?

A Different Image

Here's another scene to consider:

After nine years of marriage, a couple splits up. The wife has won sole custody of their two children, despite the man's efforts to get a joint custody arrangement. He takes an apartment a couple of miles away and furnishes it sparsely. When he sees his children, it's only for a weekend, and their time together feels forced, unnatural. He tries to make up for not seeing them all week, cramming in as many activities as possible. But at the end of the weekend, when he has to return his children to their mother, they are all exhausted and tense. He longs for the small daily rituals he used to share with his children.

His days become a sort of fog, and he is unable to concentrate on anything. At work, his performance begins slipping. He has no one to talk to about what he's going through, and nowhere to turn to for help. Fear and tremendous sadness overwhelm him.

> ➤ **Study after study strongly and consistently suggests that, while both parents suffer substantial emotional distress during divorce, mothers fare far better than fathers once the marriage has ended.**

As surprising as it may seem, this story is indeed the statistical reality according to a number of respected studies, which strongly and consistently suggest that, while both parents suffer substantial emotional distress during divorce, mothers fare far better than fathers once the marriage has ended.[3]

Perhaps the most definitive study, conducted by University of Colorado psychologists Bernard Bloom, Ph.D., Shirley Asher, Ph.D., and Stephen White, Ph.D.,[4] found that while divorced mothers experience a fourfold increase in such symptoms as depression, hospital admissions, and work problems, divorced fathers experience a *ninefold increase.* And divorced men had substantially higher rates of hospital admissions to psychiatric facilities than divorced women.

This is not a fleeting difference that evens out over a period of months. Rather, these gender imbalances in coping can last as long as ten years.[5] Even more disturbing, another study found that suicide rates for divorced men were five times higher than for married men and significantly higher for divorced men than for divorced women.[6]

> One study found that suicide rates for divorced men were five times higher than for married men, and significantly higher for divorced men than for divorced women.

George, a father from Texas, is not unlike many of the fathers we've interviewed over the years. "I got really depressed," he says of the months immediately following his divorce. "For a period of time I contemplated killing myself and actually planned on doing so. But when I finally confided my plans to my therapist, he asked me what I wanted to leave to my children as a legacy. Did I want to leave them a legacy that Daddy taught them that when things got tough you check out, or did I want to leave my children something more important and live my life as a gift to others?"

Another father confided, "I was a basket case emotionally. I began to have suicidal thoughts. I was worried that I might use my gun on myself, so I took it to a bank and locked it in a vault. The only thing that stopped me from killing myself was what it would do to my daughter."

This is not to say that women escape unscathed. On the contrary, several researchers have noted they may have a harder time than men in the period *before* the divorce, as they try desperately to hold their marriage together, while at the same time realizing the futility of their efforts.[7] But when the inevitability finally dawns, according to the book, *Lifeprints: New Patterns of Love and Work for Today's Women,* by G. Baruch, R. Barnett, and C. Rivers (McGraw-Hill), "Freed from the tension of [a conflicted, unhappy] marriage, the divorced woman often finds she is beginning to feel better about herself than she has in years."[8] For these women, who go to great lengths in trying to salvage a failing marriage, finally getting out of the relationship may actually be a relief, offering an opportunity for personal growth.[9]

Even Lenore Weitzman, whose economic analyses we critiqued in Chapter 4, found the "ironic result" that women "are likely to find their lives after divorce better and more satisfying." She reports that women outstrip men in "feeling better about themselves," and that they feel "more competent in their work . . . more physically attractive . . . [and] possessed of better parenting skills."[10]

Psychologists Judith Wallerstein, Ph.D., and Joan Berlin Kelly, Ph.D., in their landmark book, *Surviving the Breakup,* found that, at eighteen months post-divorce, "the average mother . . . had experienced a moderate increase in overall sense of well-being and general happiness—more so than her former husband."[11] Constance Ahrons, whose Binuclear Family Study was reported in the important recent book, *The Good Divorce,* says she found divorced women "much happier several years post-divorce than they had been during the marriage. . . . They enjoyed the new control over their lives . . . not being dependent on their partner's behavior or goodwill."[12] Even more compelling evidence comes from a 1985 *USA Today* poll, which found that 85 percent of divorced women say they are happier since the dissolution of their marriage, compared with 58 percent of the divorced men.[13]

Why Men Have More Trouble Recovering Emotionally

Since there appears to be surprisingly little disagreement in the empirical studies, it is harder to fathom than for any of the other erroneous beliefs we discuss in this book how the belief came to be that divorced fathers have an easier time emotionally than divorced mothers. Why do we hold this unsubstantiated image of divorced fathers?

It may be that it's hard to imagine men going through such emotional turmoil following a divorce. After all, men get the message that they must be the "strong" sex when it comes to emotions, taught from the time they are little boys to "be a man," to "take it on the chin," and not to be a "crybaby." The popular image of the man not given to emotionality is regularly examined by such entertainers, authors, and psychologists as comedian Rob Becker *(Defending the Caveman)*, linguist Deborah Tannen *(You Just Don't Understand),*[14] and psychologist John Gray *(Men Are From Mars, Women Are From Venus).*[15] But, as we've seen, the evidence is unmistakable that men *do* have a harder time than women coping with the emotional after-effects of divorce. It seems clear beyond debate that the feelings of unrecoverable loss divorced fathers experience are more profound and inescapable than those impacting divorced mothers. Why should this be true? Why should women actually be more content than men after divorce, completely contradicting the accepted image? There appear to be six reasons.

1. Women Are Most Often the Ones Who Make the Decision to Leave the Marriage

In *The Good Divorce,* Ahrons reports that between two-thirds and three-quarters of all divorces are initiated by the wife.[16] She found that no matter how it was measured, whether it was who made the decision, who actually filed for divorce, who brought up the suggestion of separation, or who made the first visit to a lawyer, it was the woman who most often was the initiator.[17] (The next chapter further documents these findings with our own sample.)

> The one who leaves the marriage holds all the power. Consequently, the one being left—most often the man—feels utterly powerless because he can do nothing to prevent the breakup of the marriage.

The one who leaves holds all the power. Consequently, the one being left feels utterly powerless because he or she can do nothing to prevent the breakup of the marriage. And since women more often initiate the breakup, men are the ones who experience this loss of power, along with a loss of self esteem. Women, on the other hand, frequently *gain* a sense of power.

One mother told us: "When I was married, we followed traditional sex roles; he earned the money, I tended the house. And *he* was lord and master of the household. He left no room for question about that! The first assertive thing I think I ever did in my life was to take the initiative to leave him. What a sense of power! *I* finally was in control of my life. *I* was finally the one who could make my life's story turn out good or bad."

Added to this sense of powerlessness is the fact that men are often totally unprepared for news of the divorce and may not even be aware of any marital problems. One study found that 18 percent of husbands compared with only two percent of wives said they "were not sure what happened" when asked to explain the divorce.[18] As one father related, "We were married for nineteen years. I never thought there was any problem. Then suddenly she wakes up one morning and decides she wants a divorce. I couldn't understand it. Much later on, I found out it was because she was having an affair."

Even when the men recognized that their marriage had problems, they were still surprised that their wives left them: "We were miserable for a long time, but her leaving so suddenly and taking the kids caught me completely off guard. . . . I was devastated by hearing that my wife wanted a divorce—it was a shock! Even though we didn't have a happy marriage, I would have been happy to stay together. . . . Sure, we were battling all the time, but I didn't want this divorce—I *sure* didn't. I came from a family where no one ever divorced. It never seemed imaginable to me. Besides, I loved her."

That many men are caught so unaware is most likely related to the problems these women have with their marriages in the first place. In fact, this very lack of knowledge about marital problems or lack of attention to the relationship was cited by many mothers as their reason for ultimately deciding to end the marriage. As Ahrons notes:

> *Underlying many women's decisions to leave their marriage is their frustration with their men's communication style. That women in general want to talk with their men more, to share more of their feelings, while men hear women's words as complaints requiring immediate solutions rather than as avenues toward intimacy, is an all-too-familiar pattern. When recounting their breakup, women often insist that for years they tried to get their hus-*

bands to talk. Their husbands withdrew, didn't take them seriously, or told them to quit complaining. Commonly, when the women ultimately left, the men were totally surprised, shocked, and indignant. The women often responded: "I've been telling you for years. You just didn't listen."[19]

2. Women Generally Have More Substantial and Effective Support Networks with Whom They Can Share Their Feelings

It is well accepted that women are better at seeking and maintaining social support from friends, family, and associates than men, who generally have far less skill in building such networks.[20] These networks, schooled in current divorce myth, are also more sympathetic to the plight of the single mother than to that of the noncustodial father. Fathers, on the other hand, have few places to turn for help. And even when they do find a support group, it may not give them the kind of emotional ballast they need.

The experience that Manuel, a father of two, had is a fairly typical one. "There were no places to turn to for help," he recalls of the time immediately following his divorce. "I went to the Catholic church, which is supposed to have a support group. But all they do is tell you to pay your child support. That's pretty much it. Go along with the system. Don't cause problems. There was no effort whatsoever to help me. I started out talking to co-workers but they got tired of it in a hurry. So did friends. People don't want to hear that. After a very short amount of time I was reduced to going home and talking to the walls—literally."

Jim, a social worker, who has custody of his daughter, wasn't even lucky enough to find a support group. He remembers the time following his divorce as one of the lowest—and loneliest points in his life. "I was a basket case," he recalled. "I felt as if I was a Vietnam survivor, and I had no support from anybody. My parents are both gone. The neighbors didn't give a damn. There were single women in the area who had children of their own, but they would not let me become part of their group because I was single and a man. I lost my sense of humor. It was always a struggle to get through the day."

At least Jim had custody of his child. And that, in itself, can offer some emotional relief. But most men do not get custody and thereby lose out on yet another way to get some emotional support. In fact, one study found that children, who typically remain with their mothers after divorce, may be a real source of support to the parent they live with.[21] As Wendy, a mother in our study, told me, "I don't know what I would have done without my twelve-year-old son, Bobby—probably turned into a puddle on the floor. But he knew I needed him to be strong, and he let me lean on him for a while. I could cry on his shoulder, and he'd say, 'Don't worry, Mom. Everything will be all right. We'll get through this. It'll be Okay.' Later, when I had recovered from the shock and got some counseling, I had the strength to return to letting him be the child and me be the parent."

➤ **Most men do not get custody of their children, and thereby lose out on yet another way to get some emotional support.**

---

3. Men Typically Lose Both Daily Involvement with Their Children and Their Guidance and Authority Position with the Family

These two problems have been consistently reported to be the two single biggest stressors on divorced fathers. And neither of them exists for the custodial mother.

➤ **Whereas a mother who has lost custody of her children elicits immediate sympathy for the hurt the loss must cause her, fathers are somehow expected not to suffer equally when the same happens to them.**

First, the overpowering pain of losing daily contact with their children is the price of divorce most overwhelming to the fathers we have interviewed. Father after father gets choked up when they describe the profound emptiness this "child hunger," as David Blankenhorn calls it,[22] causes in them. Considering how regularly we hear this, it is curious that society has yet to acknowledge the deprivation fathers experience. Whereas a mother who has lost custody of her children elicits immediate sympathy for the hurt the loss must cause her (as well as suspicion, perhaps, that she was somehow an unfit mother), fathers are somehow expected not to suffer equally when the same happens to them.

As Alex Hall and Kevin Kelly, who have run support groups for divorced fathers, write in the book, *Men in Groups:* "Fathers must deal not only with the loss of their marriage and new financial strains but also with the loss of their children from their daily lives. . . . [This] is the most central issue for most newly divorced fathers. . . . For some men, it is the loss of their children (more than the loss of their marriage) that may literally make a difference . . . between life and death."[23]

This loss is compounded further if the mother moves far away with the child. Like many fathers, Eric, a freelance photographer, is coping with an imminent move by his ex-wife and her new husband that will take him even further out of his son's life. "I will have absolutely no influence in his life whatsoever," Eric lamented. "You can't be a parent if you're not there when your child falls over and cracks his knee or when he has trouble with his homework or gets picked on by a classmate. Up until now, I've been there for him when these things happened. Now I'll be away from him for months at a time, before seeing him for only a weekend. I'm not going to be there to give him what I've given him the last ten years." Eric confessed that he felt saddened, stressed, and helpless at the anticipation of losing his son.

Fathers also face substantial ambiguity concerning how to fulfill their parenthood rights and responsibilities within the confines of the visitation relationship, for which society has never developed clear role expectations. As Judith Wallerstein (writing with Shauna B. Corbin) writes in *Family Law Quarterly,* "At its core, the visiting relationship is ambiguous and therefore stressful. A visiting father is a parent without portfolio. He lacks a clear definition of his responsibility or authority. He often feels unneeded, cut off from the day-to-day issues in the child's life that provide the continuing agenda of the parent-child relationship."[24]

According to Blankenhorn,[25] when fathers are reduced to becoming visitors in their children's lives, it "unfathers" them. He further states that "divorce, almost by definition, destroys the basis for effective paternity . . . the reality is that visiting fatherhood is a contradiction in terms. Because 'visiting' and 'fathering' do not go together, the whole idea ultimately collapses. . . . Visitation confers almost none of the predictable benefits of fatherhood because visitation is not fatherhood."[26]

➤ According to David Blankenhorn, "divorce, almost by definition, destroys the basis for effective paternity . . . the reality is that visiting fatherhood is a contradiction in terms. . . . Visitation confers almost none of the predictable benefits of fatherhood because visitation is not fatherhood."

Consider Greg's remarks: "I have no idea how I can still continue to be a father without seeing my kids every day. My father was there for me in every way. He was an authority figure and a role model. And I'd like to be there for Jordan in the same way. But I'm divorced and the system has said I *have* no authority; only my ex-wife can make parental decisions for Jordan."

Blankenhorn writes of the almost insurmountable challenge fathers have of redefining their role:

> *To devise, essentially unassisted, an entirely new household for those occasions when his children come to visit. He must start over, reinvent everything, construct an alternative family life with his children—complete with new rules, new routines, new expectations, and new father-child relationships. Most crucially, he must accomplish this feat in a home in which his children do not live . . . [and in which] virtually all parental control resides with the custodial parent. Compared to the mother, the father is largely without power or even knowledge. . . . Visiting fatherhood almost always becomes disempowered fatherhood, a simulacrum of paternal capacity.*[27]

4. Men Must Also Cope with the Loss of Valued Roles

After divorce, mothers often *gain* status-oriented roles, such as principal wage earner and head of household, although it sometimes takes time before they achieve comfort and competence in these roles. Fathers, by contrast, *lose* their most valued role: as provider and full-time protector. And any new skills fathers gain (e.g., housecleaner, cook) are not particularly valued, by fathers themselves or by society. In fact, Wallerstein and Kelly found that divorce had improved the qualities of women's lives far more than it did men's, partly from the growth in self-esteem that resulted.[28]

Along with this change of roles often comes a change in living circumstances. Men are more often the ones who must seek new housing.[29] As Bloom, Asher, and White put it: "Men seemed to undergo greater initial changes because they were usually the ones to leave familiar surroundings. Fathers felt a lack of identity, rootlessness, and complained of a lack of structure in their lives. . . . [On the contrary,] familiar surroundings and the continued presence of their children provided divorced mothers with a sense of security."[30]

5. Men Have More Trouble Giving Up the Attachment to Their Ex-spouses

One study found that, compared with women, men report feeling a greater degree of attachment and desire to reconcile with their ex-spouse.[31] In data my colleagues and I have collected, the fathers significantly more often than the mothers admitted that they didn't "see how life could have much meaning without" their ex-spouse, and that they "wished there was some way to get back together." This continued feeling of attachment, of not wanting to let go of the marriage, can make the separation even more painful. Women seem to have an easier time detaching from the marriage, most likely because they have begun the process earlier, and they have lost less that they valued.[32] Additionally, women take active steps to decrease attachment. They prefer to keep their interactions with their former spouse to a minimum and are less likely to profess love for or act on any desire to interact with their former spouse.[33]

> The continued feeling of attachment that men have toward the marriage can make the separation even more painful. Women, on the other hand, seem to have an easier time detaching from the marriage, most likely because they have begun the process earlier.

As one father confided, "I was on an emotional roller coaster. I wanted her back. The most important thing to me was that my family stay together. Even while the divorce proceedings were going on, I still thought it was a temporary situation. I believed that we would get back together."

Another father related, "After my wife left me for my business partner, I went into therapy to try to show her that I was willing to make the effort to have our marriage work. I was still clinging to the marriage, all during the separation. I still was willing to make a go of it."

6. Fathers Are Often Obsessed with What They Perceive as the Profound Bias Against Them Displayed by the Courts and the Legal System

For many fathers, this is the first time in their lives that they are confronted with a gender battleground in which they are disadvantaged. The outrage this causes them has been amply documented by sociologist Terry Arendell in her book *Fathers and Divorce*.[34]

To gauge the frustration and anger fathers have with the courts and the legal system, we gathered together a group of five fathers to hear stories of how their divorces affected them. The group was fairly diverse in terms of education, race, religion, careers, and economic background. But the one thing that united them was their belief that they had been "screwed by the system."

Randall, a former construction worker, was so upset by his treatment by the court system that he now works full-time trying to help others in a similar situation, "because New York state unfortunately feels that if you're single or divorced and you're a male, you're not a parent to your child. I was under the assumption, like so many American people are, that truth and justice prevailed. I found out that in divorce, there's a scapegoat system, where you're victimized either by race or gender. The man is automatically wrong. The law will allow a drug-addicted mother to keep custody of her child, while I as a father cannot automatically get custody—even if the mother's on drugs."

The men then each jumped into the conversation with their own tales of horror at the hands of the court system. It almost seemed as if they were trying to one-up each other with who had suffered more. Finally, Nat, a successful corporate attorney, proclaimed, "This is not law, this is lynching."

"This is lynching." These are not the words one would expect coming from this highly educated, successful lawyer. But when it comes to the experiences these fathers have had, hyperbolic statements such as this are not unusual. In fact, Mitch, a Jewish member of the group, declared, "Fathers today are like the Jews of Nazi Germany; they have no rights."

Hell Hath No Fury . . .

While men have a harder time than women in overcoming loss, sadness, and depression as a result of the divorce, there is one aspect of emotional adjustment in which men appear consistently to do better: salving their anger at their ex-spouse, an important step in moving past the divorce and getting on with life. Anger and rage are commonplace for both spouses in the early days. For example, Wallerstein and Kelly found that fully 85 percent of mothers expressed anger and bitterness toward their ex-spouse,[35] while William Goode, a prominent sociologist, reported that 48 percent of the more than five hundred women he interviewed thought that their former husbands should be punished for what they had done to them.[36]

> **Anger and rage are commonplace for both spouses in the early days. But in our data, men recovered from their anger at their ex-spouse significantly earlier than women did.**

Most people's anger abates somewhat with time, but husbands' anger appears to do so more quickly and reliably than wives'. Thus, Wallerstein and Kelly also found that while about one-third of the women had "essentially left all bitterness about the divorce behind them" by eighteen months after the divorce, fully half of the men had. "In general, more women than men hung onto the anger they felt towards their ex-spouses," they report. "Half of the mothers continued to make extremely critical or disparaging remarks about their husbands, whereas only one-fifth of the fathers were so intensely critical in front of the children."[37] These feelings of anger often did not seem to abate even over very substantial periods of time. Writing with Sandra Blakeslee in *Second Chances,* Wallerstein reports that intense anger at the ex-spouse is one and half times more frequent among wives than husbands ten years after the divorce.[38] In our data, too, men recovered from their anger at their ex-spouse significantly earlier than women did.

This gender difference in recovery from anger may seem paradoxical, in that men are the ones who are most often left, while women more often sought the divorce, and thus obtained the outcome they wanted. One would think, therefore, that men would continue to be angrier longer. While my results, as well as others', appear reliable, there is no definitive study that explains why the paradox occurs. One possibility is what has been called the "shattered dreams" theory. According to this notion, wives are enraged that their husbands behaved during the marriage in ways that caused the wife to terminate the marriage, shattering her dreams for the future. And we also have evidence that shows that women's anger for hurts done to them during the marriage seems the fuel or impetus for many of their actions post divorce, such as impeding visitation, "badmouthing," and "brainwashing" their children against the other parent, while whatever anger men continue to harbor toward their ex-wives seems not to be the driving force impelling any of their behaviors.[39]

Sometimes fathers complained that their ex-wife's desire to punish them gets taken out on the children. Nat suspected his ex-wife was making his children "pay" for the good time they had while visiting him. With the permission of the courts, he tape-recorded telephone conversations his children had with his ex-wife while they visited him. "She would ask them, 'What did you do today with your father?' They'd tell her, and she'd holler at them, making it clear that they weren't supposed to have a good time at all," he related. "That made her very unhappy, and she would do things that parents can do to children to make them regret. She even hollered at the kids because they told the psychiatrist that we were getting along fine. They weren't supposed to say that."

Added Drew, an architect, "If my sons had a good time with me, they paid a psychological price—there was some retribution exacted against them in some way that I later heard about."

Who Gets Society's Sympathies?

Once again, we see that the myth and the reality remarkably diverge. The evidence has shown that women suffer less emotionally and are more content with their lives post divorce, while men suffer more emotionally from divorce and are far more vulnerable to serious problems. But still the stereotype persists. Society wants to imbue divorced fathers with a fictitious image of well-being that is a gross distortion. Yet it is women who get society's sympathies, who are viewed as valiant innocent victims, suffering at the hands of the irresponsible male. Why has this stereotype, invalid as it is—*destructive* as it is—persisted? Simply put, it is yet another chapter in the tragedy of divorce, with the father playing the familiar role as the villain.

7.

Taking on Myth 6

Who Leaves the Marriage . . . and Why It Matters

Consider the following testimonial:

> *I tried to be as good a spouse as I could. I sacrificed my own needs for the good of the marriage. I was always understanding and respectful of my partner's needs. I believed that marriage was a lifelong commitment, that you had to make sacrifices and work at it, really work! When we started to have troubles, I tried everything I knew to save the marriage. I quietly insisted that we get marriage counseling when I realized we needed it. I never thought my spouse would leave me either. I believed somehow that we were both committed to our family. Though I was far from completely satisfied myself in the marriage, I certainly didn't consider divorce an option, because I thought it would be a disaster for me and my kids. And I turned out to be right. What kind of a system is it that will let all the work poured into a marriage go down the drain, hurting two innocent kids in the process, just because one partner got bored with the marriage and wanted more excitement?*

When I've recounted this parent's story to friends and professional colleagues, everyone assumes the storyteller is an abandoned mother.

But it wasn't; the grieving parent was a father. And we were surprised to discover that, despite the common assumption, this father was the rule, not the exception.

Are Men Really "Bad Boys"?

Myth 6 of the bad divorced dad image is the final and perhaps the most pernicious aspect of all. It states that most divorces occur because fathers are too immature and irresponsible to face the demands of family life and therefore walk out on marriage and parenthood. While women have the biological attachment to children their physiology endows them with, and the cultural maturity to be parents in every responsible sense of the word, men supposedly lack this attachment to wife and family. In this view, men are simply "bad little boys" who abandon their family to enjoy the charms of younger, more nubile paramours. According to this belief—reinforced through seemingly nightly revelations involving philandering, high-profile men—deep down most men have "zipper" or other problems and simply can't resist temptation. Their giving in to their apparently irresistible base desires threatens virtually every family. As David Popenoe, Ph.D., family sociologist and co-chair of the Council of Families in America, puts it in his recent book *Life Without Father,* "Male biology pulls men away from long-term parental investment and pair-bonding.... Men are only weakly attached to the father role ... [so] culture is central to enforcing high paternal investment."[1] This belief appears to fuel much of the vindictiveness of gender-based divorce debates, since the logical conclusion is that society should find a way to punish divorced men for their escapades and enforce constraints by imposing various sanctions.

David Blankenhorn, writing in *Fatherless America,* is a commentator generally favorable to the role of fathers. Nonetheless, he, too, believes that fathers are the ones primarily terminating marriages. He writes that while historically the principal cause of fatherlessness was paternal death, "today the principal cause of fatherlessness is paternal choice ... and paternal abandonment."[2] His unsympathetic portrayal of what he calls "the Visiting Father" betrays his belief that it is the fathers who *choose* that status. He also betrays this belief when he writes that most Visiting Fathers *"to tell it now,* never wanted the divorce."[3] He further betrays this belief when he makes the first of his twelve proposals for a cultural shift promoting fatherhood, a pledge he proposes people should take:

> Many people today believe that fathers are unnecessary. I believe the opposite. I pledge to live my life according to the principle that every child deserves a father, and that marriage is the pathway to effective fatherhood."[4]

Now, who do you think he proposes should take this pledge? "Every *man* in the United States."[5] Unless he believed that wives were largely innocent in the dissolution of marriage, shouldn't he have requested the pledge of every *parent* in America?

The assumption that it is men who are primarily responsible for dissolving families apparently extends worldwide. Eminent Australian sociologists Ailsa Burns and Cath Scott have written an important book exploring the calamitous worldwide rise in single-mother families, *Mother-headed Families and Why They Have Increased.*[6] They note that the revolutionary rise in the divorce rate is hardly restricted to our own society. After hundreds of years of constancy or very gradual increases, it has roughly doubled in the last two decades in virtually every civilized country—except those that have overwhelmingly strong religious and legal strictures preventing it, such as in the Arab world. And in every land, they note, the conventional wisdom is the same regarding its cause: "The psychology of men . . . the suspicion that many would rather readily abandon wife and children unless pinned in by moral and financial restraints."[7]

In fact, keeping the father from running out on his family seems to be one of the hoped-for benefits of higher child support awards or stricter enforcement of them. As sociologist Frank Furstenburg asserts, "As legal and social pressures for men to support their children mount, males may be less likely to desert their families, because the economic costs of doing so will be greater."[8] Feminist Barbara Ehrenreich quotes a female divorce reformer's comment that "men are going to leave their wives if they don't have to pay, because men are *this way*."[9] The tendency to think that men "will walk out of their marriages 'at the drop of a hat,' " as Burns and Scott note, is held widely by both men and women, but has a different slant depending on the gender of the speaker. "When expressed by women, the reliability of all men is commonly cast into doubt," they assert. However when expressed by men, "they usually have a class ring about them—that of respectable men of authority being aware of the need to keep less responsible men under control."[10]

Indeed, this stereotype forms the basis for our thinking and policies about divorce, resulting in laws that are passed with the seeming intention of punishing divorced fathers for walking out on their family responsibilities. A recently passed Massachusetts law, for example, requires divorced fathers to pay for their children's college educations—*but exempts married fathers from this requirement.* An Ann Landers column about this on January 10, 1995, quoted professor

Sanford Katz, a family law expert at Boston College Law School. The law in Massachusetts, he said, requires divorced fathers but not those in intact marriages to continue to support the child financially until age twenty-three if the child remains in college, because divorced fathers "give up certain rights over their children *when they petition for divorce.* In an intact family, the parents are supreme, and the judge does not supervise the parent-child relationship."[11] The law, then, assumes that it is fathers who walk out on the marriage and petition for divorce, and who therefore need to "be supervised" by the judge for their transgression.

I have personally found that lawmakers of both genders share this assumption. I conducted an informal poll among state legislators and former legislators of my acquaintance, and found that the preponderance of them were certain that it was the husband who was the initiator of most divorces.

Why We Believe Men Terminate Most Marriages

There are at least two reasons why society assumes that men are the primary initiators of divorce. The first is the power of the bad divorced dad image. Since we appear so badly to need a villain in the divorce drama, and since our current orientation is that men are irresponsible and women are innocent bystanders, the logical culmination of this image is that it *must be* men who abandon their family.

The second reason for the conventional wisdom that husbands rather than wives terminate most marriages is the notion that men benefit more from divorce than women. As we discussed in previous chapters, it is commonly—but inaccurately—thought that men fare better economically, are more satisfied with their divorce settlement, and are more content emotionally than women. If one believes these things, then it is a logical extension to think that men have the greater incentive to leave the marriage.

Gary Becker, Ph.D., a University of Chicago economics professor who was the most prominent analyst to apply the economic notions of incentives and costs to people's family behavior, won the 1992 Nobel Prize in Economics for his ideas.[12] Allen Parkman, Ph.D., J.D., a Management Professor at the University of New Mexico, and a disciple of Becker's, also expressed this line of thinking in his important book, *No-Fault Divorce: What Went Wrong?*[13] In his "economic analysis" of marriage and divorce, Parkman focuses on the incentives that operate on individuals when they decide to marry or divorce. "The decision to marry and . . . to divorce is based on the benefits and the costs associated with those choices."[14] That is to say, people are very responsive to the incentives their circumstances place on them. They decide to marry and to divorce when the advantages they see for doing so outweigh the disadvantages. In Parkman's view, "it would appear that men generally had more to gain from divorce," so it followed for him that "most divorces probably were initiated by men."[15]

Parkman saw the choice to seek divorce as emanating from the incentives operating on the spouse choosing it. And Parkman believed that these incentives on men became substantially greater when no-fault divorce laws were passed around 1970, just the time the divorce rate began to spiral out of control. (We discuss these laws in greater detail in Chapter 12.) Presumably, in a fault system, if the man wanted the divorce, in order to induce his wife to agree, he would need to negotiate and agree to alimony, attractive property settlements, generous child support, etc. With the advent of no-fault, argues Parkman, the necessity of such a husband to need to negotiate and recompense his unwilling wife to win her agreement has disappeared. He can get a divorce simply by declaring that he wants one, with no thought or recognition of her needs. As Parkman sees it, these laws were to blame for giving men too much power and incentive to divorce. "No-fault divorce statutes reduced the bargaining power of the spouse who did not want to dissolve the marriage . . . that spouse [probably is] the wife . . . because women are usually worse off after divorce than are men."[16]

The Theory of Too Many Women

Another prominent and popular social scientific theory attempting to explain the rise in the divorce rate also shares the assumption that it is men who are primarily walking out on their families. Articulated by the late feminist psychologist Marcia Guttentag, Ph.D., and finished by her surviving husband, psychologist Paul Secord, Ph.D., in their 1983 book, *Too Many Women,*[17] they theorized that a change in the birthrate associated with the baby boom in the 1950s created a population with a disproportionate number of "marriage-age women" (which they define as from twenty to twenty-four years old) relative to marriage-age men (age twenty-two to twenty-six) by the 1970s.[18] Whereas in 1960 there were 111 unmarried males of marriage age for each one hundred such females, by the 1970 Census, there were now only eighty-four.

The fact that the sex-ratio of marriageable adults dramatically changed around 1970—exactly when the divorce rate started to soar—was taken by Guttentag and Secord as substantial support for their sex-ratio theory. They argue that the gender in shorter supply has greater bargaining power in relationships because of how scarce and rare they are. They can get their way in relationships by claiming that there are plenty of willing partners available, while the more numerous gender can't make the same claim. This power enabled men to become free to "explore the market" and abandon their wives and families to pursue alternative relationships whenever the demands of family got too much for them to handle. Women, in contrast, suddenly in oversupply, abruptly became relatively powerless. They couldn't insist on fidelity or accommodation to their needs any longer. Because willing women were now in ample supply, wives were powerless to prevent men from deserting them to become "Casanovas and tomcats,"[19] as Burns and Scott put it.

Solid Evidence or Merely Gender Bias?

None of the writers or legislators I've quoted relied upon any kind of scientific data to guide them in arriving at the conclusion that families dissolve because men are the initiators of divorce. Parkman made his assumption because he believed that men benefit most from divorce, and hence have the greater incentive to leave. Guttentag and Secord felt that men leave behind their families because they have many more options than women for establishing new relationships. And Blankenhorn arrived at his conclusion without even offering an explanation.

But the following story puts another face on fathers who are in a bad marriage, a face that completely contradicts the stereotype. Here's what Steve, a father of three children, told me:

Margo and I had been having a great deal of trouble in our marriage. We argued over every imaginable topic: how we spent money, how we spent our leisure time, where we vacationed, etc. We stopped sleeping together for over two years. We went to see a marriage counselor, but it didn't help. The counselor stopped working with us together after six months of joint counseling. He asked to continue to see me alone. Once Margo was no longer present, he told me I needed to leave the marriage for my own sake. Nothing I could ever do would change things, he told me; I was heading for a lifetime of misery.

When a marriage counselor tells you it's over, to stop trying to keep the marriage together, you have to take it seriously. But every time I envisioned divorcing, my kids' faces would dangle in front of my eyes. I could see the look of anguish they'd have when I told them I was leaving. I could feel the overpowering loss I'd have if I didn't get to see them every day. I'd made an appointment with a lawyer, but I just couldn't go through with it. No matter how bad my marriage was, how empty and cold and destructive it was, I couldn't do that to my kids. I couldn't stand the guilt, the knowledge that I had so wounded the kids I loved so much. No matter what other people thought about my situation, I'd be the one who would have to bear life day after day without my kids. So I stayed in the marriage, even though it was empty.

Putting the Belief-System to the Test[20]

Could Steve be an aberration from the more normal pattern of fathers fleeing marriage? Or is Myth 6, like the others, simply another instance of gender stereotype, without any bearing in reality? By the time we came around to studying the validity of this belief, we had another reason to think that, like the previous five myths, this one, too, was at best another exaggeration, if not downright contradicted by fact.

This is because my colleagues and I *do* believe in Becker's and Parkman's notion that people divorce or stay married because of incentives.[21] But unlike what we assumed when we began our research, we were no longer convinced that *fathers* had the greater incentive to abandon their marriage. The findings reported in Chapters 4, 5, and 6 convinced us that fathers were not in fact better off than mothers, economically, emotionally, or in terms of their satisfaction with their divorce settlements. By now we had all become convinced that *mothers* had by far the greater incentive to dissolve marriages.

➤ If it's believed that fathers don't really care about their children, then the only matters weighing upon a man contemplating divorce are the splitting up of property and how much in child support he will be expected to pay. But what if fathers really care far more about their children than conventional wisdom gives them credit for? Doesn't it seem reasonable that they would remain in a less-than-perfect marriage?

We were now also coming to recognize the insufficient weight previous commentators gave to how badly fathers might feel at the potential loss of their children. If it's true that fathers don't really care about their children, then the only matters weighing upon a man contemplating divorce are the splitting up of property and how much in child support he will be expected to pay. This was the assumption of writers like Parkman and Furstenberg. But what if fathers are mostly like Steve, who really cares far more about his children than conventional wisdom gives him credit for? Doesn't it seem reasonable that they would remain in a less-than-perfect marriage? Or even stick it out in a truly bad one? Steve anticipates his life without his children as being completely unacceptable. But mothers, who would normally retain their children after divorce, and anticipate a somewhat happier life after divorce, would have no similar disincentive or barrier keeping them from ending their marriage. Even economically, our Chapter 4 analysis convinced us, mothers were at least as well-off as fathers in the short run, and likely to be even better off in the long run. On reflection, and with the hindsight that the new information we had obtained provided, we predicted that because of the greater incentives mothers had to abandon marriage, our research would reveal that they initiated divorce far more often than fathers. If this was indeed true, it would provide the ultimate demise of the bad divorced dad image.

But getting at the truth was not as easy as it might seem. Several alternative ways suggested themselves of determining who was the initiator of divorce versus who was the unwilling partner.

One way used by some previous researchers[22] is to examine the official filings in the petition for divorce. Generally, a dissolution of a marriage is sought by one of the parties, who is termed the "petitioner," while the other spouse is termed the "respondent." In keeping with this official records technique, we examined whether the husband or the wife was the "petitioner" in our sample. We found that 67 percent of those officially requesting the divorce were wives, and 33 percent were husbands. These results are in direct opposition to Myth 6.

Critics of this method believe that, though easily available to most researchers, these files might not be an apt measure of who really wanted the divorce first. In fact, this method might yield the wrong result for two entirely different reasons.

In one scenario, it could overstate the proportion of *women* wanting to terminate the marriage. In the days of fault-based divorce, the woman, even though she might want to remain married, had to file for the divorce in order to become the "injured" or "innocent" party in the divorce and preserve her settlement rights. It seemed possible that present practices might be a holdover of this tradition, one with which lawyers felt comfortable.

The second possibility was that the official records might unrealistically overstate the number of *men* who were the initiators. This is due to the possibility that filing legal papers might well devolve to the spouse with the greatest financial resources, or to the one who is most assertive or least intimidated by interactions with governmental authorities, even though that spouse would prefer the marriage to continue. This would, according to customary gender ascriptions, be the husband.

Not trusting the accepted figures for the reasons just cited, we came up with an alternative method we thought would yield a more accurate picture: we could simply ask the couples in our study to tell us who decided to initiate the divorce. The exact question we asked was, "Which one of you was the first to want out of the marriage, you or ex?" Since we had both spouses available, we could not only get the view of each, but search for disagreements or consensus. We worried, for example, that we might find that *both* spouses would claim to be the initiator, because it would "save face" to make this claim. It might be embarrassing for the unwilling partner to admit this publicly, or even privately. That's why we didn't offer them the option "or was it a mutual decision?" However, if someone spontaneously gave us this answer, we treated it as an acceptable response. But at least we would have the other spouse to either corroborate or refute that response.

Another possibility we worried about was that people might change their stories about who left whom over time. Many commentators have noted that people have a need to construct an "account" of what went wrong in the marriage. This narrative rationalizes their behavior to themselves and is a "shorthand" story to tell others.[23] University of Iowa psychologist John Harvey, Ph.D., suggests that this practice is particularly important for divorcing individuals because it serves their personal adjustment well in the future.[24] However, over time the accounts can and often do change. Shortcomings in oneself that seemed difficult to admit to initially might become more acceptable over time, with the distance of hindsight. Alternatively, accounts might harden as time progressed. Because it seemed difficult to predict the life course or trajectory of these accounts of who left whom, we decided to ask it at all three Waves, and track it empirically.

The Results

What did we find when we asked our couples "who left whom?" The results are shown in Chart 7.1. Despite our concerns with respondents changing their accounts over time, the results show remarkable consistency. No matter when the question was asked or of whom we asked the question, the *wife* was identified as the initiator in 63 to 67 percent of the couples, the husband was identified as the initiator in 26 to 34 percent of the couples, and in 4 to 9 percent of the cases, the divorce was a "mutual decision." Thus, by all measures, including the official records of who was "petitioner" in the legal action, the wife would be designated the initiator in about two-thirds of the families, directly in contradiction to the common wisdom.

➤ No matter when in the three Waves we asked respondents "who initiated the breakup?" or of whom we asked the question, the *wife* was identified as the initiator in 63 to 67 percent of the couples.

Finally, at Wave 3, three years after our couples' divorces became final, we asked, "if you could relive the last several years of your life, would you want a divorce from your ex-spouse today?" If men had the greater incentive to break up the marriage, most men would say "definitely yes," while few women would. Instead, as the figures in Chart 7.2 show, the results are the opposite. Mothers were about 20 percent more likely to say "definitely yes." Even among wives initially left by their husbands, two-thirds were now glad about the breakup, whereas only about half of male *leavers* felt as strongly. In another analysis, we found that about one in five men who initiated the breakup now felt they made a bad choice; only 1 percent of the women initiators now thought that way.

> **Our interviews with respondents three years after their divorce became final revealed that about one in five men who initiated the breakup now felt they made a bad choice, whereas only one percent of the women initiators now thought that way.**

The "Dirty Little Secret" of Divorce Research

The result that women initiate the preponderance of modern divorces is hardly unique to our investigation, we found upon further study. Rather, there is not a single study which *doesn't* find almost the same proportions.[25] The most well-known research on this matter was conducted by Judith Wallerstein, who found that 65 percent of the divorces were sought by the women, "in the face of opposition" by the other spouse.[26] Additionally, Constance Ahrons found that "between two-thirds and three quarters of all divorces are initiated by the wife."[27]

How is it that this result, while entirely consistent with previous studies, directly contradicts not only conventional wisdom, but the theories of legal and social scholars, such as Parkman and Guttentag and Secord, as well as of policymakers who write child-support and divorce laws? Though the finding that

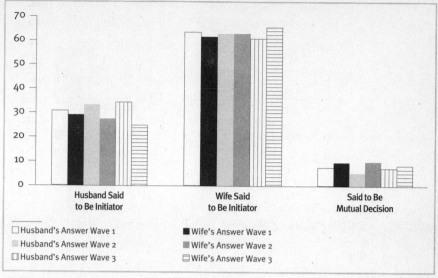

CHART 7.1   Who Divorced Whom

women are overwhelmingly the initiators in divorce is absolutely consistent among all the studies that have examined the issue, and holds up regardless of which spouse is queried or how the question is researched, it surprises almost all commentators on the divorce scene. Few policymakers in the divorce arena know or even suspect the finding.

The reason is that the result has not been well publicized (unlike the aberrant and erroneous finding of Weitzman's), perhaps because of how politically unacceptable it is. To acknowledge the result suggests that men may not be entirely to blame for divorce, and that women are perhaps not so helpless and victimized as was thought. I call the fact that women overwhelmingly initiate modern divorces the "dirty little secret" of divorce research.

Why It Matters Who Initiates Divorce

Should we really care very much about who initiated the divorce? Does it, in the end, really matter who finally put the marker on the grave of a dead marriage? Our conclusion is that it matters enormously, for three reasons.

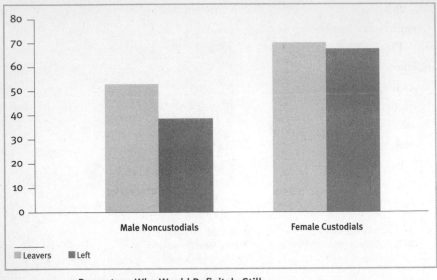

80
70
60
50
40
30
20
10
0

Male Noncustodials   Female Custodials

Leavers   Left

CHART 7.2 Percentage Who Would Definitely Still
Want a Divorce from Ex Today

First, the result provides strong vindication of all our findings presented in previous chapters that, contrary to the prevailing beliefs that fuel divorce policy, all things considered, men do less well than women after divorce. And fathers, in the waning days of their marriage, somehow know that will be true. When they factor in facing the loss of their kids, men apparently just can't bring themselves to end their marriages, as we saw with Steve. But women, who face better prospects overall, especially in the certainty that they will retain the couples' most precious commodity—the children—apparently feel that divorce would still be in their best interests. Perhaps this is why statistics show that women are even more likely to be the spouse filing for divorce when there are children than when there are not.[28]

Second, we have recently seen a number of strong arguments railing against divorce, including Blankenhorn's, Popenoe's, and Barbara Dafoe Whitehead's recent book, *The Divorce Culture*.[29] But when these exhortations are directed at men, they are preaching to the choir. According to a survey by Ohio family researchers Gay Kitson and William Holmes, "women were more likely than men to feel that 'divorce is better for children' . . . [while] men were more likely to feel that 'marriage is for life.' "[30] Thus, it appears that fathers already tend to be less receptive toward divorce than mothers do.

Finally, most remedies and reforms being discussed in the domestic-relations arena would further unlevel the playing field and provide even greater incentives than currently for women to flee marriage. In view of what we know now, it is quite possible that such changes will act to further increase the divorce rate. If most divorces are, in fact, initiated by wives, then it would appear that the best strategies for deterring divorce will be those that affect the choices wives make.

For example, Arizona State University law professor Ira Ellman is one of the leading advocates for increasing alimony payments.[31] He championed the influential American Law Institute's *Principles of the Law of Family Dissolution* draft proposals to award higher and more frequent alimony to mothers.[32] But even he had to admit, when confronting findings like those presented in this chapter, that "the goal of deterring divorce may be in tension with the goal of treating divorcing parties justly. . . . The current proposals of the American Law Institute to breathe life into the law of alimony may do further justice at the price of yet higher divorce rates."[33] Policies that coincided with the views of the judge we discussed at the end of Chapter 4 (who questioned whether it was good public policy to reward financially those divorced mothers who made the unforced choice to terminate their marriages) are more likely to curb the divorce rate, however much we otherwise find them disagreeable.

Top Ten Reasons Why Marriages Fail

When I have told audiences about the results I've presented in this chapter, that wives flee the marriages in two-thirds to three-quarters of all divorces, many are at first incredulous, because it so belies the bad divorced dad image. But many audience members who are reluctant to relinquish these beliefs assume the result must somehow arise because husbands virtually force their wives to initiate divorce by being violent or abusive or having drug and alcohol problems, etc.

We could address this issue by studying the ratings our sample gave us when we listed a series of twenty-seven possible factors and asked "how important each factor was in the breakdown of your marriage and decision to divorce." The results shown in Table 7.1 rank the top ten reasons mothers gave for seeking divorce and include fathers' ratings as well. We found that violence or abuse were strikingly absent. Rather, less dramatic factors predominated, such as "gradual growing apart," "differences in lifestyle or values," "not feeling loved or appreciated by spouse," and "spouse not able or willing to meet my needs." The only classic fault ground that made it onto wives' top ten list was "husband's extramarital affair" (37 percent of wives thought this was very important in contributing to the breakdown of the marriage, but only 9 percent of husbands agreed; conversely 30 percent of husbands gave *wife's* extramarital affair a very important rating, while only 5 percent of wives agreed). Either spouse's drug or alcohol abuse or domestic violence was rated very important by comparatively small proportions of parents.

> ➤ **According to our research, the top ten reasons mothers give for seeking divorce include such mundane factors as "gradual growing apart," "differences in lifestyle or values," "not feeling loved or appreciated by spouse," and "spouse not able or willing to meet my needs."**

These findings, which are also consistent with virtually all other studies,[34] make me skeptical about Blankenhorn's interpretations. If fathers are truly unwilling victims of divorce who haven't behaved so egregiously as to force mothers to dissolve marriages for the sake of their own survival, it strikes me as rather heartless to assail visiting fathers as he does. When a mother chooses to divorce because she is "not getting her needs met" or because of "differences in life-style or values" *and takes the children with her,* as she almost invariably does, the father truly has little choice in the matter. The only way he can father at all is to visit.

Similarly, Promise Keepers, the evangelical group that wishes men to return to traditional family values, which attracts hundreds of thousands of men for their rallies, as well as the Million Man March, exhort males to be good family men. While it's hard to find fault with this plea, these groups' efforts might inadvertently increase the divorce rate. The Promise Keepers' teachings, as ex-

Rank Order of Factor for Mothers	Factor	Percent "Very Important" for Mothers	Rank Order of Factor for Fathers	Percent "Very Important" for Fathers
1	Gradual growing apart, losing a sense of closeness	57	1	52
2	Serious differences in lifestyle and/or values	54	2	33
3	Not feeling loved or appreciated by spouse	45	6	30
4	Spouse not able or willing to meet major needs	41	4	32
5	Emotional problems of spouse	38	11	24
6	Husband's extramarital affair	37	22	9
7	Severe and intense fighting, frequent conflict	36	3	33
8	Frequently felt put down or belittled by spouse	35	13	22
9	Spouse not reliable	33	14	21
10	Problems and conflicts with roles, i.e., division of responsibility for household jobs or other chores outside of house	29	15	21
11	Husband's alcohol abuse	29	25	5
16	Violence between you and spouse	20	21	10
18	Husband's drug abuse	19	26	3
24	Wife's extramarital affair	5	5	30
26	Wife's alcohol abuse	3	23	8
27	Wife's drug abuse	3	24	6

Also in Husband's Top Ten list:
  7 Wife's jealousy of you and/or your activities   29%
  8 Wife too dependent upon or closely tied to own family   27%
  9 Sexual intimacy problems   24%
10 Wife angry, demanding   24%

TABLE 7.1   Listing of Factors Contributing to the Breakdown of Marriage and Decision to Divorce

pressed in its official guidebook, *Seven Promises of a Promise Keeper,* exhort men to "sit down with your wife and say something like this: 'Honey, I've made a terrible mistake. I've given you my role. I gave up leading this family, and I forced you to take my place.... Now, I must reclaim that role.'... [Don't] *ask* for your role back ... *take* it back.... There can be no compromise here. If you're going to lead, you must lead."[35] The backlash could well lead to even more women divorcing men.

This possibility is reinforced by a dramatic and surprising new study of why marriages fail.[36] Conducted by a team headed by renowned University of Washington psychologist John M. Gottman, Ph.D., the researchers studied a group of 130 newlyweds. They carefully observed how the couples interacted with each other, then followed them for six years, observing which marriages were stable and happy vs. which ended up in bitterness and/or divorce. To their surprise, the authors found that men "should forget all that psychobabble about active listening and validation. If you want your marriage to last for a long time ... just do what your wife says. Go ahead, give in to her.... The marriages that did work all had one thing in common—the husband was willing to give in to the wife. We found that only those newlywed men who are accepting of influence from their wives are ending up in happy, stable marriages."[37]

The researchers also appear to believe that this fact is a fairly recent development in marriage dynamics, coinciding with "the loss of power [in marriage] that men have experienced in the last 40 years."[38]

What's Soured Women on Marriage?

In view of what research indicates concerning who is initiating divorce nowadays and why, it seems plausible that most of the surge in the divorce rate could be attributed to women's increased willingness to take the first step. Prior to the upswing, wives with children were extremely reticent to abandon their marriages, and almost all divorces were initiated by dissatisfied husbands, according to Gallup's polls.[39] But something happened in the late 1960s and early 1970s to completely reverse that trend. Although trustworthy historical data are not available, if husbands today are about as willing as they always were to dissolve marriages, and wives are now six times more likely to initiate divorce as they were in the 1950s, which seems plausible, the change in women's readiness to divorce could completely account for the doubling of the divorce rate.

But what could explain this change in women? What profound cataclysm occurred to reshape the American family so radically?

Current thinking focuses on three interlocking factors. First, no-fault divorce laws came into being around the early 1970s. But most analysts discount no-fault as a truly causal factor, since the divorce rate began to rise somewhat before the repeal of fault divorce. Instead, the passage of no-fault laws is best regarded as merely another manifestation of the increased cultural acceptance of divorce. For our purposes, its real impact is that it allowed one person more easily to divorce an unwilling spouse even when that spouse had done nothing blameworthy.

Second, and more important, women gained increased financial independence because of their unprecedented entry into the workplace. In 1970 for the first time in history the majority of women were employed.[40] This allowed them to leave unrewarding marriages more easily and without having to depend on alimony or end up destitute. Women could more easily afford to divorce when they were unhappy, whereas in earlier decades they were often forced to stay in unfulfilling marriages.

While there is undoubtedly truth in this economic explanation, it is not fully convincing either. The growth in the divorce rate was discontinuous, while the growth in women's employment was regular. After a careful statistical study, University of Chicago economist Robert Michael, Ph.D., concluded that economic factors alone could not explain the divorce surge.[41] Something else happened to deepen women's unhappiness with their marital life. Economic advances allowed women *to leave when they were unhappy;* but something else must have *made them unhappy* in the first place.

The third factor, a profound cultural shift, is the most compelling explanation of all. What movement surfaced in the late 1960s that caused a sea change in gender relations? Michael McFadden, author of *Bachelor Fatherhood,* put into words that which most of us already know: "In the late 1960s, the Women's Movement began . . . and attracted a lot of young, bright wives, many of whom seemed to have ideal marriages. Since that time, I know of at least twenty marriages within that group that have broken up. And in each case it was the woman who initiated it."[42] Constance Ahrons draws a similar conclusion: "The loss of the traditional nuclear family is almost always blamed on women. It is women who left the home and entered the workplace in large numbers; it is women who demand more equality in the world and at home; it is women who initiate most divorces . . . [and] the increase in divorce coincided with the resurgence of the women's movement."[43]

There is no question that the women's movement has made fundamental positive changes in the opportunities and equality available to both women and men. I agree with most informed observers that the loosening of sex roles has increased opportunity and flexibility and widened the options offered to men as well as women, and improved the quality of lives of all members of the family. This is why I have always been a supporter of the women's movement. Despite these unmistakable benefits, according to influential author Shere Hite in her book, *The Hite Report on the Family: Growing Up Under Patriarchy,* the women's movement also contended that the traditional nuclear family was "an essentially repressive one, teaching authoritarian psychological patterns, meekness in women, and a belief in the unchanging rightness of male power."[44] Thus the movement encouraged women and men to view traditional gender relationships within marriage as unacceptable.

As David Popenoe writes: "If men in families can't be reformed, the argument goes, let's throw them out. This perspective typically envisions the nuclear family . . . as a 'patriarchal invention.' It was presumably created by men so they could 'imprison women in marriage' and have total control over their sexuality and their children."[45]

As these views took hold of the thinking of mainstream society, they undoubtedly also contributed to women's current level of dissatisfaction in marriage. Men have had their consciousness raised as well: men today are performing their roles as fathers and husbands somewhat, but not dramatically, better than in the sixties.[46] But wives' standard of acceptance of husbands' behaviors has changed far faster than most husbands' behavior. As women have raised their consciousness, their degree of tolerance for unrewarding marriages or for their husbands' behavior and shortcomings has correspondingly decreased.

> ➤ **Raising women's consciousness has correspondingly low-**
>
> **ered their degree of tolerance for unrewarding marriages or**
>
> **for their husbands' behavior and shortcomings.**

To appreciate fully how much change there has been in expectations for acceptable marital and family relationships due to the women's movement, read the following article entitled, "How to Be a Good Wife," published in the 1956 *Journal of Home Economics*:

Have dinner ready. Plan ahead, even the night before, to have a delicious meal on the table. This is a way of letting him know that you have been thinking about him and are concerned about his needs. Most men are hungry when they come home and the prospect of a good meal is part of the warm welcome needed.

Prepare yourself. Take fifteen minutes to rest so that you will be refreshed when he arrives. Touch up your make-up, put a ribbon in your hair and be fresh looking. He has been with a lot of work-weary people. Be a little gay and a little more interesting. His boring day may need a lift. Clear the clutter. Make one last trip around the house just before your husband arrives gathering up school books, toys, paper, etc. Then run a dust cloth over the tables. Your husband will feel he has reached a haven of rest and order, and it will give you a lift too.

Prepare the children. Take a few minutes to wash the children's hands and faces (if they are small), comb their hair, and if necessary, change their clothes. They are little treasures and he would like to see them playing the part.

Minimize all noise. At the time of his arrival, eliminate all noise of the washer, dryer, dishwasher or vacuum. Try to encourage the children to be quiet. Be happy to see him. Greet him with a warm smile and be glad to see him.

Some don'ts. Don't greet him with problems and complaints. Don't complain if he is late for dinner (count this as minor compared to what he might have gone through that day). Make him comfortable. Have him lean back in a comfortable chair or suggest that he lie down in the bedroom.

Have a cool or warm drink ready for him. Arrange his pillow and offer to take off his shoes. Speak in a low, soft, soothing and pleasant voice.

Allow him to relax and unwind. Listen to him. You may have a dozen things to tell him, but the moment of his arrival is not the time. Let him talk first.

Make the evening his! Never complain if he does not want to take you out to dinner or to other pleasant entertainment. Instead, try to understand his world of strain and pressure and his need to unwind and relax.

The goal. Try to make your home a place of peace and order where your husband can relax in body and spirit.

Just twelve or so years before the women's movement accelerated, these prescriptions were accepted as norms for happy families by both men and women. Today, it shocks—if not sickens—most of us.

There is also evidence that the more women accept the view of the women's movement, the more likely they are to divorce. According to a 1985 study published in the journal *Sex Roles,*[47] "the divorced population in recent years has increasingly been recruited from these ideologically inconsistent marriages in which the husband is traditional and the wife . . . [favors] non-traditional [sex roles]."[48] While women who remained married tended to have more traditional sex-role definitions, similar to both married and divorced men, divorced women insisted on much more pro-feminist ideas and egalitarian relationships. For example, 73 percent of divorced women felt that sex roles should continue to change, while the figure was near 60 percent for married women, married men, and divorced men.

This is not to say that women in more traditional marriages of the past were necessarily less happy. Working within the confines of different cultural values, they often doggedly made marriages work somehow or another, perhaps because there was no acceptable alternative. Like Cortez's men, who fought harder because their leader burned their ships behind them, precluding their retreat, older women made acceptable lives, not only for their husbands and, especially their children, but also for themselves, perhaps because they put far more energy into doing so than does the current generation. This generational difference was graphically conveyed in a scene from the movie *The River Wild.* In one scene, the maritally stressed heroine, played by Meryl Streep, is talking to her happily married mother.

STREEP: "I think my marriage is over, Mama. . . . Well, he just can't seem to make time for us anymore. He's let himself get so beaten up by his job. And he hates it. But he spends every waking minute over there. He hasn't been home one weekend since Christmas. I don't know what it is that he's trying to prove. But I'm really sick of the whole thing. I'm sick of the whole fight. Everything has become unbelievably hard."

MOTHER: "Hard? Honey, forgive me, but you don't know what hard is. That's because you give yourself an *out*. In our generation we had no *out*. That was the pact of marriage. Do you think that if I gave myself an out with your father, given his orneriness, and his deafness, that I wouldn't have taken it years ago?"

In summary, the belief that men abandon their wives and children has been shown to be not only completely erroneous, but in direct opposition to the consistent finding that wives are the ones who overwhelmingly flee marriages. No matter how initiating divorce is measured or defined, women seem to have more incentive and fewer barriers to dissolving marriages than men. Furthermore, this is a recent development, coincident with the upsurge in the divorce rate, and associated with a confluence of factors, the most important of which is the change in sex-role expectations that accompanied the growth of the women's movement.

8.

The "Parentally Disenfranchised" Dad

In the preceding chapters, we have explored every aspect of the bad divorced dad image. We have examined each of the six beliefs comprising the stereotype, and found every one is at least a serious exaggeration or caricature of the truth, and many are flatly opposite to what is true. Contrary to conventional wisdom and prevailing beliefs:

1. Divorced Dads Are *Not* Overwhelmingly Deadbeats in Terms of Child Support Compliance

They actually pay far better than assumed, especially if they remain fully employed (Chapter 2).

2. Divorced Dads Are *Not* Overwhelmingly Disappearing or Runaway Dads

Most continue a surprisingly high amount of contact with their children, and much of whatever disconnection does occur can be attributed directly to mothers impeding or interfering with visitation (Chapter 3).

3. Divorced Fathers Do *Not* End Up Noticeably More Economically Advantaged by Divorce Than Mothers

Once errors are corrected and appropriate assumptions are used, mothers' and fathers' post-divorce financial status in the short run is fairly similar, and in the long run, many divorced mothers will surpass divorced fathers in economic well-being. Divorced mothers and children do *not* disproportionately end up in poverty, and those few who do almost without exception would continue to be in that state whether or not their ex-husbands paid full child support (Chapter 4).

4. Divorced Fathers Are *Not* Far Better Satisfied or Advantaged in the Negotiations Leading to Their Divorce Settlements

In fact, fathers are significantly disadvantaged and dissatisfied compared to mothers, who feel more in control of the settlement process than fathers (Chapter 5).

5. Divorced Fathers Are *Not* More Content and Better Emotionally Adjusted After Divorce Than Mothers

In fact, overwhelming evidence suggests they are far more emotionally devastated by divorce than mothers. Only with respect to calming their anger more quickly than their ex-spouse do fathers have an emotional advantage over mothers (Chapter 6).

6. Fathers Do *Not* Generally Trigger the Marriage's Demise by Abandoning Their Wives and Families

Consistent evidence suggests that more than twice as many *mothers* initiate the termination of the marriage than fathers. Further, this is a quite recent trend precipitated by the cultural changes brought about primarily by the women's movement; this cultural trend best accounts for the unprecedented rise in the divorce rate (Chapter 7).

In our research, we came to these conclusions through more or less inadvertent discoveries. As described in the Introduction to this book, we did not set out, at the beginning of our exploration, to try to establish whether the beliefs about divorced fathers were true. As a matter of fact, we had more or less accepted the belief that many divorced fathers were disconnecting from their children—but as scientists, our acceptance was tentative. Instead, our initial goal was different:

we wanted to know *why* a divorced father would disengage from his children. We hoped we'd be lucky enough that our explorations of this issue would lead us to insights about what could be done to stem the tide. What policies and programs could be adopted that would keep divorced fathers fulfilling their important beneficial role throughout their children's lives?

Though we experienced something of a detour when we began to recognize that the beliefs about divorced fathers were questionable or even completely spurious, and we spent a great deal of our energies exploring their validity, still we were not deterred from our main quest. The question still burned in us: Though we now knew the extent of the problem to have been seriously overstated, nonetheless some fathers *do* disconnect from their children. Some curtail or completely discontinue visitation; others cease financial support. Too many dads do both. Why is that, we wanted to know? What would drive a father to become a nonentity in his child's life, or worse—to cause his child to suffer financially through his neglect or defiance of court order?

That is the question that had troubled us from the outset and, as explained, it was the primary purpose for beginning our research project. The fact that we came to recognize that a much smaller proportion of fathers than previously acknowledged became derelict in their paternal responsibilities didn't diminish the importance of the issue for us. The question of *why* remained impossible for us to ignore. So did the issue of what can be done to reduce this problem.

As with the approach to evaluating the beliefs, we attempted to answer these questions through rigorous scientific and statistical analysis, and this and the next several chapters will describe our statistical findings—which are clear and unambiguous—as well as discuss possible solutions.

As important as they are, statistical and scientific findings only create a kind of blueprint of the architecture of divorce. Through these findings we can get a general picture of emotions, economic situations, custody arrangements, how many dads visit their kids and how often, who is paying child support and who is not. But like an architectural blueprint, the picture is flat, devoid of human dimension. It's not until we hear the stories behind the findings that we can truly begin to comprehend the real picture.

Together, the following three stories of parents we encountered in the course of our research and writing this book capture the essence of our findings in flesh and blood. Reading about their cases will, we hope, convey in human and understandable terms the story *behind* the statistical and scientific findings we uncovered, details of which will be discussed later on in this chapter.

A Too-Involved Dad?

Jeremy, a landscape designer, told us he was determined to be a "new-age" father. Anxious to have a child from the beginning of his marriage, he pestered Roxanne, his wife, until she finally consented. Once she became pregnant, Jeremy read everything he could get his hands on concerning childbirth, newborns, and parenting. As soon as they were eligible, he rushed Roxanne into "husband-coached" childbirth classes. He pridefully recounted his role in cutting his son Bradley's umbilical cord at the delivery. He was the one to give Bradley baths, he said, since Roxanne was frightened she might hurt the infant; he estimated that he had done at least half of the diaper changing; and as soon as Roxanne stopped nursing, at about six weeks, he took over the three A.M. feedings. Since he and Roxanne had different work schedules, he could devote a substantial amount of time during Bradley's infancy to child-care activities, even more than Roxanne. He bought a father's chest-pack baby carrier and proudly went on neighborhood outings. He told us that he was the one who witnessed Bradley's first step and noticed his first tooth.

What he didn't notice, he sadly confided, were Roxanne's feelings about all this. While he had assumed she would welcome his involvement, she instead seemed threatened and dismayed. She complained that he had bonded with Bradley even more than she had. She began to doubt her own femininity and maternal nurturance, he surmised. She now saw Jeremy as a threat, not an ally. That he had truly become a new-age father seemed a nightmare to her, not the dream-come-true he had assumed it would be.

The hostility that emerged annihilated the foundation of their marriage. She secretly began interviewing divorce attorneys and eventually found a suitable one and served Jeremy with papers. He felt she wanted a court of law to certify that *she* was indeed the better parent. Although Jeremy felt he was conciliatory on almost every other aspect of their settlement, he could never compromise on his desire for a substantial role in Bradley's life, which he both needed and felt he deserved. He was sure that the judge would recognize his contribution as a father.

"Wrong!" he cried out, banging his fist on the table in obvious pain.

The judge just decided on the basis of traditional sex roles. She was the mother and I was "only" the father, pretty much useless, like someone's appendix. Nothing I had done in Bradley's past seemed to register at all with this guy. The lawyer I had consulted had warned me about this and told me he probably couldn't win the custody case even if I hired him and paid all his fees. He told me mothers just don't lose custody unless they are prostitutes or drug-addicts or something, so his best advice was that I should prepare myself to start a new life without Bradley. But I didn't really believe him. I trusted that the judge would see how bonded Bradley and I were. But I lost, I just lost! And Bradley lost, too.

The time after the divorce was the worst, Jeremy said. Roxanne seemed to need to justify both herself and the judge's decision in her favor by proving that Jeremy wasn't needed at all.

She's really trying to cut me out. I used to buy all the baby food because I knew what he liked and what he didn't like. I shopped for his clothes, I knew his favorite books, I knew his favorite Barney characters, I'd get on the floor and color with him. But now if she admits I have any role with him at all, it's as if that will undermine her role as the "primary parent," which the judge decreed she was. So she can't let me know what he's doing, how his health is, how he's changing, even where she takes him for childcare. She won't let me have any say in how he's being raised.

She really would prefer that I just let them be, just pay my child support and disappear. And to tell you the awful truth, I'm tempted to do just that—start a new life completely without Bradley. I don't want to be half a father, or just some guy Bradley sees. But I can't carve out a role for myself as his father with the latitude she leaves me.

Jeremy suddenly stood up and walked away toward the restroom, but I saw him take out his handkerchief on the way in and wipe his eyes.

A Controlling Factor

Brooke and Shawn were originally from rural Arizona, where her family owned substantial ranch land. The couple had traditional values, and were rooted in extended family and church, with Brooke staying home with the children—Tommy, nine, and Brandi, seven—while Shawn worked in his wife's family's business. But then they moved to the city of Phoenix, where Brooke hoped to complete a degree in accounting, while Shawn operated a bottled water delivery business. Brooke's classes were mainly at night, so she remained home with the children during the day. Shawn needed to start work quite early, before the rest of the family awoke. Because they were on such different schedules and away from their former sturdy support systems, their marital relationship became frayed.

"Shawn became very controlling," Brooke told me. "Maybe it was because he was finally his own boss; I suppose he had always resented having to take orders from my father on the ranch. But one way or another, he started needing to stick his nose in everything I did at home, or at school, or with the kids. Nothing I did was ever good enough for him. He complained about everything."

Brooke insisted they go into marriage counseling. Shawn resisted at first, but finally agreed. But it didn't help the problem. Brooke became more and more dissatisfied. Eventually, she could take no more, and decided to leave him. But then she faced a quandary: She knew that he would still try to exert influence on her even after the divorce, through the children.

That had been my problem. He was on such a power trip, he needed to control everything I did. And even divorced, he'd find a way of manipulating me, through the kids. So I made a decision, though my attorney advised me against it. I decided to forego seeking any child support. He could have afforded it, and the kids and I sure could have used the money. But I knew if he paid child support, he'd want to visit the kids, and if he was visiting the kids, he'd still want to stick his nose in how I was raising them, criticizing me and all. And that's why I was getting the divorce in the first place. If I'd have wanted him controlling me, I might as well have stayed married to him. So my dad agreed to help me enough financially to the point that I didn't need his child support, and he'd be out of my life for good.

Things worked out for a time just the way Brooke wanted. Shawn did drop out of her and the kids' life. But then she met another man, Joe, and married him quickly. "The kids can't stand Joe," she confided. "Although he is fine with me, he's always complaining about how they behave, though they are really good kids." Eventually, Tommy, who was having the most trouble with Joe, wanted to move out and live instead with his real dad. Shawn, who by then had moved away from Phoenix, was eager to renew his role as father. Despite Brooke's reluctance, Tommy did go to live with his father.

Not Letting Dad Off the Hook

Susan and Kerry were the quintessential New York couple: he was a singer and she was on the editorial staff of a highly successful magazine. Two years into their marriage Susan discovered she was pregnant. Kerry was initially angry. He felt he wasn't prepared to be a father just yet. But after the birth of their daughter, all his fears and trepidations melted away. As soon as he gazed in his daughter's eyes, he fell instantly in love. Fours years later, Susan gave birth to a son. "Kerry really loved being a father. The children were extremely fortunate," Susan recalled. "He was able to spend a lot of time with the children because of his schedule. He was usually home during the day while I was at work, so it was a good arrangement for us both."

While the children were thriving, all was not well with the marriage. Susan and Kerry began to grow apart as each wanted different things from their lives and the marriage. They began to fight. The arguments escalated into bitter battles. Both of them were miserable, but it was Susan who took the first step by informing Kerry that she wanted out of the marriage. "He was very angry and very hurt," she said. "He acted totally shocked. He was desperate to hold on, even though he had admitted we had been unhappy. It was a very bitter coming apart."

Susan moved out and took an apartment ten floors away in the same building because she liked the community they were living in and wanted to keep some continuity in the children's lives. During this time, while the divorce was still in the process of being finalized, their mutual anger was at a peak. However, Susan did not let her anger interfere with her children's relationship with their father. "I felt it was always important for the kids to know the other parent so they are grounded in reality, not drifting in a sea of fantasy," she told me. Kerry would pick the kids up after school, then take them to his apartment. When Susan got home from work at about six o'clock, he'd bring them upstairs to her apartment. "The interaction between us at that time was horrendous," she admitted. "When he'd bring them up, I would pretty much open the door and close it. Sometimes he'd have temper tantrums. And that would only make me angrier. It was hard on everyone, especially our daughter."

As angry and hurt as she was, Susan never let that become an issue over Kerry's involvement as a father. In fact, she tried to convince her children on a regular basis to sleep over at their father's, but the children had become clingy and fearful of being away from their mother for a long period of time.

"I have to say that for all the ugliness between us, I kept my head clear about the kids," Susan emphasized. "I never stood in his way of having access to the children because I felt it was good to have another parent to give me some relief. I always made sure he was involved in their upbringing. I made sure he saw their report cards. We tried to go to parent-teacher conferences together, although at first, we'd get into fights with each other."

During these first few years after the divorce, Susan helped lay the groundwork for Kerry staying involved in his children's lives. "I had come from a family where my father was alternately physically or emotionally absent and I never wanted that for my kids," she explained. This groundwork proved to be essential when Kerry moved out of New York City back to his hometown in the South. He had contracted cancer, and felt that he needed to leave the stress of the city for his health. Susan agreed with his decision. "I knew that if he wanted to live, he would have to leave New York." The children, however, were devastated at the news of his leaving. To help keep them connected to their father, Susan made arrangements for them to fly down for a visit after he got settled. In addition to their periodic visits, Kerry called his children several times a week. And Susan made sure to reciprocate. "If something great happened to either one of the kids, like winning a Little League game, I'd say, 'Let's call dad.' "

Susan contends that inviting her ex-husband to be a co-parent with her actually benefitted *her*. "When the children reached their teens, they became increasingly difficult. Kerry would often act as a mediator. When I was having some particularly tough years with our daughter, the first thing I'd do was call Kerry. He would tell me what he felt about the situation and then we'd form a plan of action. He really earned his stripes as a parent during those years."

> ➤ One mother recognized that it might have been easy to block her ex-husband from being involved as a father. "If I had given him a hard time, there's a good chance he would have dropped out and become 'the victim,' " she said. "But I wasn't about to let that happen. I and my children needed him as a parent."

Susan recognized that it might have been easy to block Kerry from being involved as a father. "If I had given him a hard time, there's a good chance he would have dropped out and become 'the victim.' But I wasn't about to let that happen. I and my children needed him as a parent." Her efforts paid off. Over the years, she and Kerry were able to put aside their differences. They worked together for the well-being of their children, who despite the upset of a divorce, developed into healthy, well-adjusted teens with a close relationship to both parents.

Solving the Puzzle of the Disconnected Father[1]

All three stories dramatize and humanize the essential point of the statistical findings we uncovered. If you want to know *why* some fathers disconnect, we found, look to the parenting role assigned to them by the legal system and/or by their ex-spouses. Look to see whether they continue to feel empowered to act as a father. In all three families, the mother's attitude toward her ex-spouse's role as a father communicated itself to the father loud and clear. Jeremy knew that Roxanne wanted no part of his role as a father to Bradley. The courts agreed. As a result, Jeremy, whose previous married life revolved around his role as father, was now on the brink of disappearing from his son's life. Brooke made a conscious effort to cut Shawn out of her life, and her children's, even giving up the child support she could have received to accomplish her goal. And it worked: Shawn completely disappeared—until one of his children clearly needed him as a father. Despite Susan's and Kerry's mutual anger, Susan recognized the importance of making sure that her ex-husband remain connected as a father to his children. By acknowledging his daily need to be involved and by sharing important aspects of their children's lives, Susan ensured that a father who might have slipped away from his children remained actively involved in their lives if given the chance.

In our attempt to statistically confirm that this was the reason why some fathers disconnected with their children after divorce, we entertained over thirty-one possible explanations of father dropout. For example, was there truth to the potential explanation that asserts that fathers who disappear are those who are fundamentally immoral and irresponsible? Are these the "bad dads" of Furstenburg's study, fathers like Gary whom we met in Chapter 3? These fathers haven't really ever connected to their kids, and they really don't care very much about them, opting instead to pursue their own pleasures selfishly. Or had dads become disconnected because they were so angry at their ex-wives that they could not tolerate being near them or have them in any way involved in their lives? Since some kind of contact with the ex-wife would be necessary to maintain a connection to their kids, these fathers instead abandoned them. Then there was another possible explanation—one raised by father's rights groups—that fathers stop paying child support because they suspect or believe the mother isn't using the money for the children, but rather for her own clothes, make-up, drinking or drugs, or to support her new "worthless" boyfriend. These fathers see their kids walking around with shabby clothes or eating poorly and vow "not to pay another dime" until it goes unerringly for their children. These dads proclaim that if they could be assured that their payments would directly benefit their children, by some system of financial accountability, then they would happily pay.

Other possibilities we looked at included:

➤ lack of strong identification with the fathering role

➤ interference with visitation by the ex-spouse (discussed in Chapter 3)

➤ father's economic hardship, i.e., too little money to pay child support (discussed in Chapter 2)

➤ competing social demands, such as a new girlfriend keeping the father too busy to stay involved with his children

➤ competing nonsocial demands, such as work commitments, recreational or athletic activities or hobbies taking up too much of the father's time to have any left for his children.

Essentially, we included in our study every possible factor that any responsible commentator or social scientist had ever proposed to explain fathers' disengagement. (The complete list is in List 8.1.)

How did we assess whether a potential explanation had scientific validity? How could we tell if the possible factor truly accounted for father dropout? For instance, if suspicions of misuse of child support were really the root cause of paternal disconnection, we reasoned, then it would be those dads who felt that their ex-wife was misusing child support who would be the primary ones to disappear. Alternatively, if anger at the ex-wife were the best and truest explanation of father dropout, then it would mainly be those dads who were most angry at their ex-wives who would disappear financially and/or emotionally from their children's lives. In short, we could go through each plausible explanation and find whether it correlated with father disengagement.

The Single Most Important Explanation of Disengagement

Our statistical results were very clear and surprisingly unambiguous. While many factors were related, one explanation turned out to be superior to all the others and literally rose to the top in terms of its ability to explain or predict which fathers would remain involved in their children's lives and which ones would disconnect. I call this factor feeling "parentally disenfranchised."

> ➤ Many of the fathers interviewed felt that everything about the divorce, especially anything concerning the way the children were raised, was completely out of their control. They felt as if the child was in no real sense *theirs* anymore. The child, in effect, belonged now to someone else, someone who, not uncommonly, despised and disparaged them.

1. Lack of a real sense of obligation to the child.

2. Lack of sense of responsibility to uphold agreements.

3. Lack of guilt about divorce.

4. Lack of a commitment to parenting.

5. Paying child support and visiting creates too much financial hardship.

6. Father doesn't enjoy visits.

7. Visits are too trying and difficult.

8. The child does not enjoy visits.

9. The father and mother fight too much.

10. The mother interferes with visits.

11. The mother opposes the idea of the father's involvement.

12. The father has too many competing nonsocial demands on his time to visit (such as work and recreation).

13. The father has too many competing social demands on his time to visit (such as friends, family, dating, or new girlfriend).

14. The father feels the amount of child support he owes is too high.

15. The father feels the mother abuses the child support he pays and doesn't use it properly for the child.

16. The father feels the terms of the decree or settlement are unfair.

17. The visits don't relieve the father's loneliness or he isn't lonely.

18. The new girlfriend objects to the father visiting.

19. The new girlfriend objects to the father's expenditures for child support.

20. The new girlfriend doesn't like the child.

21. The child doesn't like the new girlfriend.

22. The child is not communicative during visits.

23. Lack of fear of prosecution for not paying child support.

24. The father thinks the child is maladjusted.

25. Lack of support for keeping involved by friends and family.

26. The mother "bad-mouths" the father too much (to the child, the father or others).

27. The pain of being a noncustodial parent is too overwhelming to abide.

28. The father's anger at the mother interferes with his involvement with the child.

29. The pain of being divorced is too overwhelming to abide.

30. The father believes his visiting is ultimately harmful to the child.

31. The father feels he has no input into how the child is raised, feels powerless, feels parentally disenfranchised.

LIST 8.1   **Possible Reasons for the Father's Disengagement from the Child Investigated**

Many of the fathers interviewed felt that everything about the divorce, especially anything concerning the way the children were raised, was completely *out of their control*. In contrast to those fathers who felt that, despite the divorce, they shared control with the mother over child-rearing issues, these parentally disenfranchised fathers felt as if the child was in no real sense *theirs* anymore. The child, in effect, now belonged to someone else, someone who, not uncommonly, despised and disparaged them. These fathers felt they had no real rights of parenthood anymore, most especially the right to involve themselves in the way their child was raised. Like Jeremy, they were on the outside looking in. Many were extremely embittered that society demanded that they still assume the *responsibilities* of parenthood. As they saw it, society, the legal system, and their ex-wives had conspired to rip asunder their connection to their children. No longer did they have the right to share in the joys and struggles of child rearing. As one dad put it, "I can't stand being only a wallet; why can't they let me be a *father*?" Overwhelmingly it was these disempowered, embittered, despairing fathers who were the ones who discontinued contact with and support of their children.[2]

Fathers like Kerry, on the other hand, who were made to feel, either by their ex-wives or by the courts, that they still had a valuable paternal role to play overwhelmingly stayed involved and paid full child support. Shawn, when thrust out, dropped out; but when later made to feel like a father again, returned strongly to fulfilling his paternal obligations. Jeremy—for the moment at least—was still struggling mightily to hang on, fighting to find some worthwhile place in his child's life. However, he is at great risk of becoming a disengaged father.

The Experience of the "Driven Away Dad"

These parentally disenfranchised fathers who drop out of their kids' lives are the ones labeled "runaway dads," and "deadbeat dads." These terms heap all the blame on the fathers, in a sense calling into question their moral fiber. But do these terms aptly portray their experience? What would the fathers themselves tell us about what drove them to abdicate their parental responsibilities?

To attempt to go beyond the labels, we next tell the stories of three disengaged fathers in their own words. The following are what we heard from real dads who are no longer paying child support or visiting their children. We do not vouch for the accuracy of everything they told us, since we were not able to corroborate their versions with their ex-wives' or with court records.

In each case, something profound happened to them to make these formerly responsible fathers disengage. Their paternal urges were thwarted. They were somehow made to feel, either by the legal system or perhaps their ex-wives, that they had no real role to play in their children's lives. A better, more accurate label for them might be "Driven Away Dads."

Up until now, we've never heard their stories, we've never asked them their side of things, or let them speak to reporters or researchers. So it was easy to heap blame on them. But if you simply take the trouble to *listen* to a disengaged dad, this story of feeling *driven away* arises time after time. Walk a mile in such dads' shoes. Read what it feels like to be a "Driven Away Dad."

Weary of Fighting for the Right to Be a Dad

William had not seen his daughter, Jessica, age thirteen, for three and one-half years, though the court order currently grants him a very generous visitation schedule. Through five years of separation, before the divorce was granted, William and his ex-wife had agreed on a joint-custody arrangement, where Jessica would live with him on alternate weeks. The arrangement worked well for all three of them.

Then the courts got involved.

William's wife applied for welfare, claiming that William had skipped out on her, although he was still taking his daughter every other week. "We began to fight about child support, but it turned into a very ugly fight about everything," William said. "There was great mutual antagonism."

The judge rejected any possibility of William and his ex-wife continuing their custody arrangement, believing that joint-custody arrangements do not work when there is such antagonism between the couple. The judge then ordered an evaluation by a social worker, who determined that the child's mother could offer her a better home and recommended that she be awarded sole custody. "We each got a copy of the evaluation a few weeks before the final day in court for the custody decision," William told me. "When she got her copy, my ex-wife called me up and wanted to meet in a café. I didn't know why she wanted to meet, but I agreed to see her. At the café, she told me that with the evaluation, she would now be in charge and she didn't want me to make any trouble of any kind. She wanted me to affirm to the state that I was going to cooperate with her. I refused to make any kind of promise to her. I also told her that even though I lost this evaluation, I would continue to contest the decision and fight for custody."

Two days later, his ex-wife went to his child's school before it let out and attempted to get her daughter to leave with her. "The custody decision hadn't yet been put into effect, and it was my week to have my daughter," William said. Jessica refused to go with her mother, and the school officials refused to let her mother take her. "They called me, and I said, 'Don't let her take my daughter. I'm coming from work.' It's usually only a twenty-minute ride, but that day there was unusually heavy traffic and it took me an hour. And in the course of that time, the police had come to the school and said that because there was no actual order in effect at the moment, my wife could do whatever she wanted, and she left with my daughter. I had spoken with my daughter before I left work to come get her and she was screaming and crying. By the time I arrived at the school, she wasn't there."

William's ex-wife continued to hold their daughter. She told Jessica's psychologist that she would not allow William to see Jessica until he had convinced the psychologist that he would not do anything to harm his child. William let out a long sigh at this point and said,

Of course, there was no history of any abuse whatsoever by me to any member of my family. The psychologist's recommendation was that my daughter should be returned to me, and she came back to stay with me a few days later. At that point, I thought I really had something with respect to the court fight because my ex-wife had done something very harmful to my daughter. My lawyer went with me to court and went into the judge's chambers. He came out and said the judge 'couldn't care a fig' about the kidnapping, but she did remember how I had said that my daughter was better off before the court had intervened in all of our lives and that she seemed not to like me. My wife was awarded custody, and because I had never been anything but the most exemplary father, they gave me a very generous visitation, where I'd see my daughter almost 40 percent of the time.

But William knew that wasn't the end of his fight. "I predicted that my daughter's life—and my life—would be miserable from that point on. I knew that my ex-wife would stop at nothing to hurt me through Jessica. I had no hope that it would be any other way. And from my long experience with the court system, I knew that the authorities wouldn't help in any way to ensure that I would have a good relationship with my daughter. For a time, I seriously considered moving to another country, where I have relatives, but I didn't do that."

For the next eight months, William continued to visit his daughter, although he frequently had to battle with his wife to be allowed to see her even within his visitation rights. "She was incredibly ambitious when it came to thwarting my visits. She'd use obscenities and make derogatory comments. She was like a completely insane person, driven by a very intense anger."

During these eight months, William returned to court ten times for problems surrounding his visitation rights. "One of the problems occurred when I wanted to take my daughter to visit relatives in France. For my ex-wife to allow me to do that, she wanted to impose a long list of conditions, including not letting us go more than ten miles from where we'd be staying." William had to make several visits to the court to resolve this one problem.

> *I had been a full parent to my daughter for the five years after I separated from my wife. I was involved in her school life, I tucked her in bed every night that she stayed with me, I knew all her friends and all her friends' families. But now with my daughter going through so much suffering, and all the suffering that I was going through, I just couldn't live like that any longer. When you go to court, they tell you that you have to think of the best interest of the children, and when they rule against you I believe they expect you to 'take it like a man.' But I think that some people who have gone through years of fighting like this just can't take it. A lot of damage has been done. I'd have to say that my own ability to parent, which had been wonderful, was not what it should have been anymore.*

At this point in our conversation, William became very still and seemed to be in some distant place. He was clearly upset and having trouble continuing his story. Then, very quietly, he said, "It's been over three years now, since I saw my daughter. I've tried to make contact with her on several occasions during that time, but what efforts I have made have not succeeded. I have since heard through my father, who still has contact with Jessica, that she doesn't want to see me now.

She holds what happened against me. So now I don't know what to do. Maybe it's not a fair thing to hope, and maybe it's not a mature position, but I had hoped that somehow my daughter would come to *me*."

An Ironic Twist

A former child-support enforcement officer for the state of Arizona, Andrew spent years haranguing other fathers to pay up. On the occasions he went out of his way to assist a noncustodial father because he felt the system was treating him particularly unfairly, he was reprimanded by his superiors, told that his job was only to collect the money. Then he got a divorce, and he found himself on the other side of the system.

Andrew tried to get a joint legal custody arrangement, but was immediately thwarted. "My ex-wife told me at the outset that if I tried for it, she'd fight me tooth and nail; she'd dig up any dirt she could find on me," he said. "She really wanted total control over the children."

He was originally ordered to pay $560 a month in child support, based upon his salary and the income he received from a side-line business. When the business dried up, he went back to court to have his child support order lowered because he could no longer afford to pay so much. "Plus, because my ex-wife lived over thirty miles away, I had all the expenses of picking up and dropping off my children for visits, which was putting an added strain on my budget. In addition, I had gotten remarried and had a stepchild to support." He also provided his children with clothes, toiletries, toys, even bicycles that they could ride when they stayed with him.

Andrew thought it would be a fairly simple matter to get the child-support award adjusted. What he hadn't bargained on was his ex-wife's lawyer, who made "bogus" claims of child-care expenses, and claimed that Andrew was pulling in money from his business when, in fact, he had ceased operating the business. "The attorney had absolutely no documentation to substantiate their claims, but the judge believed my ex-wife because 'she was under oath.' " What was the result of Andrew's day in court? "My child support payments went *up* $200!"

While Andrew thought the ruling was unfair and would have resisted paying all the support ordered, he didn't have much of a choice, since Arizona state law requires automatic garnishment of wages. "It wasn't just because I felt the child support award was punishingly high that made me reluctant to pay," Andrew explains. "It was the fact that my ex-wife was totally inflexible with the visitation arrangements. I could never see my children outside of the prescribed schedule, which was on the first and third weekend of every month. When my current wife and I got married, for instance, I had to get a court order to allow my children to come to the wedding because it didn't fall on the scheduled visit. Yet, my ex-wife has expected me to be flexible whenever *she* wants to make a change."

Andrew began having severe anxiety attacks at work. Eventually he had to be taken to the hospital for treatment. "The doctor who was treating me said that if I stayed in my job, I would probably be dead in a year or two," Andrew said. "The psychiatrist determined that not only did the job cause stress, but that I was victimized by the same system I was trying to enforce. He felt I was basically beating myself up inside every time I took an action against a noncustodial parent."

Andrew left his job as a child-support enforcer and reopened his sideline business. Because he was no longer receiving a paycheck, the state had no way of garnishing his wages. Since he went into business, nearly a year ago, he has not paid any child support. "It's not something that I'm overly proud of," he admitted.

The Story Behind the Headlines

He was called the "King of the Deadbeat Dads." He was a precious metals analyst who owed an astonishing $640,000 in back child support. He reportedly skipped around the country and to Canada to evade authorities who had a warrant issued for his arrest. He was said to be living a life of luxury while depriving his children of the child support they rightly deserved. He was the subject of countless newspaper articles and TV reports, including a segment devoted to him on *60 Minutes*. His name is Jeffrey Nichols,[3] and from everything the newspapers had printed about him he seemed to be justly pilloried. Nichols even admitted his guilt and failed to offer any explanation. But was there more to his story, too? Could he possibly have an excuse that would make his reprehensible actions understandable?

Though he was still press shy, he agreed to meet with us in his mother's apartment in New York City, where we were immediately disarmed by this unassuming man with a dry sense of humor.

> *In 1985, my wife and I separated and I supported her and my family generously—above and beyond what was required, against the advice of my attorney, who said I would be setting a precedent that would be difficult to change. From 1985 to 1989, I paid for everything, so my children were totally unaffected financially by the divorce. My ex-wife had the credit cards and I paid the bills directly. I gave her cash every week. In 1988, following the crash of the stock market, my income from my business declined sharply and I could no longer afford to keep up the roughly $5,000 a month I was giving my ex-wife. I told her we had to economize, cut back a little bit. The next thing I knew, she was suing me for child support and alimony.*
>
> *When we went to court, the judge ordered me to continue paying the $5,000 a month, which was more than I could afford. And I continued to struggle to pay all that money. I went back to court a couple of times and asked for downward modifications, which were always turned down. Because I have my own business, the judge disbelieved anything I said about my income. She thought that I had some foreign bank account with millions hidden away, but of course the investigators were never able to find anything.*
>
> *Up until that point, my relationship with my three children was good. But once I tried to get the child support lowered, my ex-wife made it difficult for me to see them. She tried to poison them against me. I had plans of taking one of the children with me on vacation, but she prevented that.*

Around that time Nichols had begun a relationship with a woman he would later marry named Suzan. After their apartment had been broken into ("The only things that were taken were canceled checks and bank statements," he claims), they moved to Toronto to start a new life. He came back to New York every two weeks to visit his children. His business continued to remain in a slump, and he fell farther and farther behind on his child-support payments. His ex-wife went back to court and had a warrant issued for his arrest. This effectively prevented him from visiting his children, since he knew that if he set foot in New York, he would be arrested. Unable to see his children and with his financial troubles mounting, Nichols slipped into a severe depression.

"I started taking Prozac, but it didn't help much. I became a real basket case. Suzan basically took over a lot of aspects of my business because I couldn't handle them. I had already cashed in my retirement accounts and whatever savings I had had. Suzan was contributing money for our living from her savings, and I couldn't see my kids because of the arrest warrant. In frustration, I threw up my hands and said, what's the point of paying anything? So I stopped paying everything."

Nichols and his fiancée were not happy in Toronto and moved to Florida, where Suzan had originally wanted to live. With her help, his business picked up and they started to do well financially. In fact, in later years, they were doing well enough that he could have afforded the $5,000 in child support. But he continued not to pay. "I was still so angry, and I was clinically depressed, taking antidepressants and seeing one therapist after another, and I was not thinking straight," he explained.

Shortly thereafter, his ex-wife went back to court and got the child-support award doubled.

The judge decided that $5,000 wasn't enough, that I should be paying $10,000 a month. All this in my absence and without any evidence of my financial situation and ability to pay. And she made that retroactive, so that the meter was running at $10,000 a month, since 1990. And at the same time, as icing on the cake, my ex-wife, who hadn't heard from me or seen me in the last couple of years, decided that I was dangerous and asked the judge to issue an order of protection prohibiting me to come near the kids. I've never done anything violent. I'm basically a gentle person. I don't know where this idea of violence came from.

Eventually Nichols was jailed for failure to pay alimony and child-support evasion and, because the meter kept ticking even while he served time in jail, he was forced to sell off his house and most of his belongings to help meet his back child-support payments. His once-prosperous consulting business no longer exists, due to the widespread negative publicity associated with his case and more than a year in prison. Though he now pays what he can toward the more than $600,000 in past due support, his children refuse to see him. He is only able to keep up with their lives through his mother, who still has a close relationship with them.

"Looking back, would you have done anything differently?" I asked him.

"In retrospect, I made a lot of bad decisions along the way," he admitted. "I should have always paid something, if only so I could have said to my kids that I did the best that I could have done. I look back and think that no man in his right mind could shun all financial responsibility for the children he loved so much."

As disparate as their stories are, all these disengaged fathers have one thing in common: their feeling that they were kicked out, dislodged from their kids' lives by the system and by their ex-wives. These weren't the ogres I was prepared for, they are flesh-and-blood men who seem to be genuinely despairing over their loss of family. Not one of them started off being a deadbeat or runaway dad, so it is difficult to impugn their general lack of paternal concern. Rather, something happened to each one that motivated his later withdrawal, some series of events that, rightly or wrongly, told him his value as a complete father was nil.

Corroboration of Our Findings

While our study was the first to interview divorced fathers and get their spin on things (and to this day it is still the largest, best funded, and we'd like to think, most scientifically rigorous), later researchers have begun to follow suit. And the tale that fathers tell of being driven away, feeling lack of control over how their child is raised, feeling parentally disenfranchised, has arisen in virtually every later study.[4]

> ➤ The tale that fathers tell of being driven away, feeling lack of control over how their child is raised, feeling parentally disenfranchised, has arisen in virtually every study conducted since ours.

Sociologist Terry Arendell, Ph.D., finds it, too. In her recent book *Fathers & Divorce,* she writes:

> *"As long as children are minors," many [fathers] insisted in various ways, "fathers risk disenfranchisement as parents" and can be reduced to being "only faceless money machines" for former wives. Lost in divorce, they claimed, were their rights to fatherhood, discretionary control of their earnings, exercise of familial authority, and autonomy to plan and handle their futures. . . . The majority of men perceived themselves to be victimized and their rights violated by divorce.[5]*

It is worth noting that Arendell corroborated our finding using a complementary research technique called the "qualitative" method, rather than the statistical, "quantitative" methods that were employed in our study. Unlike the comparatively objective quantitative method, the more "interpretive" (to use Arendell's term) qualitative method leaves more room for researchers' judgments, biases, and ideologies to color their interpretations. Arendell recognized that she "was not a neutral observer," and that she was "influenced by" a perspective that holds that "male dominance within families . . . occurs at woman's cost."[6] Perhaps as a result, she proceeds to dismiss experiences of the fathers she interviewed as mere "rhetoric" and "masculinist discourse." One expert (female) reviewer, too, found her book "value-laden throughout," offering "misinterpretations of the father's own comments, casting fathers in a more negative light than need be."[7]

All of these more recent researchers have heard stories about feeling parentally disenfranchised from divorced father after divorced father, as I have. And with the clarity of hindsight, the explanation that fathers disconnect from their children for the simple reason that they feel robbed of their fatherhood has the compelling ring of truth.

Think about the comparison of divorced fathers to those still married. In still-married families, where mothers and fathers *both* feel connected to children, fathers virtually always feel concern and love for them, they voluntarily always take pride in their provider role, and make every sacrifice for them—as mothers do. Clearly, we don't feel any need to legislate or try to coerce fathers' care for their children in intact families. Why does this support stop when parents divorce? Because in these cases, our findings explain, the fathers feel that their children have been wrenched from them by their ex-wives and by the system, and that there is absolutely nothing they can do about it—they are powerless. No one endows them with real fatherhood anymore. In this perspective, it is easy to see why some will feel such incredible loss that they drop out.

An interesting phenomenon occurs when we speak with fathers from intact families, including judges, or lawyers or men in the child-support enforcement industry. Initially these men feel anger and outrage at the irresponsibility shown by "deadbeat" or "runaway" dads, and don't see how any responsible father can pull away from his children. But then I tell them what Jared told me:

I, too, always looked with disdain on fathers who didn't live up to their family obligations, especially deadbeat dads. I assumed if you were a good middle-class father who loved his wife, who gave up on the fast track at work so you could have more family time, who didn't drink or do drugs or beat his wife, who was the Little League and Pop Warner coach, nothing bad could happen to you or your kid. But my wife had an affair with some guy from her office. She left me for him and the two of them now live with my kid, and there was nothing I could do to stop it. My lawyer laughed when I said, "But she's the one who did wrong!"

I want to tell all the smug dads out there: This could happen to you. You have no rights—none that will be enforced, anyway. Your kid who you love so much can be ripped away from you, and nothing you did in the past can protect that. People think that if you're basically a good dad, it can't happen to you. But I am proof that it can.

I no longer look down on fathers who just quit the scene, because I've come within inches of doing it myself. In order to stay in my kid's life, I tiptoe, I bend, I swallow my pride. She is the gatekeeper, and she can be very arbitrary. I say or do whatever's necessary to keep her from getting mad, and cutting me off from my kid. To stay and try to play anything approaching the father role under these circumstances is the hardest thing I've ever done.

The Chicken or the Egg?

One of the things we noticed clearly was that paying child support and visiting the child tend to go hand in hand. For example, the association between Wave 2

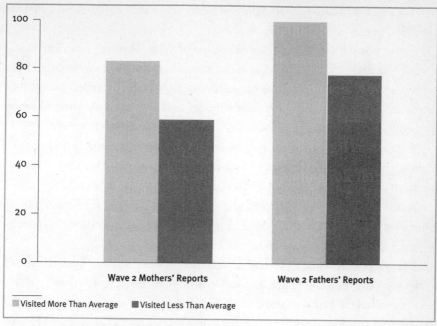

100

80

60

40

20

0

Wave 2 Mothers' Reports   Wave 2 Fathers' Reports

■ Visited More Than Average   ■ Visited Less Than Average

CHART 8.1   Percentage of Child Support Paid
by Visitation Frequency

mothers' report of how much the father visited and how much child support he paid, as well as the Wave 2 fathers' report of his visitation and how much child support he paid, is displayed in Chart 8.1.[8] Do parents visit because they pay child support, or do they pay child support because they visit? Like the eternal puzzle of which came first, the chicken or the egg, this question is one that has intrigued many.

Some researchers have argued for the first scenario, believing that fathers visit because they pay child support.[9] They contend that dads who feel compelled by enforcement machinery to pay will want to visit to look in on their investment. The alternative scenario, that fathers pay because they visit, makes the argument that once they see their children, they feel so connected to them that they are willing to support them financially. While both of these explanations are plausible, and various experts have argued for each, so is a third possibility: that both paying and visiting are each caused by some third factor. The third factor, we realized, could well be the feeling of being parentally enfranchised we had identified in our earlier analyses.

So we posed a somewhat different version of the chicken-egg problem. In analyzing our findings, we wanted to know this: Do fathers feel enfranchised because they pay child support or begin to visit? Or is the situation completely reversed? Do fathers both pay child support and visit their children because they come to feel enfranchised?

It's inappropriate to attempt to answer this question by simply asking people; they can't be counted upon to answer honestly since they may not even understand what unconsciously motivates them. But when the data are longitudinal (collected at multiple time periods, sequentially), as ours are, sophisticated statistical techniques can help us determine cause and effect. We used these techniques, called causal analyses, with our study.

Here's how it works: the researcher specifies alternative "mini-theories" about what causes what. For example, two mini-theories were discussed earlier: what we called the first scenario is that a father visits because he has been forced to pay child support. Another mini-theory is that noncustodial parents begin to feel parentally enfranchised because they visit. In other words, a father feels he has some say in how his child is raised because he has been around to exercise that say. Yet another is that a father feels parentally enfranchised for some other reason, such as that his ex-wife wanted his involvement as a father (as with Susan and Kerry), and as a result, he both determines to pay and visit. In this way, each plausible mini-theory is considered. The researcher then sees which of all the theories fits the patterns of the data better.

In employing this technique, we began to get a clear picture of the cause and effect of fathers' visiting and paying, empowerment and disaffection. Our data strongly suggested one primary causal sequence: Fathers both pay child support and maintain emotional involvement *because* they feel parentally enfranchised, not vice versa. Chart 8.2 shows these patterns that best fit our findings. In this *path diagram*, the arrows—which visually represent the causal relationships—go *from* enfranchisement *to both* payment and visiting, rather than vice versa. If a father comes to feel parentally enfranchised, he will *as a result* come both to visit his children and to pay child support.

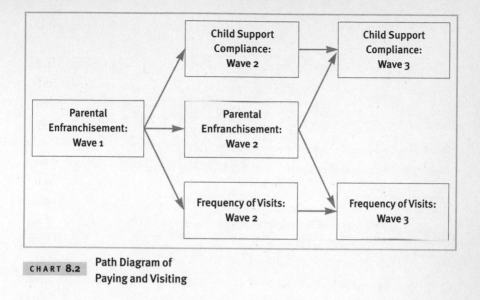

CHART 8.2   **Path Diagram of Paying and Visiting**

Reciprocal Weapons of Engagement

The opposite side of the coin was true in our data as well: we found a correspondence between the mothers' denial of visitation and the fathers' refusal to pay child support. As eminent law professor David Chambers has noted: "For many divorcing couples, visitation is the one event within the mother's control that she knows the father cares about, and child support is the one event within the father's control that he knows the mother cares about."[10] Thus, many writers have noted that if the father fails to make, or is late with, a child-support payment, the mother may "help" herself by denying him access to the children. Similarly, if the mother is not home with the child at the father's scheduled pickup time for a visit, or interferes with visitation in other ways, he may stop paying child support.[11] These feuding, retaliating patterns of mutual withholding are far more common than exercising whatever legal remedies are available. We termed visitation denial and child-support nonpayment "reciprocal weapons of engagement" in the war some divorced parents wage. For example, Chambers writes, "Nearly all [of the] ... enforcement officers ... we surveyed believed that squabbles over visitation resulted in lower payments."[12]

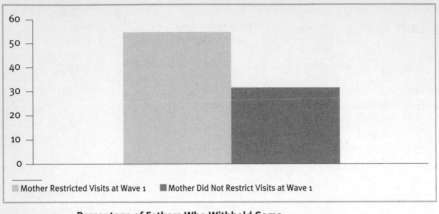

60
50
40
30
20
10
0

☐ Mother Restricted Visits at Wave 1　　■ Mother Did Not Restrict Visits at Wave 1

CHART 8.3 **Percentage of Fathers Who Withheld Some Child Support at Wave 2**

➤ Our results showed that if a mother had *previously* restricted visitation, the father was significantly more likely to withhold some child support *later.*

In our data, we found the two weapons indeed mutual.[13] And we found suggestive evidence that visitation denial was more likely to result in subsequent withholding of child support than vice versa. In Chart 8.3, we present our results that showed that if a mother had *previously* restricted visitation, the father was significantly more likely to *later* withhold some child support. Recall the truckdriver we described in Chapter 3 who stopped paying only after his wife arbitrarily refused to let him visit his children? He said he would rather go to jail than pay child support if his right to see his children weren't upheld. While this view shows little sensitivity to his children's needs, only his own, it is understandable and we encountered many fathers who agreed with this stance.

Should Visitation Be Strictly Enforced?

In view of the association just documented, many have felt that it would be a good idea to enforce visitation rights as vociferously as we enforce child-support non-payment. It has been particularly rankling to fathers that if they renege on child support, an entire billion-dollar machinery for enforcement exists, but no real remedies are available to them if a mother commits an equally serious infraction by withholding court-decreed visitation. It is undeniably true that the system is unable to redress a father's grievances the way it redresses a mother's, since, as Brian, the father whose story we told in Chapter 3, found out, the court has few tools to ensure a mother readily permits paternal access. As the agency official in the truck-driver case agreed, "Fathers should pay, and they will be seriously punished if they don't. Mothers should allow visitation, but—but nothing, at least for now." Among other things, this sends the wrong messages to fathers: that their worth to children is entirely financial, not at all emotional or psychological.

There aren't many effective sanctions available to the court, after all. Whereas garnishing a wage can be an effective means of collecting a duly owed debt of child-support money, this won't work when the infraction involves something other than money: time with the child. As a result, these programs must try to sound tough, but they are undoubtedly more bark than bite. This difference has unfortunately convinced fathers that there is a gender bias at work in the system in upholding their concerns. As we have seen, child-support nonpayment and interference with visitation are highly linked events: if one parent withholds one, the other retaliates, taking the law into his or her own hands, as it were, by withholding the other.

➤ **The fact that there aren't many effective sanctions available to the court when a mother has interfered with visitation has unfortunately convinced fathers that there is a gender bias at work in the system in upholding their concerns.**

Yet, the law generally holds that the two are disconnected: a father cannot successfully raise as a defense to a child-support payment infraction that the mother wouldn't let him visit the children. While the law probably makes sense, it ignores the reality of the linkage.

Nevertheless, some localities have begun to experiment with programs to enforce visitation. The Visitation Intake Program in Wayne County, Michigan, for instance, uses a multipronged attack to try to resolve the issue, including trying to educate the parents through telephone and personal conferences, mediation interventions, documentation of visitation arrearages, and instituting civil contempt procedures. The Expedited Visitation Services in Maricopa County, Arizona (which we discussed briefly in Chapter 3), monitors visitation compliance through telephone calls with each parent following each scheduled visitation episode, and sets up supervised visitation exchanges at a neutral location. Another program, based in Los Angeles, provides six hours of classes for groups of parents, educating them about custody and visitation law and the effects of parental conflict and litigation on children.

While some improvements have been made in visitation access, the results from these and other programs like them have been moderate, at best. A comprehensive study of five such programs, led by Jessica Pearson, Ph.D., director of the Center for Policy Studies in Denver, Colorado, found that once the program ended, about half the parents reported continuing visitation problems, with about one-third reporting no resolution or improvement of any type. Furthermore, when participants were asked to rate the programs, few felt that the program would lead to improvements in the other parent's behavior, either through upholding child-support payments or noninterference of visitation.[14]

My colleagues and I believe these systems are of value, and should be replicated elsewhere, but are no panacea. Most of them rely on *enforcement;* and enforcement is a poor cousin to education and prevention when it comes to changing people's behavior (see Chapter 12). Ultimately, then, the primary value of such programs is to convince visiting parents that their concerns are being addressed, that the playing field is more level than they had supposed and that their worth to children is broader than merely the financial.

What Makes Fathers Feel Empowered—or Disempowered?

We had discovered an important and previously unrecognized truth: Feeling parentally disenfranchised was the key to father dropout. The next question we asked was what causes this feeling of parental enfranchisement? Why do some fathers feel it?

> ➤ The most important pathway to a father's feeling parentally enfranchised, we found, is having an ex-wife who *desires* the father to be connected to the child, who supports and encourages his involvement, as compared to one who wants the father altogether out of the way.

To answer this question, we went through another series of causal analyses, and the results were once again clear and unambiguous. There are two primary routes to the father's feeling parentally enfranchised, we found. The most important pathway is having an ex-wife who *desires* the father to be connected to the child, who supports and encourages his involvement, as compared to one who wants the father altogether out of the way.

Brooke, whose story you read in the beginning of this chapter, is typical of a great many mothers. In a large proportion of divorces, the mother sees little value in any contact between child and father. She doesn't *want* to have to accommodate his desires or tastes as a father. Instead, she wishes to be rid of him and his influence that she found so onerous.

Even if such mothers don't directly interfere with visitation and permit it to take place, they can place obstacles, make it unpleasant, or let the father know in either obvious or subtle ways how unwelcome he is, as Jeremy felt Roxanne did to him. As Jared complained, "[My ex-wife] . . . is the gatekeeper, and she can be very arbitrary. I say or do whatever's necessary to keep her from getting mad, and cutting me off from my kid."

As University of Wisconsin demographer Judith Seltzer, Ph.D., wrote in the *Annual Review of Sociology*:

> *After divorce, [mothers] . . . orchestrate men's relationships with children. . . . Mothers are reluctant to relinquish authority over children even when they would be relinquishing it to the children's father. . . . For many women, divorce is a step toward autonomy and greater independence from men. . . . By facilitating divorced fathers' independent involvement with children, divorced mothers may fear that they will lose many of their own decision-making rights."*[15]

This pattern of interference is not so surprising in view of the fact that mothers often set up roadblocks to fathers' participation even during the marriage. As John Gray, Ph.D., author of the best-selling *Men Are from Mars, Women Are from Venus*[16] opined to me:

> *Many women overtly prevent fathers from parenting. They will do all sorts of things to prevent the father from taking charge of the children, then they'll turn around and say the father doesn't participate. The man does something with the children and the woman is immediately there to tell him what he is doing wrong and how he should do it better. She will start interrogating him, involving herself in the process, not allowing him to take charge and feel more responsible for the kids. She's coming from a place that he doesn't know how to do it, so she'll have to do it. But what man wants to have his wife or ex-wife correcting him all the time, particularly in front of his children? So, quite automatically then, many men back off from the situation.*[17]

Not just the need for autonomy, but lingering feelings of anger can propel mothers to impede visitation. Mary Ann Forgatch, a psychologist who conducted a longitudinal study of divorced mothers and developed an intervention program, has consistently seen this dynamic in action. In an interview,[18] she told me that "Mothers, because of their own anger in the marital relationship, can prevent fathers from being involved with their children, and I see that all too often. There are a lot of fathers who would very much like to be involved with their children, but the mothers prevent that from happening. And that's unfortunate for the child."

When a mother sees little value and only hassle in her ex-husband remaining involved, she communicates her feelings quite well to her ex-spouse. This appears to be one arena where the communication appears relatively unimpaired. If the mother reports that she does not really want the father to remain connected to the child, this gets communicated loud and clear; the father almost always agrees that that's how his ex-wife feels.[19] And when she does *not* want his involvement, the typical response in many cases is the father's withdrawal from his child, both emotionally and financially.

> ➤ When a mother sees little value and only hassle in her ex-husband remaining involved with the children, she communicates those feelings to him. This appears to be one arena where the communication appears relatively unimpaired.

Many other mothers, in contrast, *do* want their children to continue having a father. Susan, despite her bitter feeling toward her ex-husband, recognized that Kerry was still important for their children. Far more often than not in such families, the father welcomes the invitation, and stays "hooked in." He feels enfranchised, visits frequently, and pays child support at admirable rates, just as Kerry did with his children. And ultimately, the children come out the winners. In her book *Families Apart,* award-winning journalist Melinda Blau talks about the importance of ex-spouses working together in cutting down on the harmful effects on the children. She writes:

> *Co-parenting . . . eliminates another major risk factor: father absence. Although some fathers in my survey were active participants in their children's upbringing before the divorce, an equal number had relegated the parenting spotlight to their wives—until divorce forced them into center stage, too. A man who co-parents doesn't necessarily turn into "Mr. Mom," . . . but he will become more intimately involved in the details of his children's lives.[20]*

> ➤ When the mother communicates that she *does* want the father's involvement, far more often than not, he welcomes the invitation, visiting frequently and paying child support at admirable rates.

Certainly not all fathers whose ex-wives want their involvement remain good fathers. Remember Gary, from Chapter 3. But statistically, Gary is the exception and not the rule. In fact, we estimated that fathers who faced no unemployment, who lived in the same city as their children, *and felt parentally enfranchised* visited their children from 7.6 to 11.1 days a month and paid from 84 percent to 96 percent of the child support they owed.

But what happens when fathers gain more control in their children's upbringing? Does that diminish the mothers' sense of empowerment that they typically gain post-divorce? We were very heartened by our finding that *mothers did not lose power* when they helped fathers to feel enfranchised; on the contrary, mothers actually felt *more* power themselves. Parental control did not turn out to be an I-win-you-lose situation, what game theorists call a zero-sum game. Instead, if in a certain family the father felt enfranchised, so did the mother.[21] As Susan found out, allowing her ex-husband Kerry to feel parentally enfranchised had considerable benefit, and relatively little or no cost, for her and her children.

Another such story was told by Pam and Drake, her husband. When we spoke to Pam at Wave 1, prior to her divorce, she was livid about Drake. "He wants to trade in his sports car for a mini-van," she told me. "But I'm not going to let him. My lawyer says she thinks she can stop him."

"Why don't you want him to buy a mini-van?" I asked.

"Because then he'll want to participate in taking the boys to their activities in the car pool. He's never done this before! I always drove car pool. I was the soccer mom. He was always too busy, too interested in his job. Couldn't be bothered. Now, we're getting divorced and he suddenly wants to show off that he's such a great dad. It's a naked power grab, and I'm not going to let him do it."

Drake, too, felt pretty irritated. "What's the big deal?" he wanted to know.

"Me driving car pool once in a while doesn't make her less of a great mom. But she doesn't want to let me have equal standing with being a parent."

Neither parent was winning this little tug-of-war, for the moment, and both felt frustrated, angry, and powerless as a result. When we saw the parents at Wave 2, a year later, the legal process had played itself out. Drake was prevented from buying his vehicle for about six months, but finally permission was negotiated for him to make the purchase. "I was really peeved at first," Pam said. "But one Saturday morning, I was sick, and just couldn't make it to drive my turn in car pool. I called Drake and asked him if he could do it. Because he had just bought his mini-van, he was in a position to drive all six kids. I got to nurse myself back to health instead of schlepping the kids around. And I stopped and said, 'What was I resisting for? His having a mini-van means I have to drive less, and I can take it easier and get more of my own stuff done.'"

Having resigned herself to the inevitable, Pam was now in a position to see the benefits of working cooperatively rather than competitively with Drake. In this way, they both could win. He got to participate in his son's activities, and she got relief from always having to be the available parent. This, apparently, is how it works on average. If the father comes to feel enfranchised, the mother ultimately feels more control. This is a very encouraging finding, one that we will return to in Chapter 12.

The Paradox Resolved

Our research has unraveled the mystery and resolved the paradox of the disconnected dad. Divorced fathers disengage when they are driven away, made to feel like they don't matter. Yet they almost always act like good fathers when they are empowered, made to feel that their fatherhood is still necessary in bringing up their children. But how do we ensure that fathers *do* retain their rights as full parents? A simple, cost-free solution already exists, the second pathway to parental enfranchisement, and we'll discuss it in detail in the next chapter.

9.

Joint Legal Custody

Keeping Dad Involved

After I made a presentation in Montreal at the 1995 meeting of the Association of Family and Conciliation Courts to a group of court professionals, psychologists, and interested family members about the findings presented in the last chapter, a woman approached me. She appeared agitated. "Let me tell you something about my ex-husband . . ." she began. The woman, Cindy, went on to tell me about her bad experiences with her ex-husband, Ray.

> *He's a liar and very domineering. If you interviewed him, he'd tell you that he felt he had no control over our daughter's upbringing after the divorce. He would have claimed that he felt parentally disenfranchised—just like the other fathers you interviewed. But what he wouldn't have told you was how controlling he was as a husband and father. That's why I wanted out of the marriage—to be free of his domination. After our divorce I never denied him visitation or interfered in any way with his relationship with our kid. But once he learned he couldn't completely control my life or our daughter's life like he used to, he totally disengaged. He stopped visiting and stopped paying child support.*

Ray would have fit our findings "to a tee," she claimed, because his perceived control diminished *and* he disconnected, but he was not in any real sense *driven away*. That wasn't the *cause* of the disengagement, Cindy believed. She finished by saying, "His words might lead you to believe otherwise, but they're just that—meaningless words."

Cindy had well expressed the very same concerns I had had with the stories we were hearing about why some fathers abandon their children. We knew they made compelling sense and gave us some clues to fathers' disengagement, but we were well aware of the possibility that the stories could be shadings of the truth devised by the fathers to rationalize their irresponsible behavior. Even if all the fathers in our study were given and passed lie detector tests, we'd still have no way of knowing what part of what they told us was the complete truth, and what part they came to believe simply because it cast their actions in a better light.

But there *was* a way we could determine with much greater certainty whether feeling parentally disenfranchised was truly the reason some divorced fathers dropped out of their children's lives. And that was to look at fathers who had joint legal custody.

As we discussed in Chapter 6, divorce decrees for couples with children generally provide for *both* the legal and residential custody arrangements. Legal custody refers to which parent has the legal authority to make decisions concerning the child's welfare. For instance, what school will he attend? What extracurricular activities, such as sports, music lessons, and camps will she participate in? What doctors will the children use? Joint legal custody dictates that *both* parents retain these fundamental rights and responsibilities of parenthood, while sole legal custody terminates them for the noncustodial parent. Residential custody arrangements, on the other hand, indicate where children will primarily live. Nationally, less than 10 percent of divorced fathers have both legal and residential custody of their children.[1]

For ten years or so, joint or shared custody has been permitted and even encouraged in many states.[2] However, almost all awards of joint custody involve only joint *legal* custody. Joint residential decrees, specifying that children should reside about equally with each parent, are awarded to less than 5 percent of families nationally. But many more (around 20 percent) specify that the couple share joint legal custody.[3]

In bestowing joint legal custody, society tells the father in an official way that he is still his child's parent. He gets to participate in the same kind of decision-making concerning the child that fathers from intact families must deal with. He gets the right to continue to look out for his child's interests. In a sense, it is the most forceful way of enfranchising a father.

> ➤ In bestowing joint legal custody, society tells the father in an
> official way that he is still his child's parent. In a sense, it is
> the most forceful way of enfranchising a father.

In reviewing our data, if we were to find a great many fathers acting irresponsibly and dropping out despite obtaining joint legal custody, it would imply to us that what we learned from fathers in the last chapter was in fact just "meaningless words," as Cindy claimed. As we discussed in Chapter 8, sociologist Terry Arendell, too, disbelieved the claims of fathers she interviewed, labeling them merely "masculinist discourse" and "rhetoric." If those fathers who described themselves as feeling parentally disenfranchised were simply using the assertion as a convenient excuse, just rhetoric, meaningless words, or rationalizations, redressing this feeling in such an obvious way as telling the father that "you can still share in making decisions on behalf of your child; you are still the father" shouldn't affect paternal disengagement at all. Irresponsible fathers would just find some other excuse.

On the other hand, suppose we were to find that those fathers who received joint legal custody remained significantly more involved and were far more likely to act like "good dads" by paying all the child support owed and upholding the visitation schedule. What if obtaining joint legal custody turned out to be the second pathway for fathers to become paternally empowered, a pathway that didn't depend on the mother's good will? If this was the case, it would more or less prove that making fathers feel parentally enfranchised was the ultimate weapon in keeping them from dropping out.

The Joint Versus Sole Debate

What kind of custody arrangement should the judicial system encourage couples to choose? Which is the better option for parents and children alike: *joint legal* or *sole legal?* Policymakers have debated long and loudly over this issue. Advocates for joint custody have contended that fathers, by virtue of the increased legal responsibility and authority bestowed on them, will take a more active and involved role in child rearing, to the entire family's benefit. Every member of the family, according to those who advocate for joint legal custody, will have an easier time adjusting after divorce because of the parents' mutual commitment to child rearing and the fact that their responsibilities as parents are divided more equitably. Proposed benefits to fathers include less emotional loss, depression, anger, and "role discontinuity." As we see it, this should translate into more perceived control and less parental disenfranchisement. The parent who has primary physical custody, meanwhile, gets a more committed co-parent, a respite from full-time child rearing and all its attendant responsibilities (thus more time for professional and personal development), as well as potentially greater compliance with financial child support. In turn, children are expected to experience higher quality residential parenting, richer relationships with the nonresidential parent, more cooperative coparenting, and, ultimately, should adapt better to the new family configuration as a result.[4]

➤ **The idea that joint legal custody is actually a benefit for *custodial mothers* is championed by many feminists. Karen DeCrow, a former national president of NOW, claims, "It's going to be difficult for women to achieve equality in the workplace or the political arena if they are left with all the responsibility of raising their children."**

In fact, the idea that joint legal custody is actually a benefit for *custodial mothers* is championed by many feminists. Karen DeCrow, a former national president of the National Organization for Women, for example, has long advocated the presumption of joint legal custody as a benefit to women. "If it's assumed that women are the primary parent at the time of divorce, then it's going to be difficult for women to achieve equality in the workplace or the political arena if they are left with all the responsibility of raising their children," she told us.[5] "If a couple is getting divorced and they approach their parenting as a joint venture, then the woman will have a lot more time and energy to attend to her own life. When you have joint legal custody, it's not just *her* burden, it becomes *their* burden; it's not *her* responsibility, it's *their* responsibility."

Carla and Randy had as messy and acrimonious a divorce as anybody. But amidst all their turmoil, they were both clear from the outset that it would be in the best interests of their daughter if both parents had an equal say over her up-bringing. "We realized the most important thing to us is that our daughter deserves the best parents we can be, and we should work together for her benefit," Carla told me.

"I knew that Randy would feel less threatened about the divorce and that he would be a more responsible father and would be an integral part of our daughter's life," Carla gave as the reason she agreed to joint legal custody. She realized that *she* would benefit, as well. "I knew that he'd be there legally, actively, and psychologically to back me up when I needed him. I can call on him any time I need." When I asked how his child-support compliance has been, she quickly said, "Fantastic. He sends checks ahead of time, dated for the proper dates, so he's never behind. Plus, he always chips in a good amount for the larger things our daughter needs."

Carla also appreciates the benefits of joint custody to her child. Though Randy lives a four-hour drive away, he sees his daughter regularly and makes sure that he attends every important event in her life, including parent-teacher conferences and school events. "Having his support and being able to work with him without a lot of animosity has been helpful, because we've been able to make decisions as a coherent body. It's allowed her to excel in school and be accepted into a talented and gifted program. He was there physically when we were talking to the teachers, to show a united front both to our daughter and to the school. We were both supportive at the same time instead of pulling in different directions."

While Carla and Randy's experience gives credence to advocates for joint legal custody, not all divorce experts agree that joint legal custody is a beneficial arrangement for every couple. Critics cite the potential for continued conflict between parents who are forced to maintain frequent communication, contact, and coordination, but who may well be unable to get along well or resolve issues pertaining to their children's welfare. After all, their conflict was of such a magnitude that divorce resulted. We spoke via telephone to Minna R. Buck, a former Family Court Judge in Onondaga County, New York,[6] who said she believes that joint legal custody should be considered first. However, she told us she did not recommend it when the issues between the divorcing spouses were so elemental that the couple could never be expected to agree. "For instance, if the couple is splitting up because one partner joined a Fundamentalist church and the other one is firmly opposed to that religion, then I think joint legal custody doesn't make any sense," she asserted. "They will never be able to agree on really basic issues and there will be constant pushing and pulling of the children."

➤ **Critics of joint legal custody cite the potential for continued conflict between parents who are forced to maintain frequent communication, contact, and coordination, but who may well be unable to get along well or resolve issues pertaining to their children's welfare.**

Critics also warn of the risk that children will develop loyalty conflicts when they have strong attachments to feuding parties. And, some claim, the residential parent may suffer mental health difficulties if she's deprived of sole responsibility for the children. These risk factors, argue opponents of joint custody, may ultimately result in poorer child adjustment.[7]

One parent wrote me a letter expressing some of the concerns many mothers feel at the prospect of sharing custody with their ex-spouse:

> *We struggle and sacrifice for our children. And then the other parent comes along and buys all kinds of goodies, takes the kids on special outings—and it hurts like hell because we know we can't do it on our income. We worry that our children are going to want to go live with the other parent, and it scares*

the bejeebers out of us. We worry about losing control. We feel manipulated and controlled by the anger of the other parent in some cases.

But then, this parent, who finally agreed to sharing joint legal custody with her ex-husband, goes on to talk about what that decision meant to her.

Then we realize that maybe it's not such a bad thing that the other parent loves our children as much as we do. And I suppose in the long run, we learn that, beyond all the anger and distress, it is the children *who benefit from the loving interaction they have with both parents, and we learn to "let go" a wee bit. And for the children, that is the best thing that can happen.*

Which view is right? Is joint legal custody a panacea—a cure-all for the ills of father dropout, resulting in better parenting, higher child-support compliance, and well-adjusted children? Or is it a sham—a solution that promises everything and delivers nothing, resulting in emotional distress for both parents and poorly adjusted children?

The Trouble with Past Research

In fact, there exists a rather substantial body of past research comparing the outcomes of sole versus joint legal custody families.[8] For example, Sharlene Wolchik, Irwin Sandler, and I found in 1985 that children in joint legal custody had higher feelings of self-esteem, a key ingredient to leading a successful and fulfilling life, than children in sole maternal custody.[9] That may be due, in part, to having fathers who are actively and regularly involved and pay their child support. This sends a message to the child that "you are so important that *both* parents are going to continue to be supportive of your activities." However, almost all past studies—including the one of ours just mentioned—suffer from a serious methodological shortcoming we labeled "self-selection."

The problem of self-selection stems from the fact that custody arrangements are not randomly assigned by judges or agreed upon in equal proportion in all types of families. Instead, different types of families either *choose* various custody arrangements, or they have custody arrangements *suggested to or imposed* upon them by judicial authorities based (at least in part) on the facts of their particular case.

Imagine that you were the divorce attorney for a woman we'll call Claire, advising her as to whether she should pursue joint or sole legal custody of Whitney, her eight-year old. Claire is an art teacher. Her husband, Alex, is a professor of social work, who teaches courses on child welfare. He has been an admirable father, heavily involved in Whitney's child rearing since birth. The marital break-up was relatively amicable; both parents realized they just grew apart. They attempted a trial separation for a year to see if they could work things out. During this time, Whitney has stayed with Alex two to three nights per week. Because of his flexible work schedule and the fact that his apartment is pretty close to Claire's place and Whitney's school, he often picks his daughter up after school. Also, during their separation, Alex has willingly been generous with expenses for Claire and Whitney.

Given these circumstances, wouldn't you be likely to recommend joint legal custody to Claire, as most attorneys and experts would, and many judges would mandate?

Now consider what your recommendation would be to Jill, a manicurist, considering custody for her eleven-year old son, Scott. Cory, the father, works in a furniture warehouse, and has had some minor bouts with the law, due to a bad temper when drunk. Jill became pregnant at seventeen with Scott, and after some stormy times, Cory eventually married her six years ago. Their marriage came apart as a result of his not being able—or willing—to tame his drinking problem. While Scott clearly loves his father, Cory has been an irregular presence in both of their lives for the last year. He now lives forty-five minutes away, but doesn't have a driver's license, due to a DWI conviction. Jill and Cory have constant conflict when they interact, and Cory seems delighted to have Scott watch while his yelling reduces Jill to tears.

Hardly anyone would advise joint custody for Jill. It's also extremely unlikely that any judge would compel her to accept joint legal custody.

Now consider: Which child, Whitney or Scott, do you predict will have more emotional and other problems three years from now? Which child is at higher risk for such ills as poor academic performance, delinquency, and drug use, *regardless of the custody outcome?*

This illustration epitomizes the self-selection problem: the same factors that should lead Claire and Alex to joint custody would likely augur well for Whitney's future development, regardless of whether or not they actually obtain joint custody. The same factors that make joint custody unlikely for Jill and

Cory put Scott at risk, regardless of whether or not they actually end up with joint custody.

In short, it's highly plausible that the factors that lead some families to a joint legal custody award might be the very same factors that lead to better outcomes for the family. These can be called *predisposing factors*. For example, highly educated couples are known to adopt joint custody more frequently than those with less education. Similarly, families in which the fathers were very highly involved in child rearing prior to divorce are also overrepresented among those with a joint custody award. Joint custody is also more likely for couples who experience relatively little post-divorce hostility. It is plausible that these or similar predisposing factors, rather than the joint-custody arrangement in and of itself, are responsible for the more favorable outcomes of joint-custody families. This type of problem is familiar to social scientists: we refer to it as not being able to "prove the cause" from correlational data, and it is the critical problem in evaluating evidence to resolve the joint-custody debate.

> **It's highly plausible that the factors—such as low post-divorce hostility—that lead some families to a joint legal custody award might be the very same factors that lead to better outcomes for the family.**

One possibility is that the predisposing factors might cause the better outcomes for such families *whether or not* they actually obtain the joint-custody award. If so, the actual award is superfluous. These families, like Claire, Alex, and Whitney, would thrive anyway. If the actual award was indeed superfluous, there would be no need to enact policies that express preference for joint custody.

A second possibility is that the award of joint custody actually detracts from the natural benefits of the predisposing factors. Forcing the joint-custody couple to interact more to coordinate schedules, accommodate each other's needs, and jointly attend school events, could cause more open friction between the parents, ultimately resulting in negative influences on the child. If this were the case, the most reasonable policy would be one that discouraged or disallowed joint custody.

A final possibility, the one that appeared most likely to us if fathers were telling the truth, is that joint legal custody might have a beneficial impact *over and above* the predisposing factors. If this were true, it *would be* necessary to encourage such an award. Because all three possibilities are plausible and consistent with existing evidence, most social scientists researching family issues have recognized that determining the impact of joint custody *per se,* over and above the predisposing factors, is an extremely critical, if thorny, issue remaining to be answered by good research.

Putting Our Findings to the Test[10]

We knew that until we answered the question of whether an award of joint legal custody in and of itself was a large determinant of fathers remaining connected to their kids, all the research we had done thus far about the motivation for father dropout would have to be considered inconclusive. In order to know the truth, we would need to establish that most of the fathers in our sample who received joint legal custody came to feel parentally enfranchised as a result, and acted like "good dads," and that this effect was over and above the effect of any self-selection or predisposing factors.

To do this, we completed two different statistical analyses that address the problem of self-selection, in different and complementary ways. We believe that our resulting findings provide the most trustworthy information available to inform policy concerning joint legal custody.

In the first of these analyses, we explored the impact of joint legal custody *by imposing statistical controls* for predisposing factors. This technique allows us, in effect, to determine what differences would be present *if the two groups of families had been equal on all of the predisposing factors.* In these analyses, we assessed the families on a large number of potentially predisposing factors that were measured prior to the couple obtaining the divorce decree. In the pre-divorce period, the divorce terms are not yet legally finalized and are subject to change. Because legal custody, by definition, is not set until the court awards it in the final decree of divorce, any factor measured prior to this time could plausibly be considered predisposing. The factors that we looked at included such variables as educational level, fathers' pre-divorce involvement in child rearing, each of the parent's anger level at the other, and their psychological health. In all, we included sixty-three such factors. We then identified which of these statistically differentiated the families that subsequently obtained joint custody. Of the sixty-three factors assessed, seventeen met this criterion, including fathers' education level, parents' race, and the fact that joint-custody mothers were more supportive of their children. Next, we statistically equated the two groups of families—those with joint legal custody and those with sole maternal legal custody—on all of these factors (plus three more included for theoretical reasons) simultaneously, so that we were comparing families that had essentially the same educational, economic, and familial background. We then contrasted their Wave 3 (long term) outcomes.

> **Even after adjusting our results to account for all differentiating predisposing factors, we still found considerable benefits to recommend joint custody. Children in joint custody were significantly better adjusted and exhibited less antisocial and impulsive behavior than sole custody families.**

Our results, presented in Chart 9.1, bear out the claims of advocates for joint custody. Even after adjusting our results to account for all differentiating predisposing factors, we still found considerable benefits to recommend joint custody. Children in joint custody were significantly better adjusted in that they exhibited less behavior problems, impulsive behaviors, depression,[11] and antisocial tendencies[12] than children in sole custody families. Fathers also visited more, according to the mothers' reports. Mothers, however, were significantly less satisfied with the arrangement in joint custody families, perhaps because they felt they had

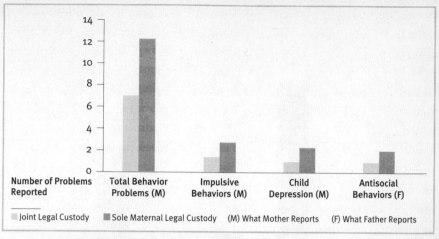

| | CHART 9.1 | Significant Child-Adjustment Differences Due to Legal Custody Arrangements |

to give up some control. However, they were less opposed to visitation (oddly, for their daughters only), apparently acceding to the fathers' legal rights.

Just as important are associations between joint legal custody and family processes that we *didn't* find. In opposition to what joint-custody critics had feared, there were no differences found between joint and sole legal custody groups on mothers' (or fathers') adjustment to the divorce, the mothers' parenting capacities, or the general level of conflict between the couple.

In our second type of analyses, we hoped to "tease out" the effects of predisposing factors by looking at the effects of joint legal custody on couples for whom it was not the preference of *both* parents. If joint legal custody wasn't a mutual initial preference, they couldn't be said to self-select it, at least not in the same way. At Wave 1, we asked fathers what form of legal custody they would prefer in their divorce decree. We found that 74 percent of fathers wanted joint custody, 15 percent preferred themselves to have sole custody, and only 11 percent preferred their ex-wives to have sole custody. In contrast, 70 percent of the mothers wanted sole custody for themselves, and 30 percent initially preferred joint custody (Chart 9.2). Thus the majority of families did *not* initially agree on custody.

It is critical to note that these couples expressed their legal custody prefer-

Divorced Dads

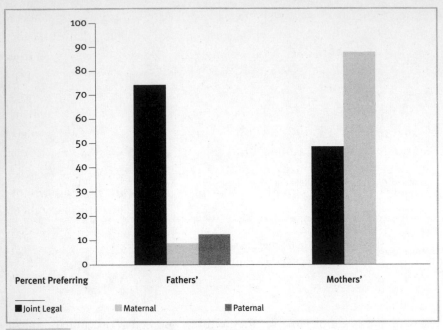

CHART 9.2 **Parents' Initial Legal-Custody Preferences**

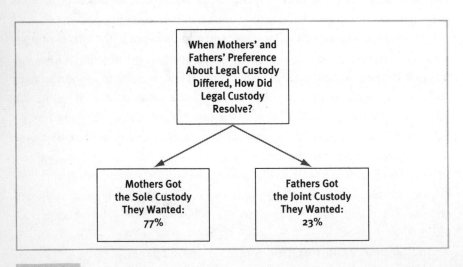

CHART 9.3

ences to us while they were still in the process of settling their divorce, well before any decisions became finalized in the divorce decree. Asking them this early in the process, we felt, would reflect a more accurate representation of their true preferences than would questioning them long after the arrangement was in effect.

We then divided the families into groups based on what they told us was their preference and their award concerning their legal-custody arrangement. Our analysis focused on three especially interesting groups: in the first group, the parents *both* initially expressed a preference for joint custody, and of course, this was awarded subsequently. The two remaining groups were the conflicted families: In these, the fathers wanted joint while the mothers wanted sole maternal custody. Of these (as shown in Chart 9.3), 77 percent ended up with sole maternal custody. The remaining 23 percent obtained joint legal custody.

Three years later, we examined the outcomes of these three groups. Comparing these groups would help us determine the impact of joint versus sole custody after the couple had disagreed initially. We hoped to find an answer to the question of which is better for the family: for the father to get *his* preference (joint) or for the mother to get *her* preference (sole)? If we were right that parental disenfranchisement was the true cause of father disengagement, and not just "rhetoric," we should find that when fathers are empowered by joint legal custody, *even when it is not the mother's initial wish,* they will stay engaged with their children.

As it turns out, the groups did differ significantly[13] in terms of how much financial child support was paid (Chart 9.4). When mothers received sole custody of the children despite the fathers' wishes, fathers reported paying 80 percent of the child support they owed; according to mothers, fathers paid 62 percent. When joint legal custody was awarded over the mothers' initial objections, child support zoomed to very high compliance: 93 percent by fathers' reports; 89 percent by mothers' reports.

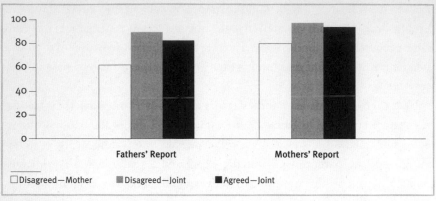

CHART 9.4   Percent of Child Support Paid by Custody Group

➤ When joint legal custody was awarded over the mothers' objections, child support zoomed to very high compliance: 93
percent by fathers' reports; 89 percent by mothers' reports.

Even more interesting, by both reports, child-support compliance was
slightly (but not significantly) greater in the latter case even than when both parents preferred joint custody initially. It could be that fathers who push for and obtain joint custody over their ex-wives' initial objections feel vindicated by the
system, and they may go to extra lengths to prove that they were right in press-
ing for joint legal custody.

A similar relationship existed for fathers' contact with the child (Chart 9.5).
It was significantly highest for the group in which joint custody was awarded despite the mother's initial opposing preference. An important point to be emphasized is that we detected no differences between the sole custody and both joint
custody groups on a number of other variables. Contrary to some critics' claims,
joint legal custody did not lead to correspondingly greater conflict between the
parents, psychological distress in the mothers, or mothers' diminished capacity
to parent.

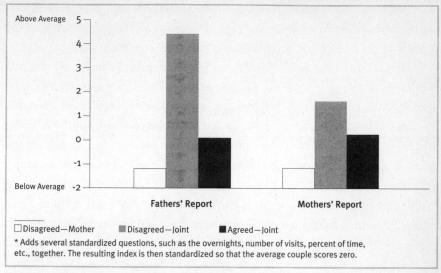

CHART 9.5   Visitation Index* by Custody Group

> ➤ Contrary to some critics' claims, joint legal custody did not
> lead to correspondingly greater conflict between the parents,
> psychological distress in the mothers, or mothers' dimin-
> ished capacity to parent.

What Joint Legal Custody Means to Fathers

Together, these two sets of analyses, which each correct for self-selection in different and complementary ways, provide convincing evidence that allowing fathers to share legal custody of their children is the second pathway to
enfranchising them, supplementing the pathway of the mother empowering him
by her supportive attitude. If a father obtains joint legal custody, we found, he al-

most always acts very responsibly; conversely, fathers who claim to be driven away seem not merely to be spouting meaningless words and rhetoric. And this process works whether or not the mother welcomes the father's involvement.

Take, for instance, the case of Nat, the lawyer we met in Chapter 6, who had much the same experience of the majority of fathers who fight for joint legal custody and lose. In his case, his wife demanded sole custody of their two children. "In this state, if a wife objects, then joint custody is denied—simply by her saying she doesn't want it. What the courts are saying to you is 'You are no longer a father. You're not anything.' And if you don't like the school your kids are going to or how they're being raised, that's too bad. You don't have any say in their lives, you're nothing to them. My ex-wife made it very clear that I was no longer any use to her or my children, except of course, for the child support. That's all I am to my children—a monthly check." After fighting and losing many legal battles, not to mention a small fortune, Nat has given up on seeing his children. "I haven't seen them in two years, and frankly, I don't think I'll ever see them again," he said, his voice edged with regret.

By contrast, a father who obtains joint legal custody becomes enfranchised. He is being told by society that we think he *matters* to his kids. The message conveyed to him is that he is still a real father, with the rights of that status, not just the responsibility. As one father confirmed, "I felt vindicated when the court awarded me joint legal custody. The decision was made by a mediator who was aware that there had been real shared parenting in the marriage up until the divorce. By allowing me to have an equal say in my children's upbringing, the mediator was recognizing the relationship that already existed between me and my children. She was valuing my role as a father. It made me feel justified for fighting."

Another father, who was awarded joint legal custody after a long and bitter fight, said he felt "relieved" because he would have continued to fight by any legal means possible. Still, he resents the fact that he had to fight for the right to be a father to his child. "The courts should recognize that it takes two to make a child," he said. "I personally love being a father. It is the greatest part of my identity—greater than anything else I've accomplished in a rather successful life. To have had that yanked away from me would have been devastating."

Joint legal custody should not be accepted as a panacea. For example, many mothers do not welcome the "interference" that comes with fathers having a say in how their children are raised, though this fact does not seem to impair their functioning and seems to actually facilitate their child's functioning. Perhaps as a result of mothers resenting the interference, we've heard from many fathers who claim that their ex-wives are not upholding the arrangement. Several have gone back to court numerous times. As one told us, "Joint legal custody only means my ex-wife has to *consult* me before doing whatever the hell she wants with my child!"

We are hardly recommending that fathers routinely wage court battles to obtain joint legal custody. But the findings in favor of it are unmistakable, so much so that most major researchers have now joined the call to support joint custody, including Christine Nord and Nicholas Zill,[14] of Westat, Inc., a social science research organization, who were collaborators with Frank Furstenburg in the landmark study cited in Chapter 3, and Stanford child psychologist Eleanor Maccoby and legal scholar Robert Mnookin, authors of *Dividing the Child*.[15]

The Message to Policymakers

As a nation, we spend literally billions of dollars on child-support enforcement. Yet, as we showed in Chapter 2, there is little evidence that these coercive policies have any noticeable effect.[16] Here, however, is a remedy that is virtually cost-free to society that appears to make fathers *want* to pay, *voluntarily*. Coercion, punishment, garnishment are normally not needed at all. Just as important, if not more so, not only do we get paying fathers, we get fathers who visit often and who become positive forces in their children's lives. Coercive policies, on the contrary, have been completely unable to get this kind of involvement from fathers, even when authorities have been successful in collecting financial support.

If we are serious about considering the best interests of children, we think the findings in this chapter should lead policymakers to adopt a "rebuttable presumption" in favor of joint legal custody. That is, instead of the current judicial bias toward mothers having sole custody, we need a judicial preference that says *both* parents, as a general rule, should retain their rights and responsibilities toward their children post-divorce.

Nevertheless, some extenuating circumstances exist in which joint legal custody should probably not be granted, such as in families where there has been domestic violence. We explore several of these issues in the next chapter. This is why we recommend that the presumption be *rebuttable* for the mother or other interested parties, so they are given the opportunity to demonstrate that those extenuating circumstances prevail in their case. In the absence of proof of these circumstances, however, children, fathers, mothers, and society are best served if we show fathers that they still matter by awarding them joint legal custody and the chance to retain their status as real fathers to their own children.

10.

Caveat

When Joint Legal Custody Is Wrong

In the previous chapter, we illustrated how, in the vast majority of cases, continuing to allow both parents to remain legally attached to and in a parental role with their child, rather than severing one parent's rights, is in the child's as well as the family's best interest. In particular, our evidence has convincingly shown that awarding joint legal custody to fathers would go a long way toward keeping them actively involved in their children's lives, both by paying child support and through regular visitation.

But are there exceptions? What if the parent is an active alcoholic? What if there has been domestic violence or child sexual abuse in the family? And what if the parent exhibits psychopathic tendencies or other mental impairment? These we consider valid counterforces to consider in deciding custody issues. The evidence and arguments we will present in the remainder of this chapter imply that in any of these three circumstances, joint legal custody should *not* be favored.

The Psychopathic Parent

Richard is a father interviewed for one of our studies. A grain salesman who repeatedly got fired from jobs, Richard lied about his past two marriages to his new wife, Sonya. After they were married, he cheated on her persistently, always having an excuse when he was caught. The first time he claimed he was seduced. The second time he explained that he had no choice—he had to have the affair to make his new consulting business work, to "grease the skids," so to speak. His excuses always had the ring of truth. But his lying and cheating did not stop at the bedroom door. Eventually, he got caught for tax evasion. Though he was found guilty, he got off lightly, receiving a suspended sentence. Sonya filed for divorce. Hoping desperately to salvage a father/son relationship for their son, Chad, she gladly offered joint legal custody. Richard accepted, but only if Sonya would cut down his child-support obligation.

Sonya constantly encouraged Richard to get together with Chad, but he was always otherwise occupied. He failed to pay the small amount of child support he was ordered to and rarely visited. He moved away, got lost to the system, and was eventually jailed for child-support evasion.

This man appeared incapable of psychological attachment. Richard is an example of someone exhibiting what we term "psychopathic deviance." We detected dads who exhibited these tendencies by the "Psychopathic Deviance" sub-scale on the Minnesota MultiPhasic Personality Inventory (MMPI), the most established personality inventory in existence.[1] Dads who are psychopathic deviates (thought to be about 8 percent)[2] are amoral and asocial persons who act with repeated and flagrant disregard for social customs and mores, are unable to learn from their mistakes, and exhibit an emotional shallowness in relating to others.

Our analyses have shown that psychopathic deviance tendencies lead to irresponsible parental behavior, including low child-support compliance and poor visitation.[3] *And there is no improvement in these rates even when the father feels parentally enfranchised, either through joint legal custody or a mother who supports a significant parenting role for the father.* Rather, such men are truly incapable of the mature, beneficial fathering role for which joint legal custody would give them rights. Thus, there is no compelling reason to award them joint legal custody, and their ex-wives' and children's lives will not be improved and may even be harmed by such an award. Of course, this picture is not limited to fathers; the same is true for mothers who exhibit psychopathic tendencies.

> ➤ Our analyses have shown that psychopathic deviance ten-
> dencies lead to irresponsible parental behavior, including
> low child-support compliance and poor visitation. And there
> is no improvement in these rates even when the father feels
> parentally enfranchised, either through joint legal custody or
> a mother who supports a significant parenting role for the
> father.

Although we have no data available on other forms of mental disorder besides psychopathic deviance, most authorities would oppose joint legal custody
when there are other forms of mental impairment as well, such as psychosis or serious mood disorders that might impact parenting.[4] In the jargon used by courts,
parents with such serious mental disorders may not be "parentally fit." This
would be another condition that would rebut the joint legal-custody presumption.

Drug and Alcohol Abuse

It is estimated that approximately 15.3 million people in the United States are impaired by alcohol or drug addition.[5] It would seem self-evident that fathers who
are regularly intoxicated, who are generally a slave to their drinking or drug com-
pulsions, are not going to parent responsibly. We found substantial evidence that
a serious drinking or drug problem impedes child-support payments and a rich
nurturing relationship with the child. Fathers who drank heavily visited less and
paid child support less well than nonalcoholic fathers, even when they felt enfranchised.[6] The father who abuses drugs or alcohol is simply not going to be
fully available to his child no matter how much the system enfranchises him. In
these cases, joint legal custody makes almost no difference, so it should not be the
legal presumption.

Kimberly, a Chicago-based realtor, was married to an alcoholic, and found that joint legal custody led to no improvement in his fathering. Her husband Tony's alcoholism led to their marriage dissolving in the first place. Shortly after the divorce, Tony got into a treatment program, began a new relationship, and seemed to be committed to staying sober. Kimberly, who had always valued his input as a father despite his drinking, agreed to award him joint legal custody in the hope that it would keep him connected with their son, Josh, who was six at the time. But Tony had frequent relapses. There were times when he'd come in his car to pick his son up for a visit when he was clearly drunk. In those instances Kimberly did not allow the visit to take place, an action that while in the best interests of her son, upset Josh terribly. This pattern of periods of soberness followed by episodes of drinking went on for years. All the while, Tony was able to maintain a mid-level management job enabling him to keep up his child-support payments until his drinking got so bad that he finally lost his job and ended up on public assistance. The child-support payments ceased. He lost contact with his son for months.

Then, during a period of soberness, he again attempted visitation. Kimberly arranged for him to pick up their son, who was now age ten, at her home. Tony was supposed to bring Josh to soccer practice, but he arrived drunk. An ugly scene ensued. "After that incident," Kimberly related, "Josh decided that *he* wanted a divorce from his father. He said, 'I don't want to see him again. He has nothing to offer me—only pain.'" Josh has not seen his father since, nor has Kimberly received any child support.

Here is an example of a father given every opportunity to remain an involved dad. But his inability to stay sober steadily eroded the trust his ex-wife placed in him and irreparably damaged his relationship with his son.

Domestic Violence

Domestic violence is one of the thorniest issues in the domestic relations arena. Statistics as to how widespread the problem is veer wildly depending on where the information is emanating from, how the information was obtained, and how the researcher defined domestic violence.[7] Added to that is the reluctance of many victims to admit to the abuse because of shame. Whatever its true prevalence, domestic violence is a serious problem.

Naturally, women or men continuously victimized by violence from their ex-spouses deserve the court's protection and shouldn't be subject to provisions that increase their vulnerability. In such instances, they should be awarded sole legal custody because the potential for violence and its devastating aftermath outweighs any advantages of keeping the offending parent involved.

But according to Bahney Dedolph, public policy advocate for the Arizona Coalition Against Domestic Violence,[8] because of the shame many victims feel, they are often reluctant to admit to being a "battered spouse." Often, they may have been in an abusive relationship for years and kept the abuse secret, even from their closest friends and family members. When it comes time to fight for custody, the abused spouse may not be able to articulate his or her fears or reluctance to accept a joint custody award. And this can prove devastating for both the victim and the children if the custody evaluator is not trained to detect abuse.

This was the case with Tina, whom Dedolph had worked with years ago in a Pittsburgh shelter. After ten years in a physically abusive relationship, Tina had finally gotten up the courage to leave her husband. After telling him she wanted a separation, she came home from work the next day to find that he had moved every stick of furniture out of the house and had taken their two children with him. A custody battle ensued that would last for two years. Because Tina was so ashamed of having stayed in such an abusive marriage, she was unable to articulate her fears clearly. The custody evaluator, who was not aware of this frequent tendency among domestic-violence victims, determined that Tina was merely narcissistic and histrionic. Her husband, on the other hand, was very charming to the evaluators and appeared able to get along with everybody except his ex-wife. As Dedolph stated, "He looked very good, and she looked terrible."

As a result, the couple was awarded joint legal custody, with Tina having residential custody. Since this arrangement required Tina to interact with her ex-husband regularly, it has been enormously stressful for Tina, as well as her children. "It's very difficult for her to assert herself or assert the needs of her children because she's very fearful of her ex-husband," reports Dedolph.

Since the underlying issue in domestic violence often has to do with power and control, Dedolph feels that granting joint legal custody to a person with a past history of physical abuse only serves to continue the damaging effects of that relationship. "It can also put the victim's safety in jeopardy, depending on the kind of abuser and his degree of obsession with her and inability to let go of the relationship," she warns.

Even in cases where the children have not been the direct victims of a parent's violence, allowing an abuser to have joint legal custody still puts the children in jeopardy. According to Evelyn J. Hall, Ph.D., a licensed marriage and family therapist and clinical supervisor of Temporary Assistance for Domestic Crises in Las Vegas,[9] "Even if the father never laid a hand on the *child,* if the mother gets pushed, hit, or thrown it's still child abuse because that affects the child emotionally."

Of course, when it *is* the *children* who are the victims of physical abuse, contact with the perpetrator should be eliminated or provided only with the strictest protection, such as supervised visitation, where a professional third party, typically under assignment by a court, accompanies the child on any visits with the abusing parent.

> **When children are the victims of physical abuse, contact with the perpetrators should be eliminated or provided only with the strictest protection, such as supervised visitation, where a professional third party accompanies the child on any visits with the abusing parent.**

We also need to be open to the possibility that we might need to protect the children from the *mother's* physical abuse, as well as the father's. According to figures compiled from the states' protective service agencies by the Men's Health Network, children may have more to fear from their mothers than from their fathers. In fact, mothers were found to physically abuse their children at a rate approaching or exceeding twice that of fathers.[10]

This is neither to condemn women nor to excuse violence in any circumstance. Rather, we cite these findings to put the argument in perspective. If women share in the guilt for violence perpetrated on children, we should be as diligent in protecting children from abusive mothers as from fathers.

Beware of False Claims

We also need to be aware that *false claims* of abuse are sometimes made by vindictive or desperate—or just frightened—spouses, or as a legal maneuver to gain advantage. This is the problem that makes domestic violence one of the trickiest issues in domestic relations. Once the specter of domestic abuse is raised, the accused can do little to rebut the charge, even if it is completely spurious. The court usually takes the position that even if the allegations are flimsy, it is better to be safe than sorry. And judges are taught that batterers are habitual deniers. When the accused denies the charges, he or she is rarely given the benefit of the doubt or assumed innocent until proven guilty beyond a reasonable doubt. This is understandable in a way: What judge wants a headline that a case assigned to him resulted in tragedy because he failed to safeguard the victim's security? Therefore, he acts on the allegation, sometimes even without evidence or detail. And there is commonly no speedy hearing to determine the truth.

> ➤ Once the specter of domestic or sexual abuse is raised, the accused can do little to rebut the charge, even if it is completely spurious. The court virtually always takes the position that even if the allegations are flimsy, it is better to be safe than sorry.

Not only will a false allegation of abuse win the custody fight, it could virtually annihilate the opposition. The person charged is powerless to rehabilitate his reputation. Thus, charges of domestic violence or child abuse becomes the ultimate weapon, the irresistible force. We have heard reports that unscrupulous divorce lawyers counsel their clients to make up allegations, to call the police without real provocation, or to do something to provoke the ex-spouse, simply to obtain a competitive advantage for their case. Courts rarely do much investigation and almost never will end up sanctioning a party for false allegations, since the court can never be entirely certain the allegations *are* false.

Remember the group of divorced fathers my co-author had gotten together in Chapter 6, who railed against the court system? Here, two of the fathers talk about their experiences with claims of domestic abuse they swear are bogus:

"I had been thrown out of the house on a domestic violence claim," said Drew, the architect. "I had been married for thirty years, and there was *never* any claim of domestic violence, nothing. It was totally false. She did it just to get me out of the house and to get an advantage in the litigation process."

Nat, the attorney, explained, "You understand you can easily get the husband out by going down to the court by yourself. As long as the husband is not there to deny anything. It's called *ex-parte* with provision. You go in and say, 'He hit me.' And the judge signs an order barring the man from the house without ever asking him what happened—without taking any testimony or ordering an inquiry."

Drew: "And the police come and take you away in handcuffs and that's it. There's no due process."

Nat: "There's nothing. And all of us have gone through this. It's standard practice."

Drew: "Even if she *fears* that something will happen, she can claim abuse. But you have to recognize that women couldn't do it by themselves. They have a system that's supporting them to make that happen."

It is clear from the above discussion that the prevalence of real abuse versus false allegations of abuse is one of the fiercest battlegrounds in gender warfare of divorce and requires sensitive scientific examination. Few true abusers will readily admit it. So we can't take denials or protestations as truth, either. But it's critical that our policies better protect both the victim and the innocent.

Other instances may fall short of full-fledged physical harm or allegations thereof. For example, one of the parties may unwisely make an empty physical threat that frightens the other. The victim may take the hollow threat literally, either honestly or simply strategically, as ammunition. And some mothers may simply *feel* unsafe knowing their ex-spouse is under the enormous emotional stress that separation brings, even though there is no objective threat to their safety.

Separating Serious Continuing Abuse from Isolated Incidents

There's no question that serious or prolonged abuse is damaging and warrants action to remove the abuser from contact with his or her victim. When a pattern or history of violence has typified the couple, the bully or batterer should be denied custody, and the victim given our careful protection. But domestic violence is not so black and white when its sole manifestation occurs around the time of an impending divorce, and there has been no prior history of violence. Studies document that comparatively minor and isolated violence is expressed in a higher percentage of families in the highly emotional period lasting from about six months before to six months after the physical separation (the "emotional peak"). Pushing, shoving, even throwing things becomes more common for both men and women.[11] These acts of violence are due to the extreme emotional stress of the moment and, for individuals with no history of abuse, may be unlikely to recur. In determining custody, these acts need to be evaluated against the lifetime of past and future risk to the victim. Thus, it is important to distinguish bona fide cases of continuing and dangerous abuse from discrete, isolated episodes.

> ➤ Studies document that minor and isolated violence is expressed in a higher percentage of families in the highly emotional period lasting from about six months before to six months after the physical separation (the "emotional peak"). Pushing, shoving, even throwing things becomes more common for both men and women.

Kerry, whom we met in Chapter 8, was similar to many husbands who have no history of domestic violence, but finds that the stress of a failing marriage causes him to act out his frustration through physical bullying and even attacking. Susan had never experienced any physical threat from Kerry, who happened to be physically powerful, as well as having a black belt in karate—until she told him she wanted a divorce. "He was beside himself and he was on edge all the time. He saw his world falling apart," she recalls.

Susan remembers one night in particular, while they were still living together, when she had been out with a girlfriend while he stayed home to watch the kids. She called Kerry from the restaurant and told him she'd be home around 11:00. But she got caught up in socializing with her friend and didn't arrive home until midnight. As she opened the door to her apartment, she found herself face-to-face with Kerry, who was in a white-hot rage. He accused her of jerking him around and setting him up as a figure of ridicule. "He slapped me across the face very hard. I sat up all night, afraid to go to bed. At that moment, I was so afraid of him." Susan follows up this report by emphasizing, "It was the only time he ever hit me."

We should not be quick to forgive Kerry, who needlessly caused Susan pain and terror. However, to deny him a substantial role with his children on the basis of this one isolated episode would be equally wrong—for him, Susan, and their children. In each family in which violence has surfaced, we need to evaluate the likelihood of recurrence. And it is important to distinguish between those cases in which there has been a pattern of repetitive—and often escalating—violence and those cases involving an isolated episode of pushing or slapping, especially during the "emotional peak" period.

Chart 10.1 documents the extent of violence, as reported by our sample of mothers and fathers, both of a comparatively minor nature as well as that for which medical attention was sought (our study did not explore the period of time six months after separation). As we see, both parents report about twice as much violence perpetrated against them by the ex-spouse as they themselves perpetrated.[12] Between 10 and 25 percent of couples report at least two episodes of hitting, slapping, pushing, shoving, kicking, biting, physical threats, or thrown objects in the last six months of the marriage. Less than four percent of these episodes required medical attention. While 11 percent of husbands report that police were called for their domestic disputes at any point in the relationship, 22 percent of wives report police presence.

Respected authorities such as Stanford child psychologist Eleanor Mac-

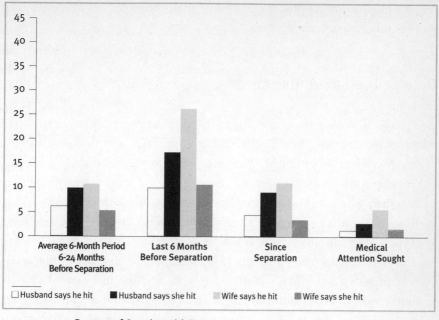

45 —
40 —
35 —
30 —
25 —
20 —
15 —
10 —
5 —
0 —

Average 6-Month Period
6-24 Months
Before Separation

Last 6 Months
Before Separation

Since
Separation

Medical
Attention Sought

☐ Husband says he hit   ■ Husband says she hit   ▨ Wife says he hit   ▨ Wife says she hit

CHART 10.1   **Percent of Couples with Two
or More Violent Episodes**

coby and legal scholar Robert Mnookin, authors of *Dividing the Child,* recommend that as long as the violence is relatively minor (for instance, if it does not require medical attention) and is confined to the emotional peak period, such incidents by mothers or fathers should carry no policy implications and should not figure into the custody or visitation determination.[13] In fact, as you may recall, Susan and Kerry eventually developed a positive co-parenting relationship.

For allegations about continuing and/or dangerous violence, however, we need better methods for judges to help them distinguish real danger from fabricated charges designed to produce competitive advantage or destroy reputations. Ironically, experienced domestic-violence professionals recognize that many genuine abuse victims will fail to make any charges because of fear, guilt, shame, or other manifestations of the victim mentality. Seasoned court mediators and mental-health professionals, trained and aware of the victim-mentality phenomenon, have acquired the skill necessary to probe sensitively in order to determine the truth in such instances.

Playing the Sex-Abuse Card

Even more damaging than false allegations of domestic violence are spurious claims of child sexual abuse. Ralph Underwager, Ph.D., a clinical psychologist in private practice in Northfield, Minnesota, who has counseled sexually-abused children for forty-four years, acts as an expert witness for the defense for fathers and mothers who have been accused of sexually abusing their children, and has conducted research and written extensively in the field. He talked with us about his experiences with the courts on this issue.[14] "When a parent accuses an ex-spouse of sexually abusing their child, what happens immediately, without adjudication, is that the child is withdrawn from the accused and, in most cases, is forbidden to have any contact with that parent. The separation can go on for years while the child is subjected to continuous interviews and therapy. And what happens during that time? The child learns to hate the accused parent—even if he or she is innocent."

We questioned Underwager as to where the fault rested in such cases.

"It's the system's fault," he declared. "It's the laws; it's the judges; it's the attorneys who set up a system whereby a parent who makes an accusation gets immediate reinforcement. He or she gets free legal advice, free support, free victims' advocacy."

While the exact figures are clearly a matter of controversy, Underwager claims that of the reports of abuse, at least 65 percent are declared unfounded. "Of the remaining 35 percent, half are declared to be inaccurate on further investigation," he added. "Of those 17 percent that are left, only about half of those go to trial. Of those 9 percent, 60 percent are determined by the justice system to be abused. Now you're down to 5 percent. Of that 5 percent, we think half are falsely convicted." The bottom line, according to Underwager, is that roughly 2.5 percent of parents who are accused of sexual abuse are likely to be guilty.

One story, which was the subject of a six-part news story that appeared in the *Detroit Free Press* in March through August, 1996, illustrates the damage that can be inflicted on parents and their children when false allegations of sexual abuse are made. In this case, the father, Ed Bielaska, was accused by the mother, Linda Orley, of sexually abusing their two daughters. According to the news report, the mother "made repeated false allegations that Bielaska had molested his daughters."[15] As a result of the unceasing barrage of accusations unleashed by the mother, the young girls came to fear Bielaska, and he was prevented by the courts from visiting them for eight months. But the allegations were eventually "found to be ludicrous by therapists and judges." In fact, one judge, in ruling that Orley "engaged in a concerted effort to alienate the father from the children," found that "She is preoccupied with sex. There is a serious flaw in her moral character." Eventually, Bielaska won full custody, and the court ordered that Orley couldn't see the girls until "after a neutral counselor reports that [Bielaska] has had time to establish his bond with the girls."

A more innocent version of false sexual abuse charges also frequently arises because some custodial mothers may not realize how normal some sexual behaviors are in young children. For example, according to a recent Mayo Clinic study, "Simply because a five-year-old boy touches his genitals occasionally, even after a weekend visit with his noncustodial parent, it does not mean he's been sexually abused. Rather, it is a behavior that is seen in almost two thirds of boys at that age."[16]

Policies to Protect Victims and Reduce False Claims

Clearly, we need to shield true victims of continuing abuse by building in a better system of protections. Orders of protection or restraining orders have often proven ineffective. Instead they have the same effect as a red cape in front of a bull. We have read all too often of newspaper headlines where an estranged husband or wife commits acts of heinous violence in fits of uncontrolled rage. Better enforcement, better training of police personnel, and better support of battered victims shelters would help protect victims before it was too late.

> ➤ We need to modify our system to provide sanctions against making accusations of domestic violence or child sexual abuse that are simply false. Parents who raise such charges, knowing they are unfounded, but making them to gain a competitive advantage, should be punished.

Just as clearly, we need to modify our system to provide sanctions against making accusations that are simply false. Parents who raise such charges, knowing they are unfounded, but making them to gain a competitive advantage, should be punished. More important, parents should *know* they will be punished for making false charges, thus reducing the incentive to make them. And lawyers who recommend such tactics should be disbarred.

Two very important caveats are in order, however. Developing sanctions against making false charges will not only deter the spurious claims, they may deter some of the factual ones, as well. In cases in which the abuse truly occurred, but the independent evidence—other than the sure knowledge of the other parent—is flimsy, the victim will be afraid to come forward, for fear of the sanctions. And abuse victims are known to be reticent enough to come forward with the present system. True abusers will have an additional weapon, the last thing we'd want.

A second issue is that if the sanctions are too severe, those making false allegations will be reticent to back down and renounce their accusations. Careful thought needs to go into the development and implementation of sanctions against false allegations of abuse in domestic relations, to appropriately calibrate the penalties.

11.

Custody Policies That Work

In previous chapters, we have made the argument that a rebuttable presumption in favor of joint legal custody is in the best interests of most children and therefore appropriate for most families. This practice would be a substantial departure from customary procedure. Many judges, subscribing to the bad divorced dad image, automatically regard mothers as the preferred custodians and decision-makers, believing that fathers have to be coerced and threatened into being responsible. An orientation that instead presumes that *both* parents are ready, willing, and able to provide the best possible life for their child, and that the child will reap huge benefits from a rich relationship with both parents, would go a long way toward righting the wrongs in the divorce system.

But is a rebuttable presumption favoring joint legal custody the only custody change necessary? Are additional remedies involving child custody needed to improve divorced families' functioning? This chapter will consider other proposals that have been made regarding custody awards. To put the arguments into perspective, however, it helps to begin by providing some historical context.

A Brief History of Custody Awards

It is important to understand that the current trends and practices are something of an aberration from that of our historical roots.

If we go back thousands of years, we see that according to Roman law, children were the property or chattel of their fathers, who had absolute power over them. Fathers could even legally force them into labor or sell them. Mothers had no rights whatsoever, even as guardians in the event of the father's death. This tradition continued into British common law, the foundation of our country's law. In England, fathers had nearly absolute power over their children, but they also had the obligation to protect, support, and educate them. If the marriage dissolved, fathers always obtained custody, regardless of circumstances, and mothers' rights to visit their children were extremely limited.[1]

This "paternal presumption" changed radically in Britain in 1839. The "tender years doctrine," advocated by Justice Thomas Noon Talfourd, chose age seven as the magic number in deciding with which parent the child would reside.[2] Custody of children beneath this age was automatically granted to mothers, while older children went to the fathers, with visiting rights to mothers.

In America, until the nineteenth century, the paternal standard was applied to custody cases.[3] By the late 1800s, as fathers increasingly sought work outside the village, mothers primarily became the caretakers. As a result, the paternal preference was gradually replaced by a strong maternal preference by the 1920s.[4] However, starting during the late 1960s and concluding by the mid 1970s, as the divorce rate began to accelerate greatly, prompted by constitutional concerns about equal protection and sex discrimination (concerns raised jointly by fathers and by feminist groups), most states abandoned the maternal presumption in favor of gender-neutral laws.[5] In 1970, the Uniform Marriage and Divorce Act, which most states adopted, provided for a "best interests of the child" standard. As renowned psychologist and divorce expert Joan Kelly, Ph.D., wrote, "For the first time in history, custody decisions were to be based on a consideration of the needs and interests of the child rather than on the gender or rights of the parent."[6] Then, in California in 1979, joint custody was permitted for the first time.[7] By 1991, 80 percent of the states either allowed or gave preference to joint custody by statute, and most of the rest permitted it by case law. Today, almost every state distinguishes between legal custody and physical (or residential) custody.

What's in the Best Interests of the Child?

At the present time, all states use the "best interests of the child" standard as the basis for custody decisions for those parents who fight it out in court. However, some courts and legislatures are considering laws that award physical custody on other bases. Although very few parents reach the point where they let the court decide custody after a hearing, agreements reached by other means are virtually always colored by what parents learn courts would do if they litigated in court (which, as we saw in Chapter 5, has been called "bargaining in the shadow of the law"). So the standards the courts use have incalculable significance.

> ➤ Critics have claimed that the "best interests of the child"
> standard is too vague and ambiguous, and that the court
> doesn't really have the Solomonic wisdom necessary to rec-
> ognize what is in any given child's best interests anyway.

Many have claimed, however, that the "best interests of the child" standard is too vague and ambiguous, and that the court doesn't really have the Solomonic wisdom necessary to recognize what is in any given child's best interests anyway. Put another way, two judges could decide the same case very differently, depending on their own biases. Among other things, this state of affairs has the serious disadvantage that, not knowing how any given judge will decide, and believing it's a crapshoot, both parties may be more inclined to pursue bitter custody battles, thinking they have a chance of winning in court. (The opposite argument is sometimes made, as well; that not knowing how any given judge will decide, the parties are *discouraged* from litigating and are more likely to settle out of court.) These critics have proposed that various other standards should replace that of the best interests of the child.

The Primary Caretaker and the Greatest Earner Standard

The most serious contender for an alternate standard is the "primary caretaker" standard, which has been promoted by, among others, an influential law professor from the University of Michigan, David Chambers.[8] This view argues that the post-divorce caretaking arrangement should provide the child stability by matching, as closely as possible, the pre-divorce arrangement. The court should look to see which parent was performing more child-care duties during the marriage, and, for the sake of as little change to the child's life as possible, continue that parent as primary caretaker after divorce. A big advantage of this standard, of course, is that it is far less ambiguous to determine which parent was doing which child-care activities prior to divorce than to decide what is truly in the child's best interests.

There are some serious drawbacks to this proposal, however, as its many critics have pointed out. By applying this standard to most divorced families, primary physical custody should actually be awarded to the day-care center, nanny, or school, which almost always has much more hands-on child-care responsibility than either parent. In fact, child-care duties almost invariably get split far differently after divorce than they were previously, particularly if the mother has to go to work or work more hours, so the consideration of maintaining stability is moot.

Other critics have pointed out that the primary caretaker standard is really a poorly disguised mother-custody standard, since the child-care activities that appear on the list of those a judge should evaluate in deciding which parent provided primary caretaking are heavily skewed toward the type of activities mothers habitually provide, such as feeding, laundering clothing, and shopping[9] rather than toward those fathers typically provide, such as coaching or repairing toys. Most notorious was the appearance on the list of "breast-feeding."[10] It has also been pointed out that most child-care activities are easily learned and adeptly performed by either parent, even if primarily performed previously by one.

One of the chief motivations driving the proponents of the primary caretaker standard is the notion of fairness to the parent who has devoted past energies to child care. They argue that that parent should be rewarded for his or her past sacrifices by winning primary custody after divorce. This argument has a certain appeal, as does the "proportional caretaker" proposal, under which the court attempts to allocate the child's time between the households as closely as possible to match the proportion of time each parent devoted to child care pre-divorce.[11] However, fairness to the parents should not be society's primary concern in custody decisions (as it might more properly be in property-division decisions, for example). Instead, the welfare of the child should be paramount.

This same reasoning should go to discredit a rival proposal based on the "greatest earner" standard. Support for this standard derives from the concern society has with the economic provisioning for the child. It is noted that if economic support is truly society's primary concern, as it appears to be, custody should be awarded typically to the parent who can best provide materially for the child. Proponents of this standard believe that if we awarded custody to the parent who earns the most, the child's standard of living would be higher, and fewer children would be in poverty. The other spouse, having only one mouth to feed, would fare better, as well. This allows for the greatest standard of living for the greatest number of people. Additionally, the standard has the advantage of being inherently fair to the parents, according to its advocates, because it rewards them for past sacrifices they made on behalf of the advancement of the family. Like the primary-caretaker standard, however, this standard weighs only one type of sacrifice—in this case, those in the service of career advancement and income—to the exclusion of other sacrifices. And as we showed in Chapter 4, few divorced children go into poverty anyway. Even more to the point, while the primary caretaker rule is a veiled euphemism for mother custody, the greatest earner standard is a transparent ruse for fathers to win custody, i.e., a return to the "paternal presumption" of 150 years ago.

➤ **While the primary caretaker rule is a veiled euphemism for mother custody, the greatest earner standard is a transparent ruse for fathers to win custody.**

The proponents of both the primary-caretaker and the greatest-earner rules tout the fact that these rules are consistent and unambiguous as their primary advantage. However, while decisions might be far easier on the court using either of these rules, it is not the judges that we should be trying to protect: it is the children. In turn, say the advocates, if the parents knew beforehand that the judge's decisions would be unambiguous and easy, favoring one parent (the primary wage earner under the greatest-earner rule) or the other (the stay-at-home parent under the primary caretaker rule) it would forestall more court custody battles.[12] Again, as we've seen, court battles don't seem to be very prevalent anyway. Joint legal custody, combined with substantial—although not necessarily identically equal—access time for both parents is a sufficiently unambiguous standard. Under this system, both parents will normally meet their responsibilities, and the children will thrive. Joint legal custody is completely compatible, then, with the best interests of the child standard that we believe should be retained.

Another advantage of the system we propose here is that it more easily adapts to changing circumstances than any rival proposal. For instance, if we use the primary-caretaker standard, what happens if the custodial parent has her work hours increased? Will custody need to change? Under the greatest-earner standard, what happens if the custodial parent's wages decrease and/or the noncustodial parent's wages increase? Need we modify custody as a result? On the other hand, if both parents have substantial time with the child and are enfranchised by the continued ability to make decisions on behalf of the child, changes in circumstances should be more easily worked out between the parties.

When Parents Can't Agree on Residential Custody

Joint legal custody and very substantial contact with both parents (a minimum of one-third of the child's nonschool hours each) should be the rebuttable presumption—which could be challenged by either party—in divorce cases. This would assure *both* parents in most families that they will retain their fundamental parental roles with the children. If one parent wished to deprive the other of this minimal level of parental enfranchisement, that parent should have the burden of proving his or her plan is more clearly in the child's best interests. We believe if this standard were the guideline, it would substantially lower the stakes for deciding the next 30 percent of the child's time, that is, which parent was declared the child's residential parent. Parents fight and argue and litigate when they feel they are being deprived of something, when they are being made to lose. With this minimum standard, few parents should feel they will suffer a loss. As a result, most couples should be able to come to an amicable physical custody and visitation agreement and define for themselves what's in their own particular child's best interests, perhaps with the help of mediation.[13]

Of course, some disagreements will inevitably arise, and the court needs to adjudicate when parents can't decide themselves, even with mediation. While the best interests standard is ostensibly gender neutral, there can be little debate that in practice, the courts favor mothers. According to Maccoby and Mnookin, the maternal presumption "has disappeared . . . in terms of the law on the books," but as a social norm "it still persists. When two competent parents—a fit mother and a fit father—each want to be primarily responsible for the child following divorce, mothers usually end up with the children."[14]

The argument typically given in defense of this practice is that mothers simply care more about children than fathers do. One study, which interviewed a sample of mothers, found that the mothers *thought* that mothers' love is different from other forms of love, is more intense and entails "a feeling that one's child is part of oneself."[15] The *mothers believed* that the fathers cared less about their children than they did. About half "did not think much of their husbands as fathers, describing them in various degrees as uninvolved and overly critical."[16]

Feminist law professor June Carbone states the obvious when she concludes that studies such as the one just mentioned "are inherently limited."[17] For example, we, too, found that mothers think they are better parents than fathers. But since we also had a sample of fathers in our study, we were able to ask them what *they* thought. These fathers on average thought *they* were better parents than the mothers. And both parents seemed to know the other's opinion.

But Carbone insists that the proposition that women care more (not differently, but more) about their children is supported both because the results "correspond to literary attempts to capture the experience of mothering . . . [and to the fact that] at divorce, mothers are much more likely to seek custody of their children than are fathers."[18] Who seeks custody should hardly be construed as an index of who cares more. Attorney Ronald Henry aptly noted the double standard when he recognized the "Catch-22 that fathers don't care enough to seek custody and, if they really cared, they would not put the children through the trauma of a court battle."[19] A recent well-publicized case brought to light the divergent views on this point.

During the O.J. Simpson trial, prosecutor Marcia Clark was so absorbed in the case that she was not as available as prior to the case to attend to her child. She filed an action to obtain greater child support from her ex-husband to help her defray the greater child-care expenses she was absorbing. He, in turn, averring that he was home and available and could care for the child for free, filed a counter-motion to switch custody to himself. "I have personal knowledge that on most nights she does not arrive home until 10 P.M. and even when she is home, she is working," Gordon Clark stated in a Superior Court declaration.[20]

Some commentators observed that if he really cared about his child he would have simply paid more instead of undermining his ex-wife's authority. This view was forcefully expressed in *Newsweek,* in an open letter to Gordon Clark from Judith Regan, a powerful New York publisher.[21]

> *Now that women have achieved some level of economic independence, there is a movement in this country to take custody away from perfectly fit mothers. It should shock the conscience of any court, because it is often a serious indication of a man's desire to control and hurt the mother of his children, rather than an indication of any sincere desire to care for his children. . . . What is in your best interests, Mr. Clark, and what* is in the best interests of your children . . . *is this: you should act according to the best interest of your wife, who, as the much loved mother of your children, has earned the right to be treated with respect and honored for the important role she has played and will continue to play as the mother of your children.*

This belief, that women are somehow "better" than fathers as post-divorce primary parents, is simply not supported by any research. According to psychologist Richard Warshak, Ph.D.,[22] author of *The Custody Revolution,* "What contradicts the gender stereotypes is that the evidence overwhelmingly demonstrates that divorced men can nurture children competently and that they're equally capable of managing responsibilities of custody. In some areas, fathers actually do a better job, particularly with boys." As far as the benefit to the children, Warshak cites his and other studies[23] that show that the gender of the parent has no bearing in predicting how well a child will function. "There really aren't any grounds to discriminate against fathers who seek custody," he emphasizes.

The Problem with Custody Evaluations

In many cases involving disputes about primary residential custody at present, the court, the parents, or the attorneys turn to *custody evaluators* for guidance.

These psychologists or social workers try to use their expertise to advise the court which parent is more fit. Unfortunately, this has turned out to be little more than guesswork. While many evaluators routinely administer expensive standardized tests such as MMPIs or Rorschachs, there is absolutely no credible evidence that these are valid predictors of which spouse will make the best primary parent.[24] In fact, there is no evidence that there *is* a scientifically valid way for a custody evaluator to choose the best primary parent. Instead, there is convincing statistical evidence that their recommendations merely follow the evaluator's own gender biases. According to an analysis of a sample of sixty-two custody evaluation reports written by professional custody evaluators, "female evaluators described fathers significantly more often in negative terms, and . . . male evaluators did the same for mothers."[25]

> ➤ There is no evidence that there *is* a scientifically valid way for a custody evaluator to choose the best primary parent. Instead, there is convincing evidence that their recommendations merely follow the evaluator's own gender biases, that "female evaluators described fathers significantly more often in negative terms, and . . . male evaluators did the same for mothers."

Perhaps the results of professional custody evaluations are so disappointing because they are attempting to split hairs over something elusive: which parent is better able to promote the child's healthy functioning, when *both* parents normally do so. Evaluators look to discipline, feeding, and bedtime habits, for example, when there is conflicting evidence that one child-rearing style is better for the child than another. In deciding disputes about which parent should have residential custody, evaluators should use some other, less-subjective indicators, factors supported by strong scientific evidence that show they relate to children's healthy adaptation.[26] They should include:

1. Which parent is more likely to encourage, support, and promote a strong relationship of the child with the other parent? We know that strong relationships with both parents predict healthy adjustment.[27]

2. Which parent is more likely to promote a civil and harmonious co-parental relationship with the other parent? Since conflict between the parents has been unequivocally shown by research to be the single most important factor hindering the child's healthy adaptation after divorce,[28] the parent who will reliably attempt to de-escalate conflict should have the advantage, since that parent is acting in the child's best interests.

3. Which parent is least likely to derogate the other parent or put the child in the middle of a loyalty conflict?[29]

4. Which parent is least likely to relocate with the child? (See "What Happens When One Parent Moves?" at the end of this chapter.)

These factors should also be the deciding ones if an initial custody arrangement—legal or residential—is found to be unsuitable and a modification is sought by one of the parties. When in dispute, the court should reward the parent most civil to the other—for that is the parent who is truly acting in the child's best interest. Our experience with divorcing mothers and fathers has taught us that the children are considered by both parents as their most precious commodity by far. Using the above factors to decide primary custody when it is in dispute can provide powerful incentives for the divorcing parents to behave civilly, responsibly, and cooperatively. And ultimately, the children will come out winners.

While initially custody evaluators were used only when primary residential custody was in dispute, increasingly they are being asked to decide other matters as well, such as the legal custody arrangement and visitation schedules. One professional custody evaluator who has handled over 1,000 evaluations, when asked, "How much of your practice would be lost if there was a presumption of joint legal custody and at least one-third time visitation?" answered, "Almost all of it. There would be relatively few disputes left." And he almost always settled upon both of these features in his recommendations to the court. Since being forced to undergo custody evaluations reliably makes the parents more inimical toward one another (as well as being costly—about $2,500 per case at present, time-consuming—averaging four to six months, and frightening to children, who are forced to recognize someone other than their parents is making decisions for them), adopting such a presumption would help the dissolution process immensely. Similarly, mediators told us that most of their *mediated* settlements concerning custody and visitation featured joint legal custody and at least one-third time visitation. And in the cases in which mediation failed, and the couple proceeded to custody evaluations, these two features were again overwhelmingly recommended by the evaluators. Wouldn't it be simpler, less expensive, and less acrimonious if that were the standard *going into* negotiations? Let the couple "bargain in the shadow of *that* law."

What About Joint Residential Custody?

As previously discussed, one advantage of joint legal custody is to keep fathers actively involved with their children. But what about joint *residential* custody, an arrangement in which the children spend virtually half of their time with each parent, typically alternating half weeks, full weeks, or months. In fact, the issue of joint residential custody being the rebuttable presumption for most divorce cases is often raised by father's rights groups as a panacea. But is this a viable solution?

Unfortunately, unlike the case for joint legal custody, there is simply not enough evidence available at present to substantiate routinely imposing joint residential custody. The reason for the lack of evidence is simple: there are too few cases adopting strict joint residential custody to perform statistical analysis. While about 7 percent of parents mutually choose a joint residential arrangement, they are a highly select sub-sample, and the sort of statistical analyses we performed for joint legal cases, in which we teased out how much of the benefit was due to the arrangement *per se*, versus how much was due to predisposing factors, is not possible. The limited analyses other researchers have performed don't strongly recommend it be imposed either.[30]

Just because there is no evidence to recommend it, should it be opposed? After all, there was limited scientific evidence to support a great many policies that have turned out, once adopted, to work well, according to the evidence that later became available. While it is recommended that the children have substantial contact with both parents, which includes time at home, time driving to and from as well as sharing the child's extracurricular activities, time feeding and clothing the child, time monitoring homework, and time spent with the child and his or her friends, it is not necessary that this time be split exactly down the middle. If each parent is empowered by joint legal custody and is allowed involvement in the full variety of child-rearing activities, few parents or children will feel deprived. A parent overly concerned that he see his child exactly the same amount of time as his ex-spouse becomes more of an accountant than a parent. Furthermore, this strict accounting of time can also set the stage for many future arguments, when arrangements must be changed because of extenuating circumstances, which routinely come up.

Finally, such arrangements are often transitional. As children get older, they frequently don't want to switch households so often. In short, insisting upon strict equality of time spent with the child may be in the weaker parent's interest, but it is rarely in the child's. As Judge Minna Buck told us in a telephone interview,[31] "Split physical custody can be devastating for school-age children—especially when they are forced to travel long distances between homes." Joint *legal* custody and *substantial* contact—though not necessarily exactly equal—with both parents appears to be an ideal solution for most children.

This was precisely the preference found among young adults who had been through divorce themselves as youngsters; the "veterans," one might say. Psychologist Bill Fabricius, Ph.D., collected responses from those of his college students whose parents had been divorced earlier, 272 students in all. Although only 14 percent of them had lived primarily with their fathers, and another 10 percent lived about an equal amount of time with both parents, when asked, "If two parents get divorced and they are both good parents and they live relatively close to one another, what do you feel is the best living arrangement for the children?" 75 percent answered "An equal amount of time with each parent," and only 11% thought the child should have less than "a substantial number of regular overnights with the father."

There is another reason for preferring substantial time with both parents. Suppose the two parents have quite dissimilar incomes and assets. One lives in a big house and the other in cramped quarters. If sole custody is awarded, the child might reside with the less well-off parent and be deprived of the affluence of the other, unless we socially engineered income and asset transfers to the other, a process that works poorly. On the other hand, if the parents shared the child, we would feel less need to arrange such transfers. The child would have *two* homes, one nice and beautiful, the other smaller. The child would automatically share in the wealth of the wealthier parent without any need for additional governmental intervention.

What Happens When One Parent Moves?

When couples divorce, not infrequently one of them finds it necessary or feels the desire to move to a different locale. For couples who have not had children, such a move might actually be beneficial. In fact, counselors often advise relocation for a childless spouse who is especially troubled by the marital breakup and having trouble recovering from the loss. In such cases, returning to the town where one's own parents live, moving near friends or other family, or starting over in a new locale that doesn't bring forth the bittersweet memories of what used to be can help hasten recovery from the grief of divorce.

➤ **When one parent moves, the other parent suddenly becomes absent from his or her child's day-to-day life. Fathers, usually the parent without custody, are particularly affected, often voicing concern about how vulnerable they feel that their ex-wives can effectively cancel out their influence any time the mother wishes, by a capricious move.**

However, things change radically when children are involved. When one parent moves, the other parent suddenly becomes absent from his or her child's day-to-day life. All the harmful consequences to the child and to the parent who can no longer regularly interact with the child ensue. In our studies, about

one-third of the families had one or both parents relocate out of the metropol-
itan area by three years after the divorce. Fathers, usually the parent without custody, are particularly affected, often voicing concern about how vulnerable they
feel that their ex-wives can capriciously cancel out their influence any time they
wish.

Louise is a mother I spoke to just before she was about to move. "I just
couldn't take dealing with Peter any longer," she said of her ex-husband. "He
makes my life miserable. He bought a house three blocks away, and now he
knows every one of my comings and goings. He knows if I have a date or am just
going out with the girls. He knows if I spent the night out of my house because
he can see my newspaper left in the front yard the next day. Every time I see him
I want to puke, he makes me so sick. And I can't avoid seeing him. We have joint
legal custody, and he thinks he needs to have a hand in every single decision I
make, even who I use as a babysitter. If I had wanted to live like that, I would have
stayed married! I can't take this any longer. I'm a good hairdresser and can get a
job anywhere I want. So I'm taking Logan and we're out of here. I can hardly
imagine how great it will feel!"

While mothers like Louise may see such a move as for their own well-being,
fathers are often bereft at the loss of contact with their children. Said one father,
"My heart really aches when I stop and think how I am missing the day-to-day
interactions with my daughter. I miss her more than I've ever missed anything in
my life. I feel that I am the one who's losing out on something that can never be
replaced or relived—my daughter's childhood."

But beyond the grief that fathers feel or the relief that mothers like Louise
feel, how does such a move affect the child? I happened to hear a radio call-in
show about this issue. The show was one in which a psychologist dispensed advice to callers with questions. In this instance, the caller was a divorced mother
who, because her grief over the divorce was overwhelming to her, and the pain
of seeing things every day that reminded her of happier times was too much to
handle, had returned to her parents' home twelve hundred miles away. In the
bosom of her parents' home, she was gradually recovering. Now, however, the
mother was starting to feel guilty that she had taken her eleven-year-old son with
her, removing him from his father, with whom the child was strongly connected.
She called the telephone therapist, no doubt hoping to hear some soothing words
that could alleviate her guilt. Since many of the questions I had heard the thera-

pist address dealt sympathetically with the callers' exaggerated sense of guilt, I fully expected the doctor to comfort the mother. We were both wrong!

"Did you find the divorce pretty overwhelming?" the therapist asked.

"Yes, it was a nightmare," the mother answered.

"Did you find yourself overpowered by feelings of loss, confusion, and depression? Did you have nightmares, anxiety, sweaty palms, and the sense that nothing would ever be right with the world again?"

The mother answered yes to these questions, most likely certain that her feelings were being well understood.

"And did you feel no one but your parents, who knew you so well and loved you so much, could provide the comfort and security you'd need to pull you through?"

Right again.

But then the psychologist unleashed her bomb: "And that's just the way your son must have felt, if not worse. But you are a grown-up; you have other ways you can cope—other defenses and resources. Your son has none; he's just a kid. His parents, both of them, are truly his only protection against a hostile world. And you, giving in to your own selfish needs, took one of them away from him. I will not speak any comforting words to you. You *should* feel guilty!"

Should policy be developed that restricts in any way the rights of one of the parents to move? This is the subject of continuing debate and court cases. Virtually all of this discussion concerns restricting the ability of a parent to relocate *with the child.* It is difficult to imagine in our country a serious movement to restrict the relocation rights of the nonresidential parent, or a parent not intending to take the child along. But as a philosophical matter, *either* parent's moving away, if that move would restrict the child's access to one of them, should be discouraged.

A law passed in Arizona in 1996[32] is a model for how states should properly treat relocation with the child. This new law gives primacy to written agreements or parenting plans that the parents may have negotiated earlier concerning relocating the child. Presumably, if negotiated freely, the parents know best, better than a judge or legislature, how to deal with the prospect of relocation. Some couples might have agreed that relocation is permissible, others that it is prohibited. The law says, "The court shall not deviate from a provision of any parenting plan or other written agreement by which the parents specifically have agreed to allow or prohibit relocation of the child unless the court finds that the provision is no longer in the child's best interests. There is a rebuttable presumption that a provision from any parenting plan or other written agreement is in the child's best interests." If there is no written agreement one way or the other, the court "shall determine whether to allow the parent to relocate the child *in accordance with the child's best interests.* The burden of proving what is in the child's best interests is on the parent who is seeking to relocate the child" (emphasis added).

Sometimes relocating to a new place with the child is necessary for health reasons or for employment reasons, such as mandatory job transfers. In many other cases, however, the move is merely a preference by the relocating parent, as in the case of Louise, not a necessity at all. A recent notorious case, in California, unfortunately set the wrong precedent. Though Paul Burgess saw his children almost daily, Wendy Burgess wanted to take another job about forty miles away. The California Supreme Court decided that Wendy did not have the burden of proving her move was necessary.[33] While Paul asserted, "The reason for the move was contrived. She wanted to get me out of her and the kids' lives," Wendy answered, "I have the right to decisions I believe will benefit my children, and I'd say if it benefits me, it benefits my children."[34] In Arizona, the law gives the court instructions to consider the reasons for wishing to move or to oppose the move, and provides a reasonable list of factors the court should consider.

Some states permit parents with sole custody unrestricted movement, just as they would give nonparents; only parents with joint legal or joint residential custody can successfully oppose a move. In fact, this may be a reason some fathers pursue joint custody with such passion: they know it will give them leverage later, should they wish to oppose their ex-wife's subsequent relocation with the child.[35] The Arizona law specifically and wisely gives no advantage or disadvantage to opposing moves based on custody status. Judges typically consider only the extent of the emotional connection between the nonrelocating parent and child and the history of contact between them when deciding what is in the child's best interests.

Finally, the Arizona law requires the parent wishing to relocate to provide substantial notice to the other parent (sixty days written notice, sent by certified mail) of the intent to relocate the child. This gives the other parent sufficient opportunity to present the argument that the move opposes the child's best interests. In those cases where the parent is required by circumstances of health or safety or employment (or to satisfy those needs in a new spouse) to relocate in less than sixty days, the court allows only a temporary relocation, with a permanent decision ultimately decided on the same basis as above.

The Only Standard That Matters

No standard other than the "best interests of the child" is necessary or desirable in awarding primary custody. And, as we saw in Chapter 9, joint legal custody fits well within that standard. Still, we need to fine-tune how custody evaluators reach their decision, and how relocation with the child is handled after divorce.

12.

Changing the Landscape of Divorce
Additional Recommendations for Reform

There is a scene near the end of the 1997 movie, *Liar, Liar,* in which Jim Carrey, who plays a slick divorce lawyer, realizes that the sleazy tactics he has used to gain his female client more than any divorcée could hope for has deprived a devoted father of his children and sentenced the children to a lesser life. The moment is unexpectedly poignant in a film filled with Carrey's usual over-the-top antics. But Carrey's character is also a divorced father, and up until this moment has fit the stereotype of the dad who consistently disappoints his son. He now realizes that he really does love his son and would do anything to prevent from happening to himself what he as a lawyer did to his client's ex-husband.

The film struck me not for what it was purportedly about, but for the subversive portrayal of a legal system that's set up to create winners and losers in divorce, a system that allows families to be ripped apart for no good reason.

This feeling is echoed among most divorce professionals, who believe that the legal context in which divorce is embedded is part of the problem, not part of the solution. It is their growing consensus that this system has created a travesty and has mortally injured the American family. Almost all the domestic-relations judges we have spoken to, and even the more candid of the lawyers, strongly agree that the adversarial legal jockeying—in which each side to a dispute hires the best advocate he can find to represent him as forcefully or brutally as possible, even distorting the facts when necessary, in the hopes that the "truth" will eventually win out—is particularly badly suited to family dissolution. That is why the call for reform is so strong: even those who have a stake in continuing the system are so sickened by it that they want it to change. As one matrimonial lawyer told me, "My fondest hope is that I can work to change the system so that it doesn't hurt families and children so much. I hope to force myself and others like me out of business."

Divorce As a Social Service Matter

Throughout the last part of this book, we have been making recommendations for easing the burden of divorce on fathers, and by extension, their children. Such measures as joint legal custody and enforcement of visitation can go a long way to improve the lives of divorced families. But they're not enough. This country needs more approaches that take place *before* the animosities build up and positions get entrenched and intransigent. The cliché that an ounce of prevention is worth a pound of cure is never more applicable than in the case of divorcing families. Nearly every thoughtful person recognizes that prevention is both cost-effective and humane because it spares human suffering. So it is surprising how often we neglect this message.

> ➤ **This country needs more approaches that take place *before* the animosities build up and positions get entrenched and intransigent.**

One solution would be to approach divorce more from a social-service perspective, as we currently do for people who are trying to adopt a child, rather than embed it strongly within a legal context. Adoption certainly has a legal aspect, but family members have the bulk of their contacts with social workers, not lawyers. These human-service caseworkers prepare the family members for the likely scenarios and problems they will confront and help them find adaptive solutions before things escalate out of control. Divorce, a far more prevalent family problem, would almost certainly benefit from this virtually nonadversarial approach.

How would a social-service system of divorce function? How could we immerse divorcing parents in a context that would maximize their well-being and that of their children? One model for a very comprehensive system has been developed by California clinical psychologists Rodney Nurse, Ph.D., and Peggy Thompson, Ph.D., and published in a 1997 article in the *Family Psychologist*.[1] Called "Collaborative Divorce," this process begins with a male-female professional team who is assigned to work with the parents at the time of separation or filing for divorce. Each parent is seen individually by a caseworker of his or her own gender for two or three sessions. During that time the team establishes a therapeutic relationship, collects basic information, helps desensitize the parents to trauma experienced during the demise of the marriage, helps them set reasonable goals for the divorce process and beyond, teaches communication skills needed to insure negotiation competency, and finally, just *listens*. The caseworkers also assess the children and identify individual needs.

Children have the opportunity to discuss their feelings and reactions with a neutral professional, which adds important new elements, all-too-infrequently heard otherwise, to the professionals' and parents' thinking. Before long the parents meet with a neutral party who assists them in developing reasonable expectations for the financial issues they will face and organizing the information relevant for their attorneys. "Parents," say Nurse and Thompson, "are usually relieved to gain some understanding and control of their financial situation."

Next, the couple meets with the team of two caseworkers in a four-way meeting. By this time, the couple has been sensitized to their habitual fighting pattern and taught some stress management and communication skills they can use. According to Nurse and Thompson, "The emphasis here is that for the well-being of their entire family, with focus on their children, they must find some ways of co-parenting in order to reshape their lives [into a well-functioning divorced family]. The children must not be caught in the middle of hostilities or they suffer damage." Only then are the attorneys brought in, to redraft the couple's agreement in legal context. Holding the entire process together are agreements signed by the couple and the professionals that none of the information discussed during the process will be available for court hearings and none of the professionals can appear in court. If the collaborative divorce process breaks down, the parties will need to seek other professionals to assist them further. The caseworkers, attorneys, and financial consultants continue to be available to assist the family throughout the time they are grappling with divorce issues.

Such an all-encompassing program, where both parents are assisted throughout the process and persuaded that their primary responsibility is to concentrate on a long-term solution for the benefit of the children, should be widely considered and adopted.

Educating Parents About Divorce

A less comprehensive alternative to Collaborative Divorce is divorcing-parent education, a fast-growing trend. Judges around the country have begun to issue court orders requiring divorcing parents to attend such programs prior to the divorce becoming final. As of 1997, at least three states (Arizona, Connecticut, and Utah) have statewide programs, but forty-five states have at least one county with such a program, 541 different counties have them, and new programs are being added by twenty counties per month.[2] By reaching the couple at an early stage, *before* their debating positions become fixed, such programs hope to prepare parents and children for what lies ahead, and encourage civil relationships. Typically, such programs last about three hours and are taught by a male/female team of mental-health professionals.[3] They teach parents the benefits of cooperation and the disadvantages of conflict, especially for the children. They help parents understand the impact of divorce on children and what parents can and should do to minimize the damage.

> ➤ By reaching the couple at an early stage, *before* their debating positions become fixed, divorcing-parent education programs hope to prepare parents and children for what lies ahead, and encourage civil relationships.

My colleagues and I have surveyed over one hundred such programs around the country.[4] Significantly, we have found that among the highest priorities of these programs, which have been independently developed by nonattorney divorce professionals, is educating custodial parents about their responsibilities in encouraging their ex-spouse's access to the children. Thus, professionals who work with divorcing families daily have independently hit upon the major theme of this book: that parentally enfranchising the fathers is good for the children. Interestingly, such programs give relatively little emphasis to educating noncustodial parents about child-support payment obligations.

In Arizona, a state law passed in 1996 made participation in such a program early in the divorcing process mandatory for all parents.[5] Couples are required to pay up to $30 for the course. Those who fail to attend are subject to a variety of judicial sanctions. Many parents are initially resentful of being ordered to spend the time and pay the money for this course. The startling thing is to note the changes that come over them by the time the course is completed. Most are grateful at having been ordered to attend, agree it should be made mandatory as a condition of divorce, and indicate that they intend to change the way they relate to their ex-spouse for the benefit of the children. They have come to recognize how their retaliative and controlling actions can hurt their kids, and realize the necessity of developing and maintaining a civil, accommodating relationship with their ex-spouse if they hope to minimize the damage to their children.

Utah is another state that has instituted mandatory divorce education. One such course, called the Divorce Education Course for Parents, runs for $2^1/_4$ hours, with a class size of anywhere from twenty to seventy-five. Some of the eleven topics covered include helping children adjust to the divorce, the correlation between parental conflict and the child's adjustment to the divorce, and how to encourage cooperative behavior with an ex-spouse. "We start with the premise that parents all love their children and don't want to do anything to harm them," says Elizabeth Hickey, the course's founder and director and the driving force behind the state law.[6] "Then we say, 'Let us show you what the research has told us about what helps children in the divorce process and what hurts them.' " The key for the success of this program, Hickey feels, is to help parents see how and why their behavior is harmful to their children. "We talk about the negative and why not to do it, and then we give them other options and alternatives to move in a different, more cooperative posture."

The class gets high marks from parents. Hickey has had participants fill out a questionnaire after they've completed the class. Nearly all—95 percent—stated that the course was worthwhile. Ninety-four percent said it helped them to understand how children are affected by a divorce, and 91 percent felt that it increased their understanding of why it's important for parents to find a way to cooperate. While there has not been any long-term study of the effects of the course to date, Hickey's associates did a six-month follow-up survey and found that many people continued to state that the class was worthwhile. "I absolutely know that people's behavior and attitudes have changed," avers Hickey. "Their motivation is greatly increased to establish a good co-parenting relationship. Many people have come to me later on and said, 'Thank you. Because of this course my ex's behavior has changed 100 percent.'"

Programs for Divorced Parents:
New Beginnings and *Dads for Life*

While such programs as divorce education are a useful first step, many parents require additional assistance to work toward healthy post-divorce relationships. The emotions unleashed by most divorces are strong ones, and many parents need programs beyond those that typify most divorce-education classes. One such program, for custodial mothers, was developed by my Arizona State University colleagues, Drs. Sharlene Wolchik, Irwin Sandler, and Lillie Weiss, and is called New Beginnings. Convincing evidence that this exceptional program results in better outcomes for mothers and children of divorce has become available.[7]

My colleagues[8] and I also developed an eight-week program for noncustodial fathers called *Dads for Life*. Our group carefully developed the program over two years, taking into account everything we had learned from our findings, the findings of other researchers, and our extensive experiences with hundreds and thousands of divorced families. During that time, we also conducted extensive focus groups with recently divorced fathers. By giving us their reactions to what we were producing, these fathers helped us ensure that we not only accurately portrayed their experience as divorced dads, but that our program would offer concrete help to them, and by extension, their children.

It is important to note that our program was *not* a standard divorce-recovery course. We were not trying to guide fathers through the minefield of grieving their loss or adjusting to their new status. Instead, *Dads for Life* was intended entirely to help them *father* effectively from within the confines of their new circumstances as divorced noncustodial parents. Thus our primary goal was to improve the well-being of the *children* of divorce. Nonetheless, we also expected that fathers would themselves benefit from our program: as they became more adept in their fathering role, and as their children profited, so would they, by recognizing that their lives as fathers were not ending, but rather entering a new phase. *Dads for Life* adopted the perspective that almost every father has the capacity to make a positive impact on his child's life, no matter what custody or visitation rights he has. As far as we are aware, *Dads for Life* is the only federally funded, research-based program of its kind in the country geared specifically to helping divorced fathers stay connected with their children and remain effective as parents, whatever the barriers.

> *Dads for Life* adopted the perspective that almost every father has the capacity to positively impact on his child's life, no matter what custody or visitation rights he has.

Divorce has frustrated fathers' basic urges to provide for and to protect their young. Few men can see how to fulfill this genetic and/or cultural imperative from within the confines of their reduced status as noncustodial fathers. Our program tries to re-empower men as protectors through all our messages and imagery.

The response from the fathers in our program has been inspiring. They seize on this message with fervor and relief.

"I think there is a natural feeling of many fathers after divorce that they're kind of out of the loop, that nobody cares about them, that they're just supposed to work and provide the money, and stay out of the way," says one graduate, a father of three. "We're not appreciated or recognized for the things we do with our family and kids. *Dads for Life* reinforced what I'd already believed, that dads *are* important to their kids."

This sentiment is eloquently expressed in Mark Bryan's book, *The Prodigal Father:*

Money isn't all of what fathering is about. Financial support of children is only part of the support we owe our children and want to give them. . . . Yet money is the only part we hear about, the part we are blamed for, judged by.

Still worse, if our culture offers men little honor in their work, unless it pays extravagantly, it offers them less for their genuine parental role. I'm thinking of the men who come home from a day on the road or working construction and roughhouse or play ball with their kids, help them with their homework, listen to their daughter's latest woes with a nasty playmate.

Many men, whose wives work, do share in taking kids to school and back, do help with the grocery shopping, and do perform some of the household chores. The fact is, men have always had to combine work outside the home with fathering. Yet the fathering aspects have rarely been honored.[9]

Perhaps the most fundamental aspect of *Dads for Life* is the basic information we provide about parenting skills, but we adapt the lessons to fit the circumstances of the divorced noncustodial father. What this means is that, during the time that the father has the child, he will have to be a solo parent, rather than the "assistant" parent many were during the marriage. He will have sole responsibility for all the child-rearing essentials, and won't be able to rely on someone else to provide the motivating directions. Many dads wish us to teach them what to do with their child, and when to do it. We help fathers learn how to tell what their child needs, how to listen effectively, and how to provide the reassurance that they will always be there for their child.

A key part of the program is teaching fathers how to discipline their children effectively. As we discussed in Chapter 3, many mothers complain that fathers are too lenient, or that they are spoiling the child, and, to an extent, the charge is accurate in many cases. Many fathers fear that if they exert any kind of discipline or punish misbehavior or even withhold something their kid wants, it will poison the little time they have with the child or make the child not want to come back. Children, for their part, are frequently skillful in manipulating this fear and exploiting the situation for their short-term advantage. But fathers are receptive to the message that discipline can still be exerted, even in the trying and artificial circumstances of a visiting relationship. We also emphasize the need to enforce rules consistently and reward appropriate behavior.

Additionally, we repeat the message most authorities attempt to impart to divorcing couples: don't fight in front of the children, put the children in the middle, or use them as a go-between or carrier of messages. But we go beyond many other programs by teaching fathers solid conflict-management techniques and effective communication skills. We then tie the topic to the message of how we are helping them emerge from the general sense of powerlessness many feel. For instance, by better managing conflict and their emotions and behaviors during negotiations with their ex-wives, they are seizing a degree of control they felt they lacked. In so doing, they can protect their children. Eventually almost all the dads see the wisdom of the strategies we advocate and adopt them to the benefit of all.

We enlist participation in our completely voluntary, free program by mailing information about *Dads for Life* to all divorced fathers in the country who, according to publicly available court records, have been divorced within the last six months. If the bad divorced dad image were valid, there would be little interest in our program among divorcing fathers. In fact, of all the eligible fathers we contacted in the previous semester, for example, an astounding 70 percent agreed to participate. No one providing social-service programming has ever heard of this kind of phenomenal response, let alone for a voluntary parenting program, and most especially for a program for men. As a point of comparison, the participation rate for divorced fathers in *Dads for Life* is about 17 percent greater than the rate of participation for that of divorced *mothers* in a comparable program we offered previously.[10]

Since the formal evaluation of *Dads for Life* is underway, we are prevented from describing its features in too much detail. The full scientific results of the formal study of the impact of *Dads for Life* on children, mothers, and fathers won't be available until we conclude the trial in 1999. However, the preliminary results are extremely encouraging. Parents, both mothers and fathers, regularly tell us that the program has changed their and their children's lives for the better. The children appear to be better adjusted and happier, and the parents seem to be more cooperative with each other. While we hardly claim that *Dads for Life* is a perfect solution to helping fathers and children adjust positively to divorce, we are so far convinced programs such as this are a substantial step in the right direction.

Mediation Instead of Litigation

Besides the programs just described, a number of other systems and/or legal changes can be made that should ensure a real role for fathers and ameliorate the problems of divorce on children. Although we have shown that most divorces are settled by the participants themselves, there still exists what we believe is an overreliance on litigation for those couples who can't come to an agreement on their own. For those couples, one important change would be to place a greater importance on mediation, as opposed to litigation. In mediation, parents decide for themselves how to resolve disputes about custody, visitation, and the like.

> ➤ **There still exists an overreliance on litigation for those couples who can't come to an agreement on their own. For those couples, one important change would be to place a greater importance on mediation, as opposed to litigation.**

A skilled mediator, usually a mental-health professional or attorney with specialized additional training and experience, helps the couple to frame the issues dealing with their divorce and finds ways of getting them to resolve differences amicably. They help to change the mentality from "one of us wins and the other loses" to a "win-somewhat" system, where each party gives a little to find an amicable compromise, resulting in both sides getting most of what they really value. Research, especially that by psychologist Robert Emery, Ph.D., at the University of Virginia,[11] sociologist Jessica Pearson, Ph.D., of Denver,[12] and psychologist Joan Kelly, Ph.D., of California,[13] has shown that such an "alternative dispute resolution" structure is especially applicable to family dissolution matters. Both participants are happier and more satisfied, agreements reached in mediation are better kept, and they return to court less often to further contest issues. More important, there is less enduring conflict between the parents.

Douglas Schoenberg, a former New Jersey divorce attorney who got so disgusted with the litigation process that he became a divorce mediator, is a firm believer in this approach. As he told me:[14]

> People who are going through a divorce are in a tremendously vulnerable, weakened state, and the litigation process—two lawyers working against each other—may not be primarily what they need. The system is so ill suited to the needs of the people going through divorce, and there's no incentive for the attorneys to tailor the system in any way to meet the particular needs of the couple. If you listen to the feedback from the people who are running through this system, you'll learn that nobody has anything good to say about it. I would bet that every experienced divorce attorney will say multiple times to his client, "What this is about is going on with your life." But the system doesn't focus people on that. It focuses them on all the recriminations of what happened before, of going over and over again the problems of the past. Mediation, on the other hand, focuses people on the present and the future.
>
> When I do mediation, I sometimes have clients say things like, "Boy you really earned your fee." The difference in the client's level of satisfaction is like night and day.

As positive as the research has been, mediation still has its critics, notably writers such as Trina Grillo in a 1991 *Yale Law Review* article.[15] She argues—without any evidence backing her up—that in mediation, women commonly accept less favorable outcomes than they would otherwise get, because men are more skilled negotiators.

On the contrary, Schoenberg sees mediation as a feminist issue. "A woman who's been disempowered in a relationship, who's always deferred to her husband, will in mediation have an opportunity to assert herself and negotiate for the things that she wants in the settlement. The mediator needs to facilitate the process and sometimes that means providing support mechanisms for empowering a spouse."

Finally, mediation seems to cut down on the violence that oftentimes breaks out between divorcing couples.[16] "A significant percentage of domestic violence occurs during litigated divorces in families who never had a history of it," Schoenberg declares. "It's the impact of the system."

While a large majority of couples successfully mediate, reaching full agreements, not all do, and of course, the court needs to be available as a last resort for such couples to resolve their disputes.

Because mediation is such a substantial improvement over the adversarial system for dealing with dissolving families, it should be expanded in scope. Many jurisdictions have mediation available to divorcing families, and some make it mandatory for couples who cannot initially agree. A better system would be to make it mandatory for *all* couples, whether they agree or not. It should universally follow universal divorce education, which sensitizes the couple to the effects of their disputes on their children. This would better approximate the social-service system umbrella discussed at the beginning of the chapter. The reason it should be required of all couples, not just those initially disagreeing, is that many fathers (or mothers) agree too rapidly to provisions they quickly regret, such as sole maternal custody, or too little in the property division. Many parents simply don't know their options, and/or are intimidated by the legal veneer of the divorce system. The mediation system, with a neutral but informed and professional third-party, guarantees more fully informed decisions that all can live with, that are therefore more likely to be in the family's long-term best interests.

Is Repeal of No-Fault Divorce an Answer?

Many men's rights organizations favor a return to a fault-based divorce system, "because fewer divorces mean fewer custody battles lost by men in the courts" says Jeffrey Leving, a Chicago divorce lawyer and President of the National Institute for Fathers and Families.[7] In fact, at least twenty-two states have been recently debating such laws. As Terry Anderson of the *Detroit Free Press,* put it in his February 20, 1996, op-ed column, "Every state has adopted no-fault divorce over the past 25 or 30 years, but the Christian right wants to roll back the tide. Current laws, they say, make it too easy for couples to divorce, and that's why we have such a high rate of family breakups, with their obvious consequences."

Would a repeal of no-fault divorce better meet the needs of the family? In the era before 1970, the divorce law of every state was based on the civil law of adversarial disputes, similar to suing a manufacturer for a faulty product that caused harm to the suing victim. Under this system, called a "fault based" approach, divorce could not be consensual. One party had to be wronged for the divorce to transpire. The basis (or "grounds") for what constituted such a wrong was spelled out in the divorce laws of every state and differed somewhat from place to place. In nearly every state, however, adultery and "cruelty" (which we now call domestic violence or abuse) were among such grounds. The divorce proceedings usually attempted to convince the judge that evidence for the grounds existed.

A quirk of this system is that no divorce could be granted if *both* parties were at fault.[18] So what happened if both parties wanted a divorce but neither or both had committed a "ground?" Under this system of law, there needed to be secret, or at least unofficial, collaboration with the spouse. In short, the couple lied, usually with the full knowledge of their attorneys and even the judge, and produced evidence, often faked or staged, that one and only one spouse had sinned. This practice, necessary under the system of law, so dismayed the practitioners that the Committee on Law Reform of the Association of the Bar of the City of New York wrote, "We . . . hope [to] eliminate what has come to be recognized as a scandal, growing out of widespread fraud, perjury, collusion and connivance which now pervade the dissolution of marriages."[19]

Partly in reaction to such unsavory deceitful practices, but also in response to various other profound pressures we explored in Chapter 7, in 1970 California passed the first state law eliminating the necessity to prove that one and only one spouse had committed a fault. Called no-fault, these laws simply require one party to want the marriage to end, without having to give a reason. If one party declares that the marriage is "irretrievably broken," the judge typically must grant a divorce, no matter what the other feels. So while fault is eliminated, mutual consent isn't necessary either. Because there seemed to be such a strong consensus against forcing people to stay married if they truly don't want to be, every one of the remaining forty-nine states also passed some form of the no-fault divorce law within the next fifteen years, in one of the fastest moving legal revolutions in history.[20]

Despite some arguments to the contrary, the great weight of evidence strongly suggests that establishment of no-fault divorce was neither the cause of the increase in the divorce rate,[21] nor the source of impoverishing women.[22] We have shown that women are generally the initiators of divorce and that this is a modern phenomenon, something that came about in the last thirty years. We have more divorces today simply because women today are far more likely to seek them than their forebears were. Not only that, we have painstakingly shown that women are less distressed about the breakup than commonly believed and, all things considered, feel they benefit from the breakup far more than do their ex-husbands.

At a national conference, a state legislator from the Midwest approached me. He said he had been largely supportive of efforts to repeal no-fault in his state until he heard the evidence we had gathered.

"My goal is to prevent divorce in as many families as possible," he said to me, "because I believe it is bad for the children in almost every case. The only exception is if there is family violence; then, even the children want their parents to end it. I want what the children want, and I think society's interests are identical. Keep marriages together whenever possible." I agreed that was a laudable goal that almost everyone could agree with.

"I had thought the reason for so many divorces was either that divorce was too easy or that men wanted to sow their oats, and no-fault divorce was allowing them to walk out on their responsibilities," the legislator said. "The fix for either was to repeal no-fault. But you have convinced me that neither is true. Am I right so far?" His reasoning was still valid, I agreed.

"Now it appears to me that the implications of your research are that, contrary to what I had believed, it is *mothers* not fathers who now seem to have less of a disincentive to divorce than they did years earlier," he continued. "That's why they are opting for it so much more than before, and that's why they are more content and satisfied than fathers afterward. My philosophy is that the best role for laws is not to force people to do this or to do that, but rather to provide people incentives to do what's in society's best interests." I wasn't sure where he was going, yet couldn't spot any flaw in his reasoning.

"But the only real incentives I see for women to divorce is that they get rid of the husband they don't like anymore and they get to keep the kids. Right?" An oversimplification, to be sure, but he was mostly right.

"So it follows for me that if we want to curb divorce, since we can't change the first incentive, we need to change the second, how likely it is that women will get the kids after divorce. So I propose we make initiating divorce one factor to consider in awarding custody. Something like . . ." He took out paper and began writing: "Since initiating divorce is presumptively opposed to the child's best interest, the parent choosing to dissolve the marriage shall have that factor counted against him or her in the award of custody. The factor can be mitigated by a showing of extenuating circumstances, such as domestic abuse, adultery, etc."

A radical proposal, to be sure, but one that would almost certainly reduce the rate of divorce substantially. If mothers thought their choosing to end the marriage would be counted against them in a custody determination, unless extenuating circumstances such as alcoholism, domestic abuse, or adultery were present, they would be far less likely to go through with the divorce. Unfortunately, the cost might be miserable mothers, who are forced to sustain unhappy and unfulfilling marriages, and, in the cases where the children are exposed to serious overt conflict and fighting or very depressed and therefore impaired parents, even more troubled kids. Would society want that trade-off?

Fortunately, evidence has very recently become available that even the far less radical custody policies recommended in this book will actually have the desired effect of lowering the divorce rate. Psychologist John Guidibaldi, D. Ed., and colleague Richard Kuhn have just released an analysis conducted on data provided by the National Center for Health Statistics. Their results show that states adopting policies that routinely award joint physical custody (which the authors define as 30 percent or more of the children's time with each parent) have lowered their divorce rate significantly more than states that don't have such policies. In explaining their findings, the authors write "On a practical level, joint physical custody makes it less likely that a parent can move to another city to eliminate interaction with the other parent.... Perhaps most significant, joint physical custody removes the capacity for one spouse to hurt the other by denying participation in raising the children.... If a parent considering divorce is told by an attorney that a judge will probably not permit him or her to relocate with the children, and that the other parent will continue to be involved, he or she may decide that it is easier to work out problems and remain married."[23] Guidibaldi and Kuhn also comment, "If a parent is able to forecast that they have total ownership of the child post-divorce, and almost all of the child's time, as usually happens in sole custody, there is little deterrent for divorce. Joint custody, according to the data, provides that deterrent."[24]

Preventing Divorce *Before* Couples Marry

Before we leave the topic of repeal of no-fault divorce, and other variants, let me point out two interesting recent offshoot proposals: One is to promote or require counseling prior to marriage. Support for counseling for couples about to marry derived from the view that, according to Ira Lurvey, head of the American Bar Association's Family Law Section, "What may help is a retraining program for all of us. We live in a world of false expectations and mixed messages. Marriage is not necessarily bells and whistles forever. It is hard work, caring, and being selfless. Those are commodities often in short supply these days."[25]

Several premarital training programs, most especially one developed by University of Denver psychologist Howard Markman, Ph.D., and discussed in his 1994 book, *Fighting for Your Marriage,*[26] have been shown to be effective, in that couples who undergo the training in problem-solving and communication techniques have a greatly reduced chance of becoming divorced years later than couples assigned to a control condition. So there is reason to think this proposal will work well to prevent divorce if implemented on a wide scale.

> ➤ **Couples who have undergone premarital training programs have been shown in one study to have a greatly reduced chance of becoming divorced years later than couples assigned to a control condition.**

Some critics of the mandated premarital counseling proposal object in principle to forcing people into counseling; other authorities believe counseling never works well unless the partners voluntarily decide for themselves. These concerns were neatly addressed by a slight modification of the proposal introduced in a bill by a legislator in my state. His proposal raised marriage license fees substantially, then allowed for them to be waived for those couples who chose to undergo counseling. Instead of coercing them into counseling, he would provide an incentive to participate.

The second variation is to allow two sorts of marriage, regular or "covenantal." Louisiana recently passed the first law of this nature.[27] Couples can choose for themselves which type of marriage they want. If they choose the former, normal divorce laws apply. However, if they choose covenantal, they can divorce only upon proof of fault of such grounds as abuse, adultery, or abandonment, or a mutually agreed-upon two-year separation. This proposal has had outspoken critics, namely Katha Pollitt, who declared in a *New York Times* op-ed piece, "You don't have to be abused or betrayed to have a bad marriage."[28] Yet public opinion seems to favor making it harder for couples to divorce, especially when children are involved. In a Time/CNN poll conducted May 7–8, 1997, when respondents were asked, "Should it be harder than it is now for married couples with young children to get a divorce?" 61 percent said "yes," and 35 percent said "no."[29]

The law's advocates predict that many couples *will voluntarily* choose covenantal marriages, because one or both of them will want to use it as a testament to the permanence of their love. They will then have to live with the consequences of their *own* choice. This consequence means they have to intensify their efforts to keep their marriage intact.

These as well as other ideas are being actively explored by legislatures who are getting the message that our current laws are too one-sided and part of the current divorce problem. Yet well-intentioned but disastrous legal changes got us into this morass in the first place. Perhaps we should rely more on education and persuasion than legal sanction. Nearly all parents want to do what's right for their kids; it's up to the professional community to educate them as to what helps them most. Without question, what helps children of divorce most is *two* involved, cooperative, and well-functioning parents who respect and dignify the parenting role of the other.

The Culture That Produces the Bad Divorce

Finally, what would help the most is an improved cultural understanding of the roots of the problem of divorced families. This book has been written to contribute to this awareness. Our children have too greatly suffered the consequences of a mythology that says most divorced men are irresponsible, dead-beat, runaway fathers. Our studies indicate that a more realistic and hopeful as-sessment of what's harming today's divorced family will, by itself, go a long way toward redressing the harm we're doing. If we relinquish our societal need to assign blame and identify a villain, if we can only recognize that real human beings are at stake here, that both mothers and fathers are trying their best under difficult circumstances, then we can be in a position to rescue our fami-lies from what Barbara Dafoe Whitehead in her recent book calls *The Divorce Culture.*[30] The pendulum has inarguably swung too far. It is time to swing it back.

Above all the statistics, what convinced us most of this fundamental but sim-ple truth was a letter we received from Joanie, a single mother of one child, who happened to attend a preliminary screening of the videos we use in our *Dads For Life* program. Joanie was particularly moved, she said, by two scenes: one where a child cries uncontrollably because his father doesn't see him anymore, and an-other where a youngster is devastated by the parental war going on over her head about a missed visit. She wrote:

> *I left the theater with tears in my eyes. Your film really struck a responsive chord because Bruce, my ex-husband, had recently stopped seeing my seven-year-old, Ben, due to our constant fighting. I have to admit to you that I truly hate Bruce for the way he repeatedly demeaned me during our mar-riage. But because of your film, I had to start looking at things through my son Ben's eyes, and even a little through Bruce's. I'm sure Bruce felt like I was keeping him away. And to be honest, this was not good for Ben, who couldn't understand why his father didn't see him anymore.*
>
> *So I called Bruce and arranged a meeting at the public library. I told him I had decided on an experiment where he could see Ben whenever he wanted for a while. I wouldn't interfere or fight with him. I'd try to be civil and supportive. If this didn't work after three months, I'd talk to my lawyer about what could be done. I doubt he believed me. But I stuck to my offer, and he finally agreed to it.*
>
> *As it turned out, the change in our relationship was dramatic. For the last two months, we are all doing better. Ben and Bruce spend a lot of time together, Bruce doesn't fight with me anymore, and Ben seems much hap-pier. Even I feel better, though every time I see Bruce I clench my teeth. I'm*

not sure what will happen as time goes on, but for now, our little family seems a lot healthier.

Joanie's story offers an encouraging scenario for a hopeful future, a future in which fathering is as valid as mothering; a future in which fathers are empowered by the courts, mothers, and society to remain positive forces in their children's lives; a future in which mothers and fathers, though no longer connected through marriage, remain equally committed to working together for the good of their children—the only constituency that ultimately matters.

Notes

INTRODUCTION

1. Henry, R. Resolution of child custody disputes. Memorandum, April 30, 1993, p. 2.
2. Phil McCombs, *Washington Post,* October 19, 1996.
3. Martin, T. C., and Bumpass, L. L. Recent trends in marital disruption. *Demography* 26:37–51.
4. *US News and World Report,* February 27, 1995.
5. National Institute of Child Health and Human Development, 1RO1-HD19383.
6. NIMH Training Grant T32 MH18387; NIMH Center Grant MH39246; NIMH Research Grant R01-MH51184.

CHAPTER 1: THE "BAD DIVORCED DAD" IMAGE

1. An exception is: Pasley, K., and Minton, C. 1997. Generative fathering after divorce/remarriage: Beyond the "disappearing dad." In *Generative fathering,* eds. A. J. Hawkins and D. C. Dollahite, pp. 118–33. Thousand Oaks, CA: Sage.
2. See, for example, U.S. Bureau of the Census. 1980. Child support and alimony: 1978. *Current Population Reports,* series P-23, no. 106. Washington, DC: U.S. Government Printing Office.
3. Furstenburg, F. F., and Nord, C. W. 1985. Parenting apart: Patterns of childrearing after marital disruption. *Journal of Marriage and the Family* 47:893–901. Furstenburg, F. F., Nord, C. W., Peterson, J. L., and Zill, N. 1983. The life course of children of divorce: Marital disruption and parental contact. *American Sociological Review* 48:656–68.
4. Weitzman, L. J. 1985. *The divorce revolution: The unexpected social and economic consequences for women and children in America.* New York: Free Press.
5. Fineman, M. 1991. *The illusion of equality: Rhetoric and the reality of divorce reform.* Chicago: University of Chicago Press.
6. Mason, M. A. 1988. *The equality trap.* New York: Simon & Schuster.
7. Wallerstein, J. S., and Kelly, J. B. 1980. *Surviving the break-up: How children and parents cope with divorce.* New York: Basic Books.

8. Ahrons, C. 1994. *The good divorce: Keeping your family together when your marriage comes apart,* p. 16. New York: HarperCollins.

9. *Harpers Magazine,* November 1985, p. 15.

10. Blankenhorn, D. 1995. *Fatherless America: Confronting our most urgent social problem.* New York: Basic Books.

11. Guttentag, M., and Secord, P. F. 1983. *Too many women: The sex ratio question.* Beverly Hills: Sage.

12. June 1, 1997.

CHAPTER 2: TAKING ON MYTH 1: DEADBEAT DADS

1. Occasionally, for literary convenience, a "composite" informant has been formed, composed of the responses of several actual people, but attributed to just one.

2. See, for example, U.S. Bureau of the Census 1980. Child support and alimony: 1978. *Current population reports* (series p-23, no. 106). Washington, D.C.; U.S. Government Printing Office.

3. See Chambers, D. 1979. *Making fathers pay: The enforcement of child support.* Chicago: University of Chicago Press; Pearson, J., and Thoennes, N. 1986. Will this divorced woman receive child support? *Minnesota Family Law Journal* 3:65–71; Quensted, R. T., and Winkler, C. F. 1965. What are our domestic relations judges thinking? *Monograph No.1, Section of Family Law,* American Bar Association; Wallerstein, J. S., and Huntington, D. S. 1983. Bread and roses: Nonfinancial issues related to fathers' economic support of their children following divorce. In *The parental child-support obligation,* ed. J. Cassetty, pp. 135–55. Lexington, MA: Lexington Books; Weitzman, L. J. 1985. *The divorce revolution;* Arthur Young & Co. 1975. *Detailed summary of findings: Absent parent child support: Cost-benefit analysis.* Washington, DC: Department of Health, Education & Welfare, Social and Rehabilitation Services; Cassetty, J. 1978. *Child support and public policy.* Lexington, MA: Lexington Books; Hill, M. S. 1984. *PSID analysis of matched pairs of ex-spouses: The relation of economic resources and new family obligations to child support payments.* Ann Arbor: University of Michigan, Institute for Social Research; Hill, M. S. May 1988. The role of economic resources and dual-family status in child support payments. Paper presented at the Population Association of America Meetings; Jones, C., Gordon, N., and Sawhill, I. 1976. Child support payments in the United States. Working paper 992–93. Washington, DC: The Urban Institute.

4. Statement in hearing before the Subcommittee on Public Assistance and Unemployment Compensation of the Committee on Ways and Means, House of Representatives, Ninety-eighth Congress, First Session, July 14, 1983, serial 98–41, pp. 34–35. Washington, DC: U.S. Government Printing Office, 1984. Quoted in Weitzman, L. J. 1985. *The divorce revolution,* p. 473.

5. *Newsweek,* January 10, 1983, p. 42.

6. Peterson, J., and Nord, C. W. 1990. The regular receipt of child support: A multistep process. *Journal of Marriage and the Family* 52:539–52; Teachman, J. D., and Paasch, K. 1993. The economics of parenting apart. In *Nonresidential parenting: New vistas in family living,* eds. C. E. Depner and J. H. Bray. Newbury Park, CA: Sage.

7. McCauley, C. 1995. Are stereotypes exaggerated? A sampling of racial, gender, academic, occupational and political stereotypes. In *Stereotype accuracy: toward appreciating*

group differences, eds. Y. T. Lee, L. J. Jussim, and C. R. McCauley. Washington, DC: American Psychological Association.

8. Traugott, M. W., and Katosh, J. P. 1979. Response validity in surveys of voting behavior. *Public Opinion Quarterly,* pp. 359-77.

9. Weinstein, N. D. 1989. Effects of personal experience on self-protective behavior. *Psychological Bulletin* 105:31-50.

10. Sherif, M., and Sherif, C. 1953. *Groups in harmony and tension: An integration of studies on intergroup relations.* New York: Harper.

11. In addition to this perhaps unconscious bias, some mothers may also have a strong incentive to lie knowingly when they under-report the amount of child support they received. A mother who is on AFDC, for example, might be reluctant to make a full report to the government via the Census Bureau for fear of jeopardizing what welfare payments she might be receiving.

12. Garfinkle, I. 1985. *Preliminary report on the effects of the Wisconsin child support reform demonstration.* Madison, WI: University of Wisconsin, Institute for Research on Poverty.

13. Ibid., p. 6.

14. A full description of the sample, and sampling methods, as well as our findings substantiating the representativeness of the sample is reported in Braver, S. L., and Bay, C. R. 1992. Assessing and compensating for self-selection bias (nonrepresentativeness) of the family research sample. *Journal of Marriage and the Family* 54:925-39.

15. Eckhard, K. 1968. Deviance, visibility, and legal action: The duty to support. *Social Problems* 15:470-77; Chambers, D. 1979. *Making fathers pay;* Cassetty, J. 1978. *Child support and public policy.*

16. The results presented in this chapter have been previously presented in Braver, S. L., Fitzpatrick, P. J., and Bay, R. C. 1988. Adaptation of the non-custodial parent: Patterns over time. Paper presented at the American Psychological Association, Atlanta, GA; Braver, S. L., Fitzpatrick, P. J., and Bay, R. C. 1991. Noncustodial parent's report of child support payments. *Family Relations* 40:180-85; and Braver, S. L., Wolchik, S. A., Sandler, I. N., Sheets, V., Fogas, B., and Bay, R. C. 1993. A longitudinal study of noncustodial parents: Parents without children. *Journal of Family Psychology* 7:9-23.

17. Personal communication from the Hon. Sylvan Brown, Presiding Judge of the Domestic Relations Bench of the Superior Court of Maricopa County, February 1984.

18. Personal communication from Judith Allen, Clerk of the Maricopa County Superior Court, March 1984.

19. Personal communication from Judith Allen, April 1984.

20. While it may appear that the index "Average of Paid Divided By Owed" should exactly equal the one above, in fact the two might differ. Consider three noncustodial parents who owe, respectively, 1000, 2000 and 3000. Suppose they pay, respectively, 0, 1000, and 3000. The average owed is 2000, while the average paid is 1333, a ratio of .66. On the other hand, their paid divided by owed ratios are 0.0, .50, and 1.00, with an average of .50. The average paid divided by owed will exceed the former figure, as it does in both this footnote example and Table 2.3, whenever there is a positive relationship between how much is owed, and the percent of that amount actually paid, which there is in our data.

21. A study conducted by Seltzer, Schaeffer, and Klawitter, three researchers at the University of Wisconsin, purports to address the issue of determining who is closer to the truth

when mothers and fathers tell us different things about child support. Their results suggested that fathers were overstating how much was paid by far more than mothers were understating it. Unfortunately, they used the Wisconsin official records of child support collection as their supposedly "objective" data source. We have already shown that most official records, including those in Wisconsin, understate how much was paid because they leave out direct payments that bypass the court. For this reason, we feel their conclusions are questionable. Schaeffer, N. C., Seltzer, J. A., and Klawitter, M 1991. Estimating nonresponse and response bias: Resident and nonresident parents' reports about child support. *Sociological Methods and Research* 20:30–59.

22. Chambers, D. 1979. *Making fathers pay;* Pearson, J., and Thoennes, N. 1986. Will this divorced woman receive child support?, pp. 65–71; Arthur Young & Co. 1975. *Detailed summary of findings;* Wallerstein, J. S., and Huntington, D. S. 1983. Bread and roses, pp. 135–55. Only one past study failed to find that noncustodial parent's income or unemployment is a sizable factor relating to child support compliance, and her study is dubious for other reasons (see Chapter 4). Weitzman, L. J. 1985. *The divorce revolution.*

23. Sonenstein, F. L., and Calhoun, C. A. 1990. Determinants of child support: A pilot survey of absent parents. *Contemporary Policy Issues* 8:75–94.

24. According to the Office's David Arnaudo, October 1997.

25. An interview with David Gray Ross, Deputy Director of the Federal Office of Child Support Enforcement. *Children Today* 24:4.

26. Klawitter, M. M., and Garfinkel, I. 1992. Child support, routine income withholding, and post-divorce income. *Contemporary Policy Issues* 10:52–64.

CHAPTER 3: TAKING ON MYTH 2: THE NO-SHOW DAD

1. Blankenhorn, D. 1995. *Fatherless America,* p. 1.

2. Furstenburg, F. F., and Nord, C. W. 1985. Parenting apart, pp. 893–904; Furstenburg, F. F., Nord, C. W., Peterson, J. L., and Zill, N. 1983. The life course of children of divorce, pp. 656–68.

3. Furstenburg, F. F., and Nord, C. W. 1985. Parenting apart, p. 903.

4. Ibid., p. 903.

5. Quoted in Wingert, P., and King, P. 1988. And what of deadbeat dads? *Newsweek,* December 19, 1988, p. 66.

6. In Furstenburg, F. F. 1988. Good dads—bad dads: The two faces of fatherhood. In *The changing American family and public policy,* ed. A. J. Cherlin, pp. 193–218. Washington, DC: Urban Institute Press.

7. Furstenburg, F. F., and Harris, K. M. 1992. The disappearing American father: Divorce and the waning significance of biological parenthood. In *The changing American family: Social and demographic perspectives,* eds. S. J. South and S. E. Tolnay. Boulder, CO: Westview Press.

8. Ihinger-Tallman, M., Pasley, K., and Beuhler, C. 1995. Developing a middle-range theory of father involvement postdivorce. In *Fatherhood: Contemporary theory, research and social policy,* ed. W. Marsiglio, p. 60. Thousand Oaks, CA: Sage.

9. Although the titles of the papers refer to "children of divorce" or "marital dis-

ruption," and the results have been regarded as applying exclusively to the divorced-separated group, a close reading reveals that never-married "families" are included: "Children whose parents never married, and hence were not at risk of marital disruption will be treated separately in the first part of our discussion. . . . Since most of these children have an outside parent, in the second part of the paper we have included them in our discussions of the patterns of parental contact along with children whose parents are separated or divorced." Furstenburg, F. F., Nord, C. W., Peterson, J. L., and Zill, N. 1983. The life course of children of divorce, pp. 658–59. "Children whose parents have never married also are included in the discussion that follows." Furstenburg, F. F., and Nord, C. W. 1985. Parenting apart, p. 894.

10.   Furstenburg, F. F., and Seltzer, J. A. 1983. Divorce and child development. Paper presented at the Orthopsychiatric Association, Boston.

11.   See Seltzer, J. A. 1991. Relationships between fathers and children who live apart. *Journal of Marriage and the Family* 53:79–101.

12.   Jacobson, D. S. 1978. The impact of marital separation/divorce on children: II: Interparental hostility and child adjustment. *Journal of Divorce* 2:3–20; Bloom, B. L., Hodges, W. F., and Caldwell, R. A. 1983. Marital separation: The first eight months: In *Lifespan developmental psychology: Non-normative events,* eds. E. J. Callahan and K. A. McKlusky, pp. 218–39. New York: Academic Press; Berkman, B. G. 1986. Father involvement and regularity of child support in post-divorce families. *Journal of Divorce* 9:67–74; Petronio, S. 1988. Communication and the visiting parent. *Journal of Divorce* 11:103–10; Koch, M. A. P., and Lowery, C. R. 1985. Visitation and the noncustodial father. *Journal of Divorce* 8:47–65; Fulton, J. A. 1979. Parental reports of children's post-divorce adjustment. *Journal of Social Issues* 35:126–39; Hetherington, E. M., Cox, M., and Cox, R. 1978. The aftermath of divorce. In *Mother-child, father-child relations,* eds. J. H. Stevens, Jr., and M. Matthews. Washington, DC: National Association for the Education of Young Children.

13.   The Wave 1 results reported in this chapter have been previously published in Braver, S. L., Wolchik, S. A., Sandler, I. N., Fogas, B. S., and Zvetina, A. 1991. Frequency of visitation by divorced fathers: Differences in reports by fathers and mothers. *American Journal of Orthopsychiatry* 61:448–54. The Wave 3 results were published in Braver, S. L., Wolchik, S. A., Sandler, B. A., Sheets, V. L., Fogas, B., and Bay, R. C. 1993. A longitudinal study of noncustodial parents, pp. 9–23. The visitation problems results were published in Wolchik, S. A., Fenaughty, A. M., and Braver, S. L. 1996. Residential and nonresidential parents' perspectives on visitation problems. *Family Relations* 45:230–37.

14.   This was the view admitted by Judith Seltzer, when she (with Yvonne Brandreth) wrote: "Ideal data for a problem of this type would include a sample in which both parents reported about child rearing after separation. . . . These data requirements can not be met by large national surveys." Seltzer and Brandwith's own analysis uses *un*matched data from fathers and mothers, attempting as best as possible to make the reports correspond. Their fundamental results, that fathers report far more contact with children than mothers report, matches that of this chapter. See Seltzer, J. A., and Brandreth, Y. 1995. What fathers say about involvement with children after separation. In *Fatherhood,* ed. W. Marsiglio.

15.   We defined this as four or more days of contact per month (equivalent to his "at least fifty-two times last year").

16. The result is virtually identical if *all* mothers and fathers, not just those in which their matched ex-spouse was also included in the sample, are considered.

17. Bray, J. H., and Berger, S. H. 1990. Noncustodial father and paternal grandparent relationships in stepfamilies. *Family Relations* 39:414–19; Depner, C. E., Maccoby, E. E., and Mnookin, R. H. 1988. Assessing father participation in the post-divorce family. Paper presented at the Annual Meeting of the American Psychological Association, Atlanta, GA; Maccoby, E. E. Depner, C. E., and Mnookin, R. H. 1988. Child custody following divorce. In *Impact of divorce, single parenting and step-parenting on children,* eds. E. M. Hetherington and J. D. Arasteh, pp. 91–114. Hillsdale, NJ: Lawrence Erlbaum; Seltzer, J. A. 1991. Relationships between fathers and children who live apart, pp. 539–51.

18. This pattern of results is consistent with what sociologist Constance Ahrons found in her paper. Ahrons, C. A. 1983. Predictors of paternal involvement postdivorce: Mothers' and fathers' perceptions. *Journal of Divorce* 6:55–69. Her finding also was that noncustodial parents claimed to be more involved with their children than custodial parents reported them to be. A distinction between her methodology and the present one concerns the nature of the questions asked. The questions in the present study called for numeric responses to items like "How many different visits did non-custodial parent have with child last month?" In principle, at least, there is a "correct," "objectively valid" answer to such questions. In contrast, Ahrons' items called for verbal subjective responses ("very much," "pretty much," "a little") to items such as "How involved are you (is your ex) in dressing and grooming the children?" ". . . running errands for and with the children?" Such responses are inherently subjective, with no correct or valid answer even in principle. Because of the less-subjective nature of the current items, it might have been expected that they would be less susceptible to response bias, and that as a result Ahrons' pattern of findings might not have been replicated. Instead, it is apparent that even less subjective responses are vulnerable to distortion in reports.

19. Furstenburg and his colleagues comment on the possibility that mothers contribute to paternal disengagement, but suggest that such denial is generally in "retaliation" for child-support noncompliance: "Lest this observation be taken as a judgment about the motives of the outside parent, we should point out that . . . outside parents are sometimes discouraged or actively barred from seeing their children, especially when custodial mothers are dissatisfied with the level of material support provided by the fathers." Furstenburg, F. F., Nord, C. W., Peterson, J. L., and Zill, N. 1983. The life course of children of divorce, p. 665.

20. Pearson, J., and Thoennes, N. 1988. The denial of visitation rights: A preliminary look at its incidence, correlates, antecedents and consequences. *Law & Policy* 10:363–80.

21. Wallerstein, J. S., and Kelly, J. B. 1980. *Surviving the breakup.*

22. Weiss, R. S. 1979. *Going it alone: The family life and social situation of the single parent,* pp. 134, 141, 146. New York: Basic Books.

23. Lee, C. D., Shaughnessy, J. J., and Bankes, J. K. 1995. Impact of Expedited Visitation Services, a court program that enforces access: Through the eyes of children. *Family and Conciliation Courts Review* 33:495–514.

24. In a telephone interview, August 4, 1997.

25. Gardner, R. 1987. *The parental alienation syndrome and the differentiation between fabricated and genuine child abuse.* Cresskill, NJ: Creative Therapeutics.

26. Wolchik, S. A., Fenaughty, A. M., and Braver, S. L. 1996. Residential and nonresidential parents' perspectives, pp. 230–37.

CHAPTER 4: TAKING ON MYTH 3: STANDARDS OF LIVING

1. Weitzman, L. J. 1985. *The divorce revolution.*

2. She has since moved to George Mason University.

3. Katherine Webster, AP newswire article, May 1996.

4. Ibid.

5. Peterson, R. R. 1996. A re-evaluation of the economic consequences of divorce. *American Sociological Review* 61:528–36.

6. Hoffman, S. D., and Duncan, G. J. 1988. What *are* the economic consequences of divorce? *Demography* 25:641.

7. Weitzman, L. J. 1985. *The divorce revolution.*

8. Garfinkel, I., and Klawitter, M. 1990. The effects of routine withholding of child support collections. *Journal of Policy Analysis and Management* 9:155–77; Office of Child Support Enforcement. 1990. *Child support enforcement, fifteenth annual report to Congress, for the period ending September 30, 1990.* Washington, DC: US Department of Health and Human Services; Pearson, J., Thoennes, N., and Tjaden, P. 1989. Legislating adequacy: The impact of child support guidelines. *Law and Society Review* 23:569–90.

9. Weitzman, L. J. 1985. *The divorce revolution.* Ellman, I. M. 1989. The theory of alimony. *California Law Review* 77:1–81; Fineman, M. 1983. Implementing equality: Ideology, contradiction, and social change. *Wisconsin Law Review,* 789–886; Kay, H. H. 1987. Equality and difference: A perspective on no-fault divorce and its aftermath. *Cincinnati Law Review* 56:1–90; Singer, J. 1989. Divorce reform and gender justice. *North Carolina Law Review* 67:1103–21; Rutherford, J. 1990. Duty in divorce: Shared income as a path to equality. *Fordham Law Review* 58:539–92.

10. Mahoney, K. 1996. Gender issues in family law: Leveling the playing field for women. *Family and Conciliation Courts Review* 34:198–218.

11. Day, R. D., and Bahr, S. J. 1986. Income changes following divorce and remarriage. *Journal of Divorce* 9:75–88.

12. Katherine Webster, AP newswire article, May 1996.

13. The findings are from, respectively: Duncan, G. J., and Hoffman, S. D. 1985. Economic consequences of marital instability. In *Horizontal equity, uncertainty, and economic well-being,* eds. M. David and T. Smeeding, pp. 427–71. Chicago: University of Chicago Press; Weiss, R. S. 1984. The impact of marital dissolution on income and consumption in single-parent households. *Journal of Marriage and the Family* 46:115–27; Hoffman, S. D., and Duncan, G. J. 1985. A reconsideration of the economic consequences of marital dissolution. *Demography* 22:485–97; Braver, S. L., Gonzalez, N., Wolchik, S. A., and Sandler, I. N. 1989. Economic hardship and psychological distress in custodial mothers. *Journal of Divorce* 12:19–34; Bianchi, S. 1991. Family disruption and economic hardship; U.S. Bureau of the Census, series P-70, no. 23; Sorenson, A. 1992. Estimating the economic consequences of separation and divorce: A cautionary tale from the United States. In *The economic consequences of divorce: The international perspective,* eds. L. Weitzman and M. MacLean, pp. 264–82. New York: Oxford University Press; and Weitzman, L. J. 1985. *The divorce revolution.*

14. Faludi, S. *Backlash: The undeclared war against American women,* p. 21. New York: Doubleday.

Notes

15. The work whose outcome is depicted in the graph is Braver, S. L., Gonzalez, N., Wolchik, S. A., and Sandler, I. N. 1989. Economic hardship, pp. 19–34.

16. Peterson, R. R. 1996. A re-evaluation of the economic consequences of divorce, pp. 528–36.

17. Weitzman, L. 1996. The economic consequences of divorce are still unequal. *American Sociological Review* 61:537–38.

18. Katherine Webster, AP newswire article, May 1996.

19. As of this writing, it has not been established that the error I suggested was precisely what was responsible for her incorrect figure. However, it appears to be the most plausible and understandable way to account for her huge mistake.

20. Even the analyses presented in this book potentially contain errors, of course, though every effort has been made to avoid them. A certain measure of protection against errors is afforded when scientific work is previously published in professional journals. There, the "peer review" process, in which neutral professionals critically scrutinize the work prior to publication, can generally be counted on to catch some mistakes. As noted in this book's notes, most of the analyses presented here have been previously published in professional journals and have therefore undergone critical scrutiny (unlike Weitzman's finding, which was never previously peer reviewed). In addition, my data files have already been shared with fellow professionals, and I make them readily available to other social scientists. The work in this chapter, though not previously published professionally, has been reviewed by, among others, Greg Duncan, economists Elizabeth Peters and Judi Bardfeld, and law professor Ira Ellman.

21. Allen, M. 1992. Child-state jurisdiction. *Family Law Quarterly* 6:293–318.

22. Butler, S. S., and Weatherly, R. A. 1992. Poor women at mid-life and categories of neglect. *Social Work* 37:510–15.

23. Fineman, M. L. 1986. Illusive equality: On Weitzman's *Divorce revolution. American Bar Foundation Research Journal* (1986):781–90.

24. Haffy, M., and Cohen, P. M. 1992. Treatment issues for divorcing women. *Families in Society* 73:142–48.

25. Hewlett, S. 1996. *A lesser life.* New York: Morrow.

26. Lonsdorf, B. J. 1991. The role of coercion in affecting women's inferior outcomes in divorce. *Journal of Divorce and Remarriage* 16:69–106.

27. Melli, M. 1986. Constructing a social problem: The post-divorce plight of women and children. *American Bar Foundation Research Journal* (1986):759–72.

28. Seiling, S. B., and Harris, S. H. 1991. Child support awards: links with alimony and in-kind support. *Divorce and Remarriage* 16:121–35.

29. Woodhouse, B. B. 1990. Towards a revitalization of family law. *Texas Law Review* 69:245–90.

30. Polikoff, N. D. 1986. Review of *The divorce revolution,* by Lenore J. Weitzman. *American Bar Association Journal* 72:112–16.

31. Okin, S. M. 1991. Economic equality after divorce. *Dissent* 38:383–87.

32. This list is originally given in Peterson, R.R. 1966. A re-evaluation of the economic consequences of divorce.

33. Braver, S. L. Gonzalez, N., Wolchik, S. A., and Sandla, I. N. 1989. Economic hardship, pp. 19–34.

34. Peterson, R. R. 1989. *Women, work, and divorce,* NY: SUNY Press.

35. U.S. Bureau of the Census. 1989. *Current Population Reports,* series P-60, no. 163. Poverty in the United States: 1987. Washington, DC: U.S. Government Printing Office.

36. From the Census Bureau's Web page: http://www.census.gov/ftp/pub/hhes/poverty/thresld/thresh96.html

37. Weitzman, L. J. 1985. *The divorce revolution,* pp. 481–82.

38. Watts, H. W. 1980. Special panel suggests changes in BLS Family Budget Program. *Monthly Labor Review* 1–10.

39. Roby B. Sawyers, memorandum dated April 27, 1989.

40. Espenshade, T. J. 1979. The economic consequences of divorce, *Journal of Marriage and the Family* 41:615–25.

41. Burkhauser and associates purport to take taxation into account, but their article provides almost no detail about this; thus, it's impossible to know whether they have compensated for taxes properly, for example by taking state taxes and the child-care credit into their computations. Burkhauser, R. V., Duncan, G. J., Hauser, R., and Berntsen, R. 1991. Wife or frau, women do worse: A comparison of men and women in the United States and Germany after marital dissolution. *Demography* 28:353–60.

42. The parties can, of course, negotiate who receives this exemption, but unless the custodial parent signs a special form allocating the exemption to the other parent, the Federal tax code assumes she receives the benefit.

43. In an interview conducted July 2, 1997.

44. There is some confusion among experts about whether the poverty thresholds do or do not account for child-care expenses. Most scholars seem convinced that child-care expenses are not included in the poverty levels. On the other hand, rather than just lumping together parents and children into the total number in the household, the tables distinguish how many of the household are parents and how many are children. In 1987, for example, if a three-person household has *no* minor children, the poverty level is $8,885, while if two of the three household members are children, the figure is higher, $9,151. Since three adults undoubtedly *eat more* than one adult and two children, etc., one would think the poverty level would be higher in the former than the latter case unless child-care expenses had been taken into account. Instead, the $266 additional dollars are plausibly the net effect of less food, etc., costs but more child-care costs.

45. The needs-adjustment method can be further adapted to account for this contingency by adopting the Arizona approach, which estimates that 31.5 percent of a household's extra expenses that are due to its children are fixed expenses, like mortgage payments. For families in which the fathers also keep up a residence large enough to accommodate substantial visitation, *both* parents will pay this extra expense. For Rachel and Jeff, ($9,151 − $5,909) = $3,242 are the extra expenses due to their children. They each need to have 31.5 percent of this amount, or $1,021, incorporated into their needs. The remaining 68.5 percent, or $2,221, will be split among their needs in proportion to their time with the children, in this case 32.3 percent to 67.7 percent. Thus Jeff's needs are $5,909 plus $1,021 plus $717 for a total of $7,647, yielding a net post-divorce standard of living loss of 27 percent. According to this computation, Rachel's needs are $8,434, yielding neither a net post-divorce standard of living loss or gain (the same as before). We did *not* make such an adjustment in any of the analyses in this

chapter, which means we assumed *no* fathers maintained a residence large enough to accommodate substantial visitation. Many states assume there is some relatively high level of visitation where a father's larger residence is necessary and adjust the child support amount downward when visitation reaches this threshold. However, no data exist, including our own, about what percentage of fathers actually keep up a household large enough to accommodate visitation (e.g., extra bedrooms, TVs, etc., for the children.)

46. Citro, C. F., and Michael, R. T. 1995. *Measuring poverty: A new approach.* Washington, DC: National Academy Press.

47. In an e-mail message, March 31, 1998.

48. In theory, marital assets should normally be divided 50-50. Thus, if she kept the house, he would receive cash or other considerations to be bought out for his share of the equity. Similarly, if she kept most of the household items, he would be monetarily compensated for half of their value. Few of our fathers, however, felt that was how the system worked in practice. The fact that mothers more often keep the family home was also noted by Sugarman, S. 1990. Dividing financial interests at divorce. In *Divorce reform at the crossroads,* eds. S. Sugarman and H. Kay. New Haven, CT: Yale University Press.

49. Amounts for pre-separation were obtained within twelve weeks of filing for dissolution and for post-separation were calculated one year after the first interview.

50. If we calculate the percent gain or loss for each individual and then take the median of all these gains or losses, fathers show a 7 percent decrease, and mothers a 3 percent decrease.

51. For example, some commentators who believe our figures are biased *for* fathers and *against* mothers told us that we didn't properly take into account child-care expenses the mother pays. Our data show an average paid of $1,800 per year, resulting in an average childcare tax credit of $444 per year. It is not clear whether this expense is already figured into the needs tables (see note 42), whether it should be subtracted from income, or added to needs. If one subtracts it from income, mothers are shown to experience an 8 percent loss in standard of living. Others indicated that we needed to find out whether the tax exemption for children was actually taken by the mothers. Meanwhile, commentators who believe our figures are biased *against* fathers and *for* mothers told us that Arizona fathers in 1987 paid proportionately far less child support than most fathers in other states are now ordered to pay (the next year, the Arizona Child Support Guidelines were increased an average of $900 per year), and that we didn't take into account the capital gains exclusion on the sale of the family home (that only mothers often benefit from). We hope our findings stimulate other analysts to redo our analyses with national data sets, using their own assumptions about these matters, but taking into account visitation and taxes.

52. As Greg Duncan wrote me in an October 16, 1997, letter, a "Vital point to make is *not* what happens to the *average* father and mother following divorce. There is a wide distribution of experiences following divorce, some favoring fathers, and yes, a substantial number favoring mothers. No single stereotype fits all, and judges, policy-makers and the public need to be aware of the diversity of circumstances." While this statement is no doubt true, few past analysts emphasized the *diversity* of circumstances, preferring to focus on the average. See Peterson, R. R. 1989. *Women, work and divorce* for an exception.

53. Teachman, J., and Paasch, K. 1993. The economics of parenting apart.

54. Duncan and Hoffman found that the poverty rate doubled for women in the year following divorce but then declined subsequently, but never quite to the pre-divorce levels. Duncan, G. J., and Hoffman, S. D. 1985. Economic consequences of marital instability, pp. 427–71.

55. Sugarman, S. 1990. Dividing financial interests at divorce, p. 150.

56. Peterson, R. R. 1989. *Women, work and divorce.*

57. Cherlin, A. 1981. *Marriage, divorce, remarriage,* p. 29. Cambridge, MA: Harvard University Press.

58. Duncan, G. J. and Hoffman, S. D. 1985. Economic consequences of marital instability, pp. 427–71. For women with children, the increase is not as great in their "all women" analyses, since the gain is offset by a decline in child support received. They also find that men's standard of living increases 14 percent. Moreover, children seem to cost more as they get older, though child-care costs may decline (but so does the income tax offset of the child-care credit).

59. Day, R. D., and Bahr, S. J. 1986. Income changes following divorce and remarriage, pp. 75–88.

60. Though we had hoped to complete a post-remarriage analysis of our own, taking into account taxation and visitation, we realized that we hadn't asked the proper questions on our Wave 3 measure to complete it satisfactorily; for example, we did not obtain information about how much child support the mother's new husband was paying to *his* former spouse, nor how many, if any, of the new wife's children were living with the father.

61. A similar sentiment was expressed by law professor Steven Sugarman, who argued that nonfinancial consequences, including most notably satisfaction with custody arrangements, needs also to be taken into account if the law attempts to redress any gender-based inequities: "Where women have physical custody of the children and men feel that they have, as a result, lost something terribly important to them, it is deeply troubling to compare the former spouses . . . in terms that treat the children solely as a liability," as the needs adjustment method does. Sugarman, S. (1990). Dividing financial interests at divorce, p. 151.

62. See Chapter 7, Table 7.1.

CHAPTER 5: TAKING ON MYTH 4: TERMS OF DIVORCE

1. In, respectively: Fineman, M. (1991). *The illusion of equality;* Mahoney, K. 1996. Gender issues in family law, pp. 198–218; Weitzman, L. J. 1985. *The divorce revolution;* Arendell, T. 1986. *Mothers and divorce: Legal, economic and social dilemmas.* Berkeley: University of California Press; Arendell. T. 1995. *Fathers and divorce.* Thousand Oaks, CA: Sage; and Mason, M. A. 1988. *The equality trap.*

2. Maccoby and Mnookin put the national rate of alimony awards at 8 percent. Maccoby, E. E., and Mnookin, R. H. 1992. *Dividing the child: Social and legal dilemmas of custody.* Cambridge, MA: Harvard University Press. The U.S. Census puts it at 15 percent; U.S. Bureau of the Census. 1986. Child support and alimony: 1985. *Current Population Reports,* series P-23, no. 152. Washington, DC: U.S. Government Printing Office.

3. On rare occasions, the two types of support, spousal and child supports, are combined into "family support."

4. In the remaining 1 percent, both spouses continued residing in it.

5. Koel, A., Clark, S., Straus, R., Whitney, R., and Hauser, B. 1994. Patterns of relitigation in the postdivorce family. *Journal of Marriage and the Family* 56:265–77.

6. Mnookin, R. H., and Kornhauser, L. 1979. Bargaining in the shadow of the law: The case of divorce. *Yale Law Review* 88:950–97. See also Mnookin, R. H. 1985. Divorce bargaining: The limits of private ordering. *University of Michigan Journal of Law Reform* 18:1015–37.

7. Mahoney, K. 1996. Gender issues in family law, pp. 198–202.

8. Ibid., p. 203.

9. Ibid., p. 202–3.

10. At least one divorce researcher who has intensively studied the matter found reason to disagree. Child psychologist Eleanor Maccoby observed, "Yes, many men are directly power-assertive and women self-abnegating in their domestic interaction, but ... having studied a large group of divorcing couples over a number of years ... I cannot fail to be aware of how coercive *women* can be when a relationship disintegrates." Maccoby, E. E. 1991. Gender and relationships: A reprise. *American Psychologist* 46:539.

11. Weitzman, L. 1985. *The divorce revolution;* Seltzer, J. A., and Garfinkel, I. 1990. Inequality in divorce settlements: An investigation of property settlements and child support awards. *Social Science Research* 19:82–111; Lonsdorf, B. 1991. The role of coercion in affecting women's inferior outcomes in divorce, pp. 69–106; Okin, S. M. 1989. *Justice, gender and the family.* New York: Basic Books; Erlanger, H. S., Chambliss, E., and Melli, M. S. 1987. Participation and flexibility in informal processes: Cautions from the divorce context. *Law & Society Review* 21:585–604; Beuhler, C. 1989. Influential factors and equity issues in divorce settlements. *Family Relations* 38:76–82; Mason, M. A. 1988. *The equality trap;* Fineman, M. 1991. *The illusion of equality;* Mahoney, K. 1996. Gender issues in family law, pp. 198–218.

12. The results presented in this chapter have been previously presented in Sheets, V., and Braver, S. L. 1993. Gender differences in satisfaction with divorce decrees. Paper presented at the Western Psychological Association Conference, Phoenix, AZ, and appearing in *Family Relations* 45 (1996):336–42; and Braver, S. L., and Griffin, W. A. The involvement of fathers in the post-divorce family. Paper presented at the Conference on Father Involvement, October 1996, Bethesda, MD.

13. For this analysis, only subjects whose divorce action was complete by one-year post-petition (when they were first asked about their decree satisfaction) were included. This resulted in a sample of 477 respondents (223 women and 254 men) from 312 different families. Longitudinal analyses are necessarily restricted to those who were reinterviewed at the final wave of data collection (three-years post-petition); this includes 418 respondents (199 women and 219 men) from 282 different families. Note that the actual sample sizes used in analyses may vary with missing data.

14. Although we could match 69 percent of our respondents to their ex-spouses, they were treated as independent samples for the present analyses. Treating the ex-spouses as independent (uncorrelated) samples was justified by the lack of inter-spousal correlations in satisfaction ratings: $rs = -.10, .02, -.08, -.04, .02$, all $ps > .15$, for custody, visitation, child-support, financial, and property division stipulations, respectively, at Time 1. Nonetheless, we also conducted analyses parallel to the ones in the text that utilized the *paired* re-

sponses of husbands and wives and resulted in paired t-tests. These analyses revealed substantively identical differences in satisfaction, but they are not presented in detail because of the complexity they introduce to the explanatory analyses presented below.

15. This difference was statistically significant for satisfaction with the custody, $t (475) =$ 5.94, $p < .001$; visitation, $t (470) = 2.42$, $p < .05$; child financial provisions, $t (468) = 2.38$, $p < .05$; and property settlements, $t (467) = 3.16$, $p < .01$, specified in the decree. However, the difference in satisfaction with child-support awards, while also showing that women are more satisfied, did not reach conventional levels of significance, $t (472) = 1.56$, $p < .12$.

16. Koel, A., Clark, S., Straus, R., Whitney, R., and Hauser, B. 1994. Patterns of relitigation in the postdivorce family, pp. 265–277.

17. The statistical reliability of these trends was examined with a 2 × 2, Gender (a between subjects factor) × Time (a two-level repeated measures factor) mixed-factor multivariate analysis of variance (MANOVA). Main effects were noted for Gender, $F (5, 383) = 12.65$, $p < .001$, and Time, $F (5, 383) = 2.76$, $p < .05$; and the interaction was also significant, $F (5, 383) = 3.09$, $p < .01$. Univariate tests (i.e., 2 × 2 ANOVAs) were employed to identify further longitudinal patterns in decree satisfaction. Overall satisfaction with custody, $F (1, 413) = 1.66$, ns, visitation, $F (1, 407) = 1.94$, ns, child-support, $F < 1$, and other financial provisions of the decree, $F < 1$, did not change (i.e., no Time main effect) over the two-year post-divorce interval. However, satisfaction with the property division increased slightly over this period, Time $F (1, 404) = 6.63$, $p < .05$. Further, the absence of significant Gender × Time interactions confirmed that women's *relative* satisfaction with custody, $F < 1$, visitation, $F (1, 407) = 2.87$, ns, and property settlement provisions, $F < 1$, was also unmodified during this period: Even after two years, women in our sample continued to be more satisfied than men with the custody, [Gender simple main effect at Time 2 $F (1, 413) = 43.41$, $p < .001$, visitation, $F (1, 407) =$ 12.79, $p < .001$], and the property division, [Gender simple main effect at Time 2 $F (1, 404) =$ 10.04, $p < .01$], stipulations in their decree. As there was no gender-based change in satisfaction with child-support stipulations, Gender × Time interaction $F < 1$, there was still no significant difference in satisfaction with child-support awards at three years post-petition, Gender simple main effect at Time 2 $F < 1$.

18. This difference was statistically significant, $F (1, 408) = 12.51$, $p < .001$ (for the Gender × Time interaction).

19. This difference approached statistical significance, $F (1, 408) = 2.91$, $p < .10$.

20. The interested reader is referred to Sheets, V. L., and Braver, S. L. 1996. Gender differences in satisfaction with divorce decrees, pp. 336–42.

21. This difference was highly significant, $t (412) = 12.42$, $p < .001$. The dependent measure was a variable where "0" indicated that the individual received neither the legal nor residential custody they preferred, a "1" indicated that they obtained either the legal or residential custody they preferred, and a "2" indicated that they received both the legal and residential custody preferred. Only stipulations for maternal, joint, or paternal custody were scored; other arrangements were too difficult to classify.

22. The means are 3.28 for women, and 2.82 for men; $S_{pooled} = .96$, $t (474) = 5.2$. This difference is statistically significant at $p < .001$. The result that mothers feel substantially more in control of post-divorce events than fathers do, albeit calculated somewhat differently from the measure described here, was also reported in Bay, R. C., and Braver, S. L. 1990. Perceived control of the divorce settlement process and interparental conflict. *Family Relations*

39:382–87. Feeling in control of the process accounted for the difference better than did being the initiator of the divorce.

23. In other words we found significant *positive correlations* with satisfaction with the various terms of the decree, ranging from .28 to .58.

24. Arditti, J., and Allen, K. 1993. Understanding distressed fathers' perceptions of legal and relational inequities post-divorce. *Family and Conciliation Courts Review* 31:461–76. See also Kruk, E. 1992. Psychological and structural factors contributing to the disengagement of noncustodial fathers after divorce. *Family and Conciliation Courts Review* 30:81–101; and Arendell, T. 1995. *Fathers and divorce.*

25. Bay and Braver found it increased the average award by $75 per month. Bay, C., Braver, S. L., Fogas, B. S., Fitzpatrick, P. J., and Wolchik, S. A. 1988. New child-support guidelines: Changes and perceived fairness. Paper presented at the Western Psychological Association Convention, Burlingame, CA. Jessica Pearson's data confirms this figure. Pearson, J., Thoennes, N., and Tjaden, P. 1989. Legislating adequacy, pp. 501–22.

26. The difference is statistically significant, $t(94) = 4.92$, $p < .001$.

27. The difference between fathers' and mothers' views is statistically significant, $t(94) = 10.41$, $p < .001$. Even mothers' views alone suggest a statistically significant advantage for mothers; for the test that the mean differs significantly from the "not slanted" value of 3, $t(92) = 2.83$, $p < .01$.

28. Arendell, T. 1995. *Fathers and divorce;* Buehler, C. 1989. Influential factors and equity issues in divorce settlements, pp. 76–82; Erlanger, H. S., Chambliss, E., and Melli, M. S. 1987. Participation and flexibility in informal processes, pp. 585–604; Lonsdorf, B. 1991. The role of coercion in affecting women's inferior outcomes in divorce, pp. 69–106; Okin, S. M. 1989. *Justice, gender, and the family;* Seltzer, J. A., and Garfinkel, I. 1990. Inequality in divorce settlements, pp. 82–111; Walters, L. H., and Abshire, C. R. 1995. Single parenthood and the law. *Journal of Divorce and Remarriage* 20:161–88. Weitzman, L. 1985. *The divorce revolution.*

CHAPTER 6: TAKING ON MYTH 5: EMOTIONAL ISSUES OF DIVORCE

1. Holmes, T. H., and Rahe, R. H. 1967. The social readjustment rating scale. *Journal of Psychosomatic Research* 11:213–18; Dohrenwend, B. S., and Dohrenwend, B. 1974. *Stressful life events: Their nature and effects.* New York: Wiley.

2. *The Washington Post,* September 24, 1996.

3. Albrecht, S. L. 1980. Reactions and adjustment to divorce: Differences in the experiences of males and females. *Family Relations* 29:59–68; Asher, S. J., and Bloom, B. L. 1983. Geographic mobility as a factor in adjustment to divorce. *Journal of Divorce* 6:69–84; Bloom, B. L., and Caldwell, R. A. 1981. Sex differences in adjustment during the process of marital separation. *Journal of Marriage and the Family* 43:693–701; Chiraboga, D. A. 1982. Adaptation to marital separation in later and earlier life. *Journal of Gerontology* 37:103–14; White, S. W., and Bloom, B. L. 1981. Factors related to the adjustment of divorcing men. *Family Relations* 30:349–60; Zeiss, A. M., Zeiss, R. H., and Johnson, S. M. 1980. Sex differences in initiation and adjustment to divorce. *Journal of Divorce* 4:21–33.

4. Bloom, B. L., Asher, S. J., and White, S. W. 1978. Marital disruption as a stressor: A review and analysis. *Psychological Bulletin* 85:867–93.

5. Keith, P. M. 1985. Financial well-being of older divorced/separated men and women: Findings from a panel study. *Journal of Divorce* 9:161–72; Wallerstein, J. S. 1986. Women after divorce: Preliminary report from a ten-year follow-up. *American Journal of Orthopsychiatry* 56:65–77.

6. Price, S. J., and McKenry, P. C. 1988. *Divorce.* Newbury Park, CA: Sage.

7. Albrecht, S. L. 1980. Reactions and adjustment to divorce, pp. 59–68; Bloom, B. L., and Caldwell, R. A. 1981. Sex differences in adjustment during the process of marital separation, pp. 693–701; Chiraboga, D. A., and Cutler, L. 1977. Stress responses among divorcing men and women. *Journal of Divorce* 1:95–106.

8. Baruch, G., Barnett, R., and Rivers, C. 1983. *Lifeprints: New patterns of love and work for today's women.* New York: McGraw-Hill.

9. Ibid.

10. Weitzman, L. J. 1985. *The divorce revolution,* pp. 345–46.

11. Wallerstein, J. S., and Kelly, J. B. 1980. *Surviving the break-up,* pp. 154–55.

12. Ahrons, C. 1994. *The good divorce,* p. 16.

13. *Harper's Magazine,* November 1985, p. 15.

14. Tannen, D. 1990. *You just don't understand: Women and men in conversation.* New York: Ballantine.

15. Gray, J. 1992. *Men are from Mars, women are from Venus: A practical guide for improving communication and getting what you want from relationships.* New York: Harper-Collins.

16. Ahrons, C. 1994. *The good divorce,* p. 35.

17. Ibid., p. 92.

18. Kitson, G. C., and Sussman, M. B. 1982. Marital complaints, demographic characteristics, and symptoms of mental distress in divorce. *Journal of Marriage and the Family* 44:87–101.

19. Ahrons, C. 1994. *The good divorce,* pp. 93–94.

20. Chiraboga, D. A., Coho, A., Stein, J. A., and Roberts, J. 1979. Divorce, stress and social supports: A study in helpseeking behavior. *Journal of Divorce* 3:121–35; Keith, P. M. 1986. Isolation of the unmarried in later life. *Family Relations* 35:389–95.

21. Keith, P. M. 1985. Financial well-being of older divorced/separated men and women, pp. 161–72.

22. Blankenhorn, D. 1995. *Fatherless America.*

23. Hall, A. S., and Kelly, K. R. 1996. Noncustodial fathers in groups: Maintaining the parenting bond. In *Men in groups: Insights, interventions, psychoeducational work,* ed. M. P. Andronico, p. 248. Washington, DC: American Psychological Association.

24. Wallerstein, J. S., and Corbin, S. B. 1986. Father-child relationships after divorce: Child support and educational opportunity. *Family Law Quarterly* 20:114.

25. Blankenhorn, D. 1995. *Fatherless America.*

26. Ibid., pp. 150–55, 300.

27. Ibid., pp. 156–57.

28. Wallerstein, J. S., and Kelly, J. B. 1980. *Surviving the break-up,* pp. 154–55.

29. Steven Sugarman found that in 1977 in California, wives kept the family home more than twice as often as husbands did. Sugarman, S. D. 1990. Dividing financial interests at divorce, pp. 130–65. Our results on this matter are reported in the previous chapter.

30. Bloom, B. L., Asher, S. J., and White, S. W. 1978. Marital disruption as a stressor, p. 877.

31. Bloom, B. L., and Kindle, K. R. 1985. Demographic factors in the continuing relationship between former spouses. *Family Relations* 34:375–81.

32. Berman, W. H. 1985. Continued attachment after legal divorce. *Journal of Family Issues* 6:375–92.

33. Goetting, A. 1979. The normative integration of the former spouse relationship. *Journal of Divorce* 2:395–414.

34. Arendell, T. 1995. *Fathers and divorce.* However, she dismisses this rage as mere "masculinist rhetoric."

35. Wallerstein, J. S., and Kelly, J. B. 1980. *Surviving the break-up.*

36. Goode, W. J. 1956. *After divorce.* Glencoe, IL: Free Press.

37. Wallerstein, J. S., and Kelly, J. B. 1980. *Surviving the break-up,* p. 154.

38. Wallerstein, J. S., and Blakeslee, S. 1989. *Second chances: Men, women and children a decade after divorce; Who wins, who loses—and why,* p. 29. New York: Ticknor & Fields.

39. Bay, R. C., Braver, S. L., Sandler, I. N., Wolchik, S. A., and Whetstone, M. R. In press. Child support non-compliance/visitation interference: Reciprocal weapons of engagement in interparental post-divorce conflict. In *Family differences: Conflict and its legacy,* eds. C. E. Depner and J. H. Bray. Newbury Park, CA: Sage.

CHAPTER 7: TAKING ON MYTH 6: WHO LEAVES THE MARRIAGE . . .

1. Popenoe, D. 1996. *Life without father: Compelling new evidence that fatherhood and marriage are indispensable for the good of children and society,* pp. 173, 184. New York: Free Press.

2. Blankenhorn, D. 1995. *Fatherless America,* pp. 22–23.

3. Ibid., p. 160, emphasis added.

4. Ibid., p. 226.

5. Ibid., emphasis added.

6. Burns, A., and Scott, C. 1994. *Mother-headed families and why they have increased.* Hillsdale, NJ: Lawrence Erlbaum Associates.

7. Ibid., p. 3.

8. Furstenburg, F. F. 1994. History and current status of divorce in the United States. *Future of Children* 4:38.

9. Ehrenreich, B. C. 1983. *The hearts of men,* p. 165. New York: Pluto Press.

10. Burns, A., and Scott, C. 1994. *Mother-headed families and why they have increased,* p. 3.

11. *The Charleston Gazette,* January 10, 1995, emphasis added.

12. Becker, G. 1981. *A treatise on the family.* Cambridge, MA: Harvard University Press. See also Levinger, G. 1976. A social psychological perspective on marital dissolution. *Journal of Social Issues* 32:21–47; Levinger, G. 1982. A social exchange view on the dissolution of pair relationships. In *Family relationships: Rewards and costs,* ed. F. I. Nye. Beverly Hills: Sage; Peters, H. E. 1986. Marriage and divorce: Informational constraints and private contracting. *The American Economic Review* 76:437–54; Scanzoni, J. 1972. *Sexual bargaining.*

New York: Free Press; Braver, S. L., Wolchik, S. A., Sandler, I. N., and Sheets, V. L. 1993. A social exchange model of nonresidential parent involvement. In *Nonresidential parenting: New vistas in family living,* eds. C. E. Depner and J. H. Bray, pp. 87–108. Newbury Park, CA: Sage.

13. Parkman, A. 1992. *No-fault divorce: What went wrong?* Boulder: Westview Press.

14. Ibid., p. 3.

15. Ibid., p. 85.

16. Ibid., p. 9.

17. Guttentag, M., and Secord, P. F. 1983. *Too many women.*

18. This imbalance has been called "the marriage squeeze" by demographers. See Carter, H., and Glick, P. C. 1976. *Marriage and divorce: A social and economic study,* rev. ed. Cambridge, MA: Harvard University Press.

19. Burns, A., and Scott, C. 1994. *Mother-headed families and why they have increased,* p. 3.

20. These results have been previously reported in Braver, S., Whitley, M., and Ng, C. 1991. Who divorced whom: It depends on how you measure it. Paper presented at Western Psychological Association, San Francisco; and Braver, S., Whitley, M., and Ng, C. 1993. Who divorced whom: Methodological and theoretical issues. *Journal of Divorce and Remarriage* 20:1–20.

21. Braver, S. L., Wolchik, S. A., Sandler, I. N., and Sheets, V. L. 1993. A social exchange model of nonresidential parent involvement, pp. 87–108.

22. Dixon, R. B., and Weitzman, L. J. 1982. When husbands file for divorce. *Journal of Marriage and the Family* 44:103–15; Levinger, G. 1966. Sources of marital satisfaction among applicants for divorce. *American Journal of Orthopsychiatry* 36:803–7; Goode, W. J. 1956. *After divorce.*

23. Hopper, J. 1993. Oppositional identities and rhetoric in divorce. *Qualitative Sociology* 16:133–56; Hopper, J. 1993. The rhetoric of motives in divorce. *Journal of Marriage and the Family* 55:801–13; Reissman, C. K. 1990. *Divorce talk: Women and men make sense of personal relationships.* New Brunswick, NJ: Princeton University Press; Arendell, T. 1995. *Fathers and divorce;* Coltrane, S., and Hickman, N. 1992. The rhetoric of rights and needs: Moral discourse and the reform of child custody and child support laws. *Social Problems* 39:400–420; Duck, S. W., and Sants, H. K. A. 1983. On the origin of the specious: Are personal relationships really interpersonal states? *Journal of Social and Clinical Psychology* 1:27–41.

24. Harvey, J. H., Weber, A. L., Galvin, K. S., Huszti, H. C., and Garnick, N. N. 1986. Attribution and determination of close relationships: A special focus on the account. In *The emergent field of personal relationships,* eds. R. Gilmour and S. W. Duck. Hillsdale, NJ: Lawrence Erlbaum.

25. This result strongly corroborates previous research of Pettit, E. J., and Bloom, B. L. 1984. Whose decision was it: The effects of initiator status on adjustment to marital disruption. *Journal of Marriage and the Family* 48:587–95; Beuhler, C. 1987. Initiator status and the divorce transition. *Family Relations* 36:82–86; Zeiss, A. M., Zeiss, R. A., and Johnson, S. M. 1980. Sex differences in initiation of and adjustment to divorce, pp. 21–33. Kitson, G. C., and Holmes, W. M. 1992. *Portrait of divorce: Adjustment to marital breakdown.* New York: Guil-

Notes

ford. Even in other countries (e.g., Australia, Germany) women are the initiators in two out of every three divorces: McDonald, P., ed. 1986. *Settling up: Property and income distribution in divorce in Australia.* Sydney: Prentice-Hall; Voegeli, W. 1987. Single women and their families: The case of Germany. Paper presented at the Fourth Annual Australian Family Research Conference, Sydney.

26. Wallerstein, J. S., and Blakeslee, S. 1989. *Second chances,* p. 39.

27. Ahrons, C. 1994. *The good divorce,* p. 92.

28. According to the National Center of Health Statistics, in divorces between 1982–1986, the wife was the petitioner in 56 percent of couples without children, but in 65 percent of couples with one or more children. National Center of Health Statistics, 1989.

29. Whitehead, B. D. 1997. *The divorce culture.* New York: Alfred A. Knopf.

30. Kitson, G. C., and Holmes, W. M. 1992. *Portrait of divorce,* p. 74.

31. Ellman, I. 1989. The theory of alimony, pp. 1–81.

32. American Law Institute, 1997. *Principles of the law of family dissolution.*

33. Ellman, I. 1997. The misguided movement to revive fault divorce, and why reformers should look instead to the American Law Institute. *The International Journal of Law, Policy and the Family* 11:225.

34. Booth, A., and White, L. K. 1980. Thinking about divorce. *Journal of Marriage and the Family* 42:605–16; Kitson, G. C., and Sussman, M. B. 1982. Marital complaints, demographic characteristics, and the symptoms of mental distress in divorce, pp. 87–101; for a review, see Kitson, G. C., Babri, K. B., and Roach, M. J. 1985. Who divorces and why: A review. *Journal of Family Issues* 6:255–93.

35. *Time,* October 6, 1997, p. 39.

36. Gottman, J. M., Coan, J., Carrere, S., and Swanson, C. 1998. Predicting marital happiness and stability from newlywed interactions. *Journal of Marriage and the Family* 60:5–22.

37. Quotes from *Los Angeles Times,* February 1998.

38. Gottman, J. M., Coan, J., Carrere, S., and Swanson, C. 1998. Predicting marital happiness and stability from newlywed interactions, p. 18.

39. DeWitt. 1992. Breaking up is hard to do. *American Demographics* 53:458.

40. Bergman, B. 1986. *The economic emergence of women,* p. 21. New York: Basic Books.

41. Michael, R. T. 1988. Why did the U.S. divorce rate double within a decade? *Research in Population Economics* 6:367–99.

42. McFadden, M. 1974. *Bachelor fatherhood,* p. 9. New York: Charter Books.

43. Ahrons, C. 1994. *The good divorce,* p. 14.

44. Hite, S. 1994. *The Hite report on the family: Growing up under patriarchy.* New York: Grove Press. From a book excerpt: Bringing democracy home. *Ms.,* March/April 1995, p. 57.

45. Popenoe, D. 1996. *Life without father,* p. 193.

46. Haas, L. 1982. Determinants of role-sharing behaviors: A study of egalitarian couples. *Sex Roles* 8:747–60; Douthitt, R. A. 1989. The division of labor within the home: Have gender roles changed? *Sex Roles* 20:693–704; Thompson, L., and Walker, A. J. 1989. Gender in families: Women and men in marriage, work and parenthood. *Journal of Marriage and the Family* 51:845–71.

47. Finlay, B., Starnes, C. E., and Alvarez, F. B. 1985. Recent changes in sex-role ideology among divorced men and women: Some possible causes and implications. *Sex Roles* 12:637–53.

48. Ibid., p. 641.

CHAPTER 8: THE "PARENTALLY DISENFRANCHISED" DAD

1. The findings reported in this chapter have been previously presented in: Bay, R. C., and Braver, S. L. 1989. Perceived control of the divorce process and interparental conflict. Paper presented at Western/Rocky Mountain Association Meeting, Reno, NV; Braver, S. L., Wolchik, S. A., and Sandler, I. N. 1991. Development of a social exchange model of noncustodial parent involvement. Paper presented at American Psychological Association, San Francisco; Bay, R. C., Braver, S. L., Sandler, I. N., and Wolchik, S. A. 1993. Child support non-compliance/visitation interference: Empirically disentangling the causal sequence. Paper presented at American Psychological Association, Toronto, Ontario, Canada; Braver, S. L., Whetstone, M. R., and Sheets, V. L. 1994. Custody preferences versus custody outcomes: Effects of discrepancies on divorcing mothers, fathers, and children. Paper presented at Law & Society Association, June 1994, Phoenix, AZ; Braver, S. L. 1995. Parental access and child support compliance. Paper presented at the National Child Support Enforcement Association Workshop, Washington, DC; Bay, R. C., and Braver, S. L. 1990. Perceived control of the divorce settlement process and interparental conflict, pp. 382–87; Braver, S. L., Wolchik, S. A., Sandler, I. N., Sheets, V., Fogas, B., and Bay, R. C. 1993. A longitudinal study of noncustodial parents, pp. 9–23; Braver, S. L., Wolchik, S. A., Sandler, I. N., and Sheets, V. 1993. A social exchange model of noncustodial parent involvement; Bay, R. C., Braver, S. L., Sandler, I. N., Wolchik, S. A., and Whetstone, M. R. In press. Child support non-compliance/visitation interference.

2. The correlation with visitation frequency ranged from .59 (father's report, Wave 2) to .37 (Mother's report, Wave 2); the correlation of perceived control with child support compliance ranged from .37 (father's report, Wave 2) to .29 (father's report, Wave 3).

3. His real name; he has consented to public disclosure.

4. Dudley, J. R. 1991. Increasing an understanding of divorced fathers who have infrequent contact with their children. *Family Relations* 40:279–85; Kruk, E. 1991. Discontinuity between pre- and post-divorce father-child relationships: New evidence regarding paternal disengagement. *Journal of Divorce and Remarriage* 16:195–227; Kruk, E. 1992. Psychological and structural factors contributing to the dissengagement of noncustodial fathers after divorce, pp. 81–101; Arditti, J. A. 1990. Noncustodial fathers: An overview of policy and resources. *Family Relations* 39:460–65; Arditti, J. A. 1991. Child support noncompliance and divorced fathers: Rethinking the role of paternal involvement. *Journal of Divorce and Remarriage* 14:107–19; Arditti, J. A., and Allen, K. R. 1993. Understanding distressed fathers' perceptions of legal and relational inequities postdivorce, pp. 461–76; Arditti, J. A., and Keith, T. Z. 1993. Visitation frequency, child support payment, and the father-child relationship postdivorce. *Journal of Marriage and the Family* 55:699–712; Arditti, J. A., and Kelly, M. 1994. Fathers' perspectives of their co-parental relationships postdivorce. *Family Relations*

43:61–67; McKenry, P. C., Price, S. J., Fine, M. A., and Serovich, J. 1991. Predictors of single, noncustodial fathers' physical involvement with their children. *Journal of Genetic Psychology* 153:305–19; McKenry, P. C., McKelvey, M. W., Leigh, D., and Wark, L. Nonresidential father involvement: A comparison of divorced, separated, never married, and remarried fathers. *Journal of Divorce and Remarriage* 25:1–13; Umberson, D., and Williams, C. L. 1993. Divorced fathers: Parental role strain and psychological distress. *Journal of Family Issues* 14:378–400.

5. Arendell, T. 1995. *Fathers and divorce,* p. 14.

6. Ibid., pp. 10–12.

7. Prof. Kay Pasley, Personal Communication, May 18, 1994.

8. The within Wave correlations are all statistically significant and range from .14 to .31. Similar relationships have been reported by Seltzer, J. A. 1992. Custody and visiting after divorce: The other side of child support. In *Child support assurance,* eds. I. Garfinkle, S. S. McLanahan, and P. K. Roberts, pp. 113–35. Washington, DC: The Urban Press Institute; Seltzer, J. A., Schaeffer, N. C., and Charng, H. 1989. Family ties after divorce: The relationship between visiting and paying child support. *Journal of Marriage and the Family* 51:1013–31; and Peterson, J. L., and Nord, C. W. 1990. The regular receipt of child support, pp. 539–51.

9. Weiss, Y., and Willis, R. J. 1985. Children as collective goods in divorce settlements. *Journal of Labor Economics* 3:268–92.

10. Chambers, D. 1979. *Making fathers pay,* p. 128.

11. Ibid.; Fulton, J. A. 1979. Parental reports of children's post-divorce adjustment, pp. 126–39; Goode, W. J. 1956. *Women in divorce.* New York: Free Press; Pearson, J., and Thoennes, N. 1986. Will this divorced woman receive child support?, pp. 65–71; Pearson, J., and Thoennes, N. 1988. The denial of visitation rights, pp. 363–80.

12. Chambers, D. 1979. *Making fathers pay,* p. 128.

13. Both within Wave and across Wave correlations of the questions asked of fathers, "Did your ex-spouse prevent you from visiting?" and "Did you skip one or more child support payments or make partial payments?" were all in the .2 range and statistically significant.

14. Pearson, J., and Anhalt, J. 1994. Enforcing visitation rights. *Judges' Journal* 33:3–7, 39–42.

15. Seltzer, J. A. 1994. Consequences of marital dissolution for children. *Annual Review of Sociology* 20:258–59.

16. Gray, J. 1992. *Men are from Mars, Women are from Venus.*

17. Telephone interview with John Gray, June 1997.

18. Telephone interview with Mary Ann Forgatch, February 12, 1997.

19. In our path model, the path coefficient was .62, one of the highest of any finding in our data. See Bay, R. C., Braver, S. L., Sandler, I. N., Wolchik, S. A., and Whetstone, M. R. In press. Child support non-compliance/visitation interference.

20. Blau, M. 1993. *Families apart: Ten keys to successful co-parenting,* p. 145. New York: Perigee.

21. The correlation between the two parents' sense of control was positive, .31, $p < .001$.

CHAPTER 9: JOINT LEGAL CUSTODY

1. Meyer, D. R., and Garasky, S. 1993. Custodial fathers: Myths, realities, and child support policy. *Journal of Marriage and the Family* 55:73–89.

2. Freed, D. J., and Walker, T. B. 1987. Family law in the fifty states: An overview. *Family Law Quarterly* 22:408–29.

3. Christine Nord and Nicholas Zill report that only 4 percent have a joint residential custody arrangement while 21 percent have joint legal. Nord, C. W., and Zill, N. 1997. Noncustodial parents' participation in their children's lives. *Child Support Report* 19:1–2. In California the estimates for joint residential are closer to 20 percent. Maccoby, E. E., and Mnookin, R. H. 1992. *Dividing the child.*

4. For example, see Clingempeel, W. D., and Reppucci, N. D. 1982. Joint custody after divorce: Major issues and goals for research. *Psychological Bulletin* 91:102–27; Goldstein, J. A., and Solnit, A. J. 1984. *Divorce and your child.* New Haven, CT: Yale University Press; Creif, J. B. 1979. Fathers, children, and joint custody. *American Journal of Orthopsychiatry* 49:311–19; Kelly, J. 1983. Further observations on joint custody. *University of California-Davis Law Review* 16:762–70; Luepnitz, D. A. 1982. *Child custody: A study of families after divorce.* Lexington, MA: Lexington Books; Roman, M., and Haddad, W. 1978. *The disposable parent.* New York: Holt, Rinehart & Winston; Steinman, S. 1981. The experience of children in a joint-custody arrangement: A report of a study. *American Journal of Orthopsychiatry* 51:403–14; Ware, C. 1982. *Shared parenting after divorce.* New York: Viking.

5. In a telephone interview, June 11, 1997.

6. In a telephone interview, June 18, 1997.

7. For example, see Alexander, S. J. 1977. Protecting the child's rights in custody cases. *Family Coordinator* 26:377–85; Clingempeel, W. D., and Reppucci, N. D. 1982. Joint custody after divorce, pp. 102–27; Goldstein, J. A., Freud, A., and Solnit, A. J. 1973. *Beyond the best interests of the child.* New York: Free Press; Jenkins, R. L. 1977. Maxims in child custody cases. *Family Coordinator* 26:385–90; Kelly, J. 1983. Further observations on joint custody, pp. 762–70; Steinman, S. 1981. The experience of children in a joint-custody arrangement, pp. 403–14; Steinman, S. 1983. Joint custody: What we know, what we have yet to learn, and the judicial and legislative implications. *University of California-Davis Law Review* 16:739–62.

8. Pearson, J., and Thoennes, N. 1990. Custody after divorce: Demographic and attitudinal patterns. *American Journal of Orthopsychiatry* 60:233–49; Kline, M., Tschann, J. M., Johnston, J. R., and Wallerstein, J. S. 1989. Children's adjustment in joint and sole physical custody families. *Developmental Psychology* 25:430–38; Nelson, R. 1989. Parental hostility, conflict, and communication in joint and sole custody families. *Journal of Divorce* 13:145–57; Bowman, M. E., and Ahrons, C. R. 1985. Impact of legal custody status on fathers' parenting postdivorce. *Journal of Marriage and the Family* 47:481–88; Johnston, J. R., Kline, M., and Tschann, J. M. 1989. Ongoing postdivorce conflict: Effects on children of joint custody and frequent access. *American Journal of Orthopsychiatry* 59:576–92; Maccoby, E. E., and Mnookin, R. H. 1992. *Dividing the child.*

9. Wolchik, S. A., Braver, S. L., and Sandler, I. N. 1985. Maternal versus joint custody: Children's postseparation experiences and adjustment. *Journal of Clinical Psychology* 14:5–10.

10. The research reported here has been previously presented in Gunnoe, M. L., and

Braver, S. L. 1997. The effects of joint legal custody on family functioning, controlling for factors that predispose a joint award. *Child Development,* under review; Braver, S. L., Whetstone, M. R., and Sheets, V. L. 1994. Custody preferences versus custody outcomes: Effects of discrepancies on divorcing mothers, fathers, and children. Paper presented at Law and Society Association, June 1994, Phoenix, AZ.

11. All statistically significant at $p < .05$ or less by mother's report.

12. Statistically significant at $p < .05$ by father's report.

13. The difference reached conventional levels of statistical significance only for mother's report.

14. Nord, C. W., and Zill, N. 1997. Noncustodial parents' participation in their children's lives, p. 2.

15. They "cautiously support a presumption in favor of joint legal custody." Maccoby, E. E., and Mnookin, R. H. 1992. *Dividing the child,* p. 289.

16. Klawitter, M. K., and Garfinkle, I. 1992. Child support, routine income witholding, and post-divorce income, pp. 52–64; Pearson, J., Thoennes, N., and Anhalt, J. 1992. Child support in the United States: The experience in Colorado. *Family and Conciliation Courts Review* 31:226–43.

CHAPTER 10: CAVEAT

1. Dahlstrom, W. G., Welsh, G. S., and Dahlstrom, L. E. 1960. *An MMPI handbook. Vol.1.* Minneapolis: University of Minnesota-Lund Press; Dahlstrom, W. G., Welsh, G. S., and Dahlstrom, L. E. 1975. *An MMPI handbook. Vol. 2: Research applications.* Minneapolis: University of Minnesota Press.

2. About 8 percent of them reach the clinical cutoff on the Psychopathic Deviance scale. Lanyon, R. I., and Goodstein, L. D. 1997. *Personality assessment,* 3rd ed., p. 73. New York: Wiley.

3. Dion, M. R., Braver, S. L., Wolchik, S. A., and Sandler, I. N. 1997. Alcohol abuse and psychopathic deviance in noncustodial parents as predictors of child support payment and visitation. *American Journal of Orthopsychiatry* 67:70–79.

4. Caldwell, A.D. 1996. Forensic questions and answers on the MMPI/MMPI-2. *Caldwell Report.*

5. This many people were estimated to meet the criteria for alcohol abuse, dependence or both, as defined by the Diagnostic and Statistical Manual of Mental Disorders, 3rd ed. Eighth Special Report to the U.S. Congress on Alcohol and Health. Secretary of U.S. Department of Health and Human Services, September 1993, Department of Health and Human Services, Public Health Service.

6. Dion, M. R., Braver, S. L., Wolchik, S. A., and Sandler, I. N. 1997. Alcohol abuse and psychopathic deviance in noncustodial parents as predictors of child support payment and visitation, pp. 70–79.

7. Straus, M. A., Gelles, R. J., and Steinmetz, S. K. 1981. *Behind closed doors: Violence in the American family.* Newbury Park, CA: Sage; Goodman, L. A.; Koss, M. P., and Felipe Russo, N. 1993. Violence against women: Physical and mental health effects. Part I: Research findings. *Applied and Preventive Psychology* 2:79–89.

8. In a telephone interview, September 2, 1997.

9. In a telephone interview, August 27, 1997.

10. Men's Health Network Health Data Summary. 1994. Domestic violence: A two-way street, revised October 1995.

11. Johnston, J. R. In press. *Guidelines for the resolution of disputed custody and visitation for children of domestic violence. Section 1: Final report to the judicial council of California;* Straus, M. A., Gelles, R. J., and Steinmetz, S. K. 1981. *Behind closed doors.* Depner, C. E., Cannata, K. V., and Simon, M. B. 1992. Building a uniform statistical reporting system: A snapshot of California Family Court Services. *Family and Conciliation Court Review* 30:169–84.

12. The statistical interaction of reporter X perpetrator is significant in every case, but no main effects are. These are matched parents.

13. Maccoby, E. E., and Mnookin, R. H. 1992. *Dividing the child,* p. 287.

14. In a telephone interview, June 2, 1997.

15. All quotes are from *The Detroit Free Press,* August 2, 1996.

16. Friedrich, W. N., Fisher, J., Broughton, D., Houston, M., and Shafran, C. R. 1998. Normative Sexual Behavior in children: contemporary sample. *Pediatrics* 101:8.

CHAPTER 11: CUSTODY POLICIES THAT WORK

1. Roth, A. 1976. The tender years presumption in child custody disputes. *Journal of Family Law* 15:423–61.

2. See 2 and 3 Victoria, 1839.

3. Mason, M. A. 1994. *From father's property to children's rights: The history of child custody in the United States.* New York: Columbia University Press.

4. Roth, A. 1976. The tender years presumption in child custody disputes, pp. 423–61.

5. Kelly, J. B. 1994. The determination of child custody. *The Future of Children* 4:121–42.

6. Ibid., p. 122.

7. Folberg, J. 1991. Custody overview. In *Joint custody and shared parenting,* 2nd ed., ed. J. Folberg, pp. 3–10. New York: Guilford Press.

8. Chambers, D. L. 1984. Rethinking the substantive roles for custody disputes in divorce. *Michigan Law Review* 83:477–569.

9. Crippen, G. 1990. Stumbling beyond best interests of the child: Reexamining child custody standard setting in the wake of Minnesota's four-year experiment with the primary caretaker preference. *Minnesota Law Review* 75:427–503.

10. Proposal of Professor Carol Bruch.

11. Scott, E. S. 1992. Pluralism, parental preferences, and child custody. *California Law Review* 80:615.

12. Actually, the incidence of custody litigation in Minnesota increased when it experimented with the primary-caretaker presumption, according to Crippen, G. 1990. Stumbling beyond best interests of the child, pp. 427–503.

13. However, rules that change child support drastically at levels near this 35 percent threshold needlessly increase the stakes again.

14. Maccoby, E. E., and Mnookin, R. H. 1992. *Dividing the child,* p. 283.

15. Genevie, L., and Margolies, E. 1987. *The motherhood report: How women feel about being mothers,* p. 84. New York: Macmillan.

16. Ibid., p. 319.

17. Carbone, J. R. 1994. A feminist perspective on divorce. *Future of Children* 4:186.

18. Ibid.

19. Henry, R. Resolution of child custody disputes. Memorandum, April 30, 1993.

20. *Los Angeles Times,* March 2, 1995.

21. Regan, J. 1995. An open letter to Mr. Clark. *Newsweek,* March 13, 1995, pp. 57–58. The byline indicates that Regan "lives in New York with her two children and is involved in a custody battle over her young daughter," p. 58.

22. In a telephone interview, August 27, 1997.

23. Warshak, R. A. 1992. *The custody revolution.* New York: Simon & Schuster; Warshak, R. A. 1986. Father custody and child development: A review and analysis of psychological research. *Behavioral Sciences and the Law* 4:185–202; Warshak, R. A., and Santrock, J. W. 1983. The impact of divorce in father-custody and mother-custody homes. In *Children and divorce,* ed. L. A. Kurdek. San Francisco: Jossey-Bass; Santrock, J. W., and Warshak, R. A. 1979. Father custody and social development in boys and girls. *Journal of Social Issues* 35:112–25; Warshak, R. A. 1996. Gender bias in custody decisions. *Family and Conciliation Courts Review* 34:396–409; Luepnitz, D. A. 1982. *Child custody.* Rosen, R. 1979. Some crucial issues concerning children of divorce. *Journal of Divorce* 3:19–25; Ambert, A. 1982. Differences in children's behavior toward custodial mothers and custodial fathers. *Journal of Marriage and the Family* 44:73–86; Lowery, C. R., and Settle, S. A. 1985. Effects of divorce on children. Differential impact of custody and visitation patterns. *Family Relations* 34:455–64; Maccoby, E. E., Depner, C. E., and Mnookin, R. M. 1988. Custody of children following divorce. In *The impact of divorce, single-parenting and step-parenting on children,* eds. E. M. Hetherington and J. Arasteh, pp. 91–114. Hillsdale, NJ: Lawrence Erlbaum.

24. The only known evidence regarding the MMPI and parenting effectiveness postdivorce is our work, discussed in the last chapter.

25. Bradshaw, E. R., and Hinds, R. W. 1997. The impact of client and evaluator gender on custody evaluations. *Family and Conciliation Courts Review* 35:325.

26. These factors were identified after careful reviews of ninety-two studies that provided statistical evidence by Amato, P. R., and Keith, B. 1991. Parental divorce and the well-being of children: A meta-analysis. *Psychological Bulletin* 100:26–46; Amato, P. R., and Keith, B. 1991. Parental divorce and adult well-being: A meta-analysis. *Journal of Marriage and the Family* 53:43–58.

27. Amato, P. R., and Keith, B. 1991. Parental divorce and the well-being of children, pp. 26–46; Amato, P. R., and Keith, B. 1991. Parental divorce and adult well-being, pp. 43–58.

28. Amato, P. R., and Keith, B. 1991. Parental divorce and the well-being of children, pp. 26–46; Amato, P. R., and Keith, B. 1991. Parental divorce and adult well-being, pp. 43–58; Amato, P. R. 1993. Children's adjustment to divorce: Theories, hypotheses, and empirical support. *Journal of Marriage and the Family* 55:23–38.

29. Arbuthnot, J., and Gordon, D. A. 1994. *Children in the middle: Parent's version,* 2nd ed. Athens, OH: Center for Divorce Education; Emery, R. E. 1994. *Renegotiating family relationships: Divorce, child custody, and mediation.* New York: Guilford; Kelly, J. B. 1993.

Current research on children's postdivorce adjustment: No simple answers. *Family and Conciliation Courts Review* 31:29–49.

30. Johnston, J. R. 1995. Children's adjustment in sole custody compared to joint custody families and principles for custody decision making. *Family and Conciliation Courts Review* 33:415–25; Johnston, J. R., Kline, M., and Tschann, J. M. 1989. Ongoing postdivorce conflict, pp. 576–92; Kline, M., Tschann, J. M., Johnston, J. R., and Wallerstein, J. S. 1989. Children's adjustment in joint and sole physical custody families, pp. 430–38; Maccoby, E. E., and Mnookin, R. H. 1992. *Dividing the child.* Nelson, R. 1989. Parental hostility conflict and communication in joint and sole custody families, pp. 145–57; Pearson, J., and Thoennes, N. 1990. Custody after divorce, pp. 233–49; Bowman, M. E., and Ahrons, C. R. 1985. Impact of legal custody status on fathers' parenting postdivorce, pp. 481–88; Buchanan, C. M., Maccoby, E. E., and Dornbusch, S. M. 1992. Adolescents and their families after divorce: Three residential arrangements compared. *Journal of Research on Adolescence* 2:261–91.

31. In a telephone interview, June 18, 1997.

32. Arizona Revised Statutes 301–25.

33. Burgess—California Supreme Court. 1996. *Family and Conciliation Courts Review* 34:492–507. See also Shear, L. E. 1996. Life stories, doctrines, and decision making: Three high courts decide the move-away dilemma. *Family and Conciliation Courts Review* 34:439–58.

34. Puente, M. *USA Today,* April 22, 1996.

35. Paul Burgess's attorney said, in view of the court's decision in his case, "When I go into court (for a divorcing father), there's no way . . . [now] I'm going to settle for less than joint physical custody if there's even a hint the other parent might move." And lawyers said, "The ruling will encourage more fathers to seek sole or joint physical custody. That could mean more fighting earlier in the divorce process." *USA Today,* April 22, 1996.

CHAPTER 12: CHANGING THE LANDSCAPE OF DIVORCE

1. Nurse, A. R., and Thompson, P. 1997. Collaborative divorce: Oxymoron or a new process? *The Family Psychologist* 13:21–25.

2. Blaisure, K. R., and Geasler, M. L. 1996. Results of a survey of court-connected parent education programs in U.S. counties. *Family and Conciliation Courts Review* 34:23–40.

3. Braver, S. L., Salem, P., Pearson, J., and DeLuse, S. R. 1996. The content of divorce education programs: Results of a survey. *Family and Conciliation Courts Review* 34:41–59.

4. Ibid.

5. Arizona Revised Statutes § 25–352.

6. In a telephone interview, June 11, 1997.

7. Wolchik, S. A., Sandler, I. N., West, S. G., and Anderson, E. 1997. Children of divorce: six-year follow-up of prevention efforts. Grant proposal submitted to NIMH (1RO1MH57013).

8. I enlisted the help of some extremely talented clinical psychologists and family therapists, namely my close friends and long-time collaborators Drs. Irwin Sandler, Sharlene Wolchik, as well as new colleagues Drs. Lillie Weiss, Steve Spaccarelli, and most important, William Griffin.

Notes

9. Bryan, M. 1997. *The prodigal father: Reuniting fathers and their children*, p. 4. New York: Clarkson Potter.

10. Wolchik, S. A., West, S. G., Westover, S., and Sandler, I. N. 1993. The children of divorce parenting intervention: Outcome evaluation of an empirically based program. *American Journal of Community Psychology* 21:293–331; Wolchik, S. A., West, S. G., Sandler, I. N., Braver, S. L., and Tein, J. Y. 1997. Children of divorce: Assessing the effectiveness of an intervention for custodial mothers. Manuscript in preparation.

11. Emery, R. E. 1994. *Renegotiating family relationships.*

12. Pearson, J. 1991. The equity of mediated divorce agreements. *Mediation Quarterly* 7:347–63.

13. Kelly, J. B. 1996. A decade of divorce mediation research: Some answers and questions. *Family and Conciliation Courts Review* 34:373–85.

14. In a telephone interview, June 11, 1997.

15. Grillo, T. 1991. The mediation alternative: Process dangers for women. *Yale Law Review* 100:1545–1609.

16. Davies, B., Ralph, S., Hawton, M., and Craig, L. 1995. A study of client satisfaction with family court counseling in cases involving domestic violence. *Family and Conciliation Courts Review* 33:324–41; Depner, C., Cannata, K., and Simon, M. 1992. Building a uniform statistical reporting system, pp. 169–84; Ellis, D. 1995. *Family mediation pilot project, Hamilton Unified Family Court.* North York, Canada: York University.

17. Leving, J., as quoted in Gatland, L. 1997. Putting the blame on no-fault. *ABA Journal,* p. 52.

18. Katz, S., and Raskin, M. G. 1947. The dying doctrine of recrimination in the United States of America. *Canadian Bar Review* 35:1046.

19. This passage is cited in Wels, R. H. 1950. New York: The poor man's Reno. *Cornell Law Review* 35:303–4.

20. Weitzman, L. J. 1985. *The divorce revolution;* Kay, H. H. 1990. Beyond no-fault: New directions in divorce. In *Divorce reform at the crossroads,* eds. S. D. Sugarman and H. H. Kay, pp. 6–36. New Haven: Yale University Press; Freed, D. J., and Walker, T. B. 1985. Family law in the fifty states, pp. 369–471.

21. Richards, M. 1996. Divorce numbers and divorce legislation. *Family Law* 151; Frank, A., Berman, J., and Mazur-Hart, S. 1979. No-fault divorce and the divorce rate: The Nebraska experience—An interrupted time-series analysis and commentary. *Nebraska Law Review* 58:22; Becker, G. 1981. *A treatise on the family,* Schoen, R. et al. 1975. California's experience with non-adversary divorce. *Demography* 12:223; Marvel, T. 1989. Divorce rates and the fault requirement. *Law and Society Review* 23:543; But see Nakonezny, P., Shull, R., and Rodgers, J. 1995. The effect of no-fault divorce law on the divorce rate across the 50 states and its relation to income, education and religiosity. *Journal of Marriage and the Family* 57:477–88.

22. Jacob, H. 1988. *The silent revolution.* Chicago: University of Chicago Press; Jacob, H. 1989. Another look at no-fault divorce and the post-divorce finances of women. *Law and Society Review* 25:95–97; Abraham, J. H. 1989. The divorce revolution revisited: A counter-revolutionary critique. *Northern Illinois University Law Review* 9:251–98; Sugarman, S. 1990. Dividing financial interests at divorce.

23. From the Web page http://www.vix.com/crc/sp/spcrc97.htm

24. 1998. *Speak Out for Children* 12 (Winter 1998):8.

25. Lurvey, I., as quoted in Gatland, L. 1997. Putting the blame on no-fault. *ABA Journal,* p. 54.

26. Markman, H. J. 1981. Prediction of marital distress: A 5-year follow-up. *Journal of Consulting and Clinical Psychology* 49:760–62. Markman, H. J., Stanley, S. M., and Blumberg, S. L. 1994. *Fighting for your marriage: Positive steps for preventing divorce and preserving a lasting love.* San Francisco: Jossey-Bass.

27. Louisiana House Bill 756. See Creating a more perfect union? LA's "Covenant marriage" debated. *The New Orleans Times-Picayune,* June 9, 1997.

28. Kirn, W. 1997. The ties that bind. *Time,* August 18, 1997, p. 49.

29. The *Time*/CNN Poll results were reported in Kirn, W. 1997. The ties that bind.

30. Whitehead, B. D. 1997. *The divorce culture.*

Index

Index

Index

Index

Index

Index

Index

Contagious & Non-Contagious Infectious Diseases Sourcebook

Basic Information about Contagious Diseases like Measles, Polio, Hepatitis B, and Infectious Mononucleosis, and Non-Contagious Infectious Diseases like Tetanus and Toxic Shock Syndrome, and Diseases Occurring as Secondary Infections Such as Shingles and Reye Syndrome, Along with Vaccination, Prevention, and Treatment Information, and a Section Describing Emerging Infectious Disease Threats

Edited by Karen Bellenir and Peter D. Dresser. 566 pages. 1996. 0-7808-0075-3. $78.

Death & Dying Sourcebook

Basic Information for the Layperson about End-of-Life Care and Related Ethical and Legal Issues, Including Chief Causes of Death, Autopsies, Pain Management for the Terminally Ill, Life Support Systems, Coma, Euthanasia, Assisted Suicide, Hospice Programs, Living Wills, Near-Death Experiences, Counseling, Mourning, Organ Donation, Cryogenics and Physician Training and Liability, Along with Statistical Data, a Glossary, and Listings of Sources for Additional Help and Information

Edited by Annemarie Muth. 600 pages. 1999. 0-7808-0230-6. $78.

Diabetes Sourcebook, 1st Edition

Basic Information about Insulin-Dependent and Noninsulin-Dependent Diabetes Mellitus, Gestational Diabetes, and Diabetic Complications, Symptoms, Treatment, and Research Results, Including Statistics on Prevalence, Morbidity, and Mortality, Along with Source Listings for Further Help and Information

Edited by Karen Bellenir and Peter D. Dresser. 827 pages. 1994. 1-55888-751-2. $78.

"...very informative and understandable for the layperson without being simplistic. It provides a comprehensive overview for laypersons who want a general understanding of the disease or who want to focus on various aspects of the disease." — *Bulletin of the MLA, Jan '96*

Diabetes Sourcebook, 2nd Edition

Basic Consumer Health Information about Type 1 Diabetes (Insulin-Dependent or Juvenile-Onset Diabetes), Type 2 (Noninsulin-Dependent or Adult-Onset Diabetes), Gestational Diabetes, and Related Disorders, Including Diabetes Prevalence Data, Management Issues, the Role of Diet and Exercise in Controlling Diabetes, Insulin and Other Diabetes Medicines, and Complications of Diabetes Such as Eye Diseases, Periodontal Disease, Amputation, and End-Stage Renal Disease; Along with Reports on Current Research Initiatives, a Glossary, and Resource Listings for Further Help and Information

Edited by Karen Bellenir. 725 pages. 1998. 0-7808-0224-1. $78.

Diet & Nutrition Sourcebook, 1st Edition

Basic Information about Nutrition, Including the Dietary Guidelines for Americans, the Food Guide Pyramid, and Their Applications in Daily Diet, Nutritional Advice for Specific Age Groups, Current Nutritional Issues and Controversies, the New Food Label and How to Use It to Promote Healthy Eating, and Recent Developments in Nutritional Research

Edited by Dan R. Harris. 662 pages. 1996. 0-7808-0084-2. $78.

"Useful reference as a food and nutrition sourcebook for the general consumer."
— *Booklist Health Sciences Supplement, Oct '97*

"Recommended for public libraries and medical libraries that receive general information requests on nutrition. It is readable and will appeal to those interested in learning more about healthy dietary practices."
— *Medical Reference Services Quarterly, Fall '97*

"With dozens of questionable diet books on the market, it is so refreshing to find a reliable and factual reference book. Recommended to aspiring professionals, librarians, and others seeking and giving reliable dietary advice. An excellent compilation." — *Choice, Feb '97*

Diet & Nutrition Sourcebook, 2nd Edition

Basic Consumer Health Information about Dietary Guidelines, Recommended Daily Intake Values, Vitamins, Minerals, Fiber, Fat, Weight Control, Dietary Supplements, and Food Additives; Along with Special Sections on Nutrition Needs throughout Life and Nutrition for People with Such Specific Medical Concerns as Allergies, High Blood Cholesterol, Hypertension, Diabetes, Celiac Disease, Seizure Disorders, Phenylketonuria (PKU), Cancer, and Eating Disorders, and Including Reports on Current Nutrition Research and Source Listings for Additional Help and Information

Edited by Karen Bellenir. 600 pages. 1999. 0-7808-0228-4. $78.

Domestic Violence Sourcebook

Basic Information about the Physical, Emotional and Sexual Abuse of Partners, Children, and Elders, Including Information about Hotlines, Safe Houses, Safety Plans, Resources for Support and Assistance, Community Initiatives, and Reports on Current Directions in Research and Treatment; Along with a Glossary, Sources for Further Reading, and Listings of Governmental and Non-Governmental Organizations

Edited by Helene Henderson. 600 pages. 1999. 0-7808-0235-7. $78.